D0461427

What Can I Do Now?

Film

Books in the
What Can I Do Now? Series

Animal Careers
Animation
Art
Business and Finance
Computers
Education
Engineering, Second Edition
Environment, Second Edition
Fashion
Film
Health Care
Journalism, Second Edition
Law
Music
Nursing, Second Edition
Radio and Television, Second Edition
Safety and Security, Second Edition
Science
Sports, Second Edition
Travel and Tourism, Second Edition

What Can I Do Now?

Film

Yolo County Library
226 Buckeye Street
Woodland, CA 95695
530-666-8005

Ferguson Publishing
An imprint of Infobase Publishing

What Can I Do Now? Film

Ferguson
An imprint of Infobase Publishing
132 West 31st Street
New York NY 10001

Library of Congress Cataloging-in-Publication Data

Film. — 1st ed.
    p. cm. — (What can I do now?)
  Includes bibliographical references and index.
  ISBN-13: 978-0-8160-8076-2 (hardcover : alk. paper)
  ISBN-10: 0-8160-8076-3 (hardcover : alk. paper) 1. Motion pictures—Vocational guidance. 2. Motion picture industry—Vocational guidance. I. J.G. Ferguson Publishing Company.
  PN1995.9.P75F45 2010
  791.43023—dc22
                      2009043193

Ferguson books are available at special discounts when purchased in bulk quantities for businesses, associations, institutions, or sales promotions. Please call our Special Sales Department in New York at (212) 967-8800 or (800) 322-8755.

You can find Ferguson on the World Wide Web at http://www.fergpubco.com

Text design by Kerry Casey
Composition by Mary Susan Ryan-Flynn
Cover printed by Sheridan Books, Ann Arbor, MI
Book printed and bound by Sheridan Books, Ann Arbor, MI
Date printed: April 2010
Printed in the United States of America

10 9 8 7 6 5 4 3 2 1

This book is printed on acid-free paper.

All links and Web addresses were checked and verified to be correct at the time of publication. Because of the dynamic nature of the Web, some addresses and links may have changed since publication and may no longer be valid.

Contents

Introduction

There are many people just like you who want to pursue a career in film—whether on a movie set or in a recording or animation studio, editing room, college classroom, or other setting. You may see a film-related career in your future and wonder how you can get started right away, while still in high school. There are countless areas of the film industry in which you can work and utilize your unique skills and talents. All you need to begin is a general interest in the field. Although many film careers require a combination of formal training, creative ability, and experience, there is absolutely no reason to wait until you get out of high school to "get serious" about a career. That doesn't mean you have to make a firm, undying commitment right now. Indeed, one of the biggest fears most people face at some point (sometimes more than once) is choosing the right career. Frankly, many people don't choose at all. They take a job because they need one, and all of a sudden 10 years have gone by and they wonder why they're stuck doing something they hate, like being an animator rather than being an actor. Don't be one of those people! You have the opportunity right now, while you're still in high school and still relatively unencumbered with major adult responsibilities, to explore,

to experience, to try out a work path. Or several paths if you're one of those overachieving types. Wouldn't you really rather find out sooner than later that you're not cut out to be a screenwriter after all, and that you'd actually prefer to be a film editor or a stunt performer?

There are many ways to explore film careers. What we've tried to do in this book is give you an idea of some of your options. The What Do I Need to Know About the Film Industry? section will give you an overview of the field—a little history, where it's at today, and promises of the future—as well as a breakdown of its structure (how it's organized) and a glimpse of some of its many career options.

The Careers section includes 10 chapters, each describing in detail a specific film career path: actor, animator, film director, film editor, producer, production designer and art director, screenwriter, sound worker, special and visual effects technician, and stunt performer. These chapters rely heavily on first-hand accounts from real people on the job. They'll tell you what skills you need, what personal qualities you need to have, and what the ups and downs of the jobs are. You'll also find out about educational requirements—including specific high school and college classes—advancement possibilities, related jobs, salary ranges, and the employment outlook.

In keeping with the secondary theme of this book (the primary theme, for those of you who still don't get it, is "You can do something now"), Section 3, Do It Yourself, urges you to take charge and learn about film-related careers on your own and start your own programs and activities where none exist—school, community, or the nation. Why not?

The real meat of the book is in Section 4, What Can I Do Right Now? This is where you get busy and *do something*. The chapter "Get Involved" will clue you in on the obvious volunteer and intern positions, the not-so-obvious summer camps and summer college study, and other opportunities.

"Read a Book" is an annotated bibliography of books (some new, some old) and periodicals. If you're even remotely considering a film career, reading a few books and checking out a few magazines or professional journals is the easiest thing you can do. Don't stop with our list. Ask your librarian to direct you to more materials. Keep reading!

While we think the best way to explore film-related careers is to jump right in and start doing it, there are plenty of other ways to get into the motion picture mindset. "Surf the Web" offers you a short annotated list of Web sites where you can explore everything from job listings (start getting an idea of what employers are looking for now), to film festivals, to educational requirements, to on-the-job accounts from those who work behind and in front of the camera.

"Ask for Money" is a sampling of scholarships for people who are interested in pursuing film careers. You need to be familiar with these because you're going to need money for school. You have to actively pursue scholarships; no one is going to come up to you one day and present you with a check because you're such a wonderful student. Applying for scholarships is work. It takes effort. And it must be done right and often as much as a year in advance of when you need the money.

"Look to the Pros" is the final chapter. It lists professional organizations you can turn to for more information about accredited schools, education requirements, career descriptions, salary information, union membership, job listings, scholarships, and more. Once you become a college student in a film-related field, you'll be able to join many of these; others, such as the American Film Institute, are open to people of any age. Time after time, professionals say that membership and active participation in a professional organization is one of the best ways to network (make valuable contacts) and gain recognition in your field.

High school can be a lot of fun. There are dances and football games; maybe you're in band or play a sport. Great! Maybe you hate school and are just biding your time until you graduate. That's too bad. Whoever you are, take a minute and try to imagine your life five years from now. Ten years from now. Where will you be? What will you be doing? Whether you realize it or not, how you choose to spend your time now—studying, playing, watching TV, working at a fast-food restaurant, hanging out, whatever—will have an impact on your future. Take a look at how you're spending your time now and ask yourself, "Where is this getting me?"

If you can't come up with an answer, it's probably "nowhere." The choice is yours. No one is going to take you by the hand and lead you in the "right" direction. It's up to you. It's your life. You can do something about it right now!

SECTION 1

What Do I Need to Know About the Film Industry?

When you hear the word *film*, you probably think of famous actors or actresses like Denzel Washington, Reese Witherspoon, Russell Crowe, or Nicole Kidman, or famous directors like Steven Spielberg, Spike Lee, the Coen Brothers, and Peter Jackson. Maybe you think of the stuntworkers who work behind the scenes to help create those spectacular car crashes, fight scenes, and explosions in the action movies you and your friends love to watch. The reality of a career in film today is actually much more diverse and complex than these examples. Millions of people work in the international film industry in literally thousands of different ways. There are opportunities in almost any work setting you can imagine, including Hollywood film sets and on-location at sites throughout the world, animation studios, college classrooms, editing rooms, recording studios, offices, and many others. You obviously know about actors and directors, but did you know that production designers are needed to develop the look and feel of a movie and make it seem believable to viewers? That screenwriters are needed to write plots that make you cry during a chick-flick or almost jump out of your seat while watching a nail-biting chase scene? That professors are needed to teach students about acting, animation, directing, screenwriting, and other film-making skills? That critics are needed to review movies and help you pick a movie for date night? And these examples really haven't even scratched the surface of the variety of jobs available to someone interested in this field. The qualifications for

many jobs in the film industry, such as actors, directors, composers, and screenwriters, are not based so much on formal education, but rather on creativity, talent, and years of practice and dedication. Others, such as entertainment lawyers and production designers, require college training. In short, there are opportunities for people with every interest, skill, and educational background. Now it's up to you to decide which career path is for you. The following sections provide more information on the history of the film industry, its structure, typical career paths, and the employment outlook for the field.

GENERAL INFORMATION
The film industry holds a place in the American imagination like no other, while also maintaining a firm hold on the American pocketbook. The U.S. moviegoing public spent $9.79 billion at the box office in 2008. We rent and purchase our favorite films on DVD and Blu-ray; download them to our iPods, computers, and cell phones; subscribe to many cable channels devoted to the 24-hour repeat of recent and classic productions; and, of course, head to movie theaters to see the latest blockbusters (movie theaters aren't dead yet; in fact, there were 1.4 billion theatrical admissions in 2008, according to the Motion Picture Association of America). We read magazines and books about filmmaking and visit Web sites and blogs devoted to our favorite stars and movies. And thousands of people flock to Hollywood every year to invest in a more

---

Lingo to Learn

art department A collection of professionals (production designer, art director, set director, and others) who work with the visual aspects and designs of a film.

boom mike A microphone attached to the end of a long pole and kept above the heads of actors out of view of the camera.

box office The office from which theater tickets are sold; also refers to the commercial success of a film.

casting Placing actors in roles for a film.

continuity Maintaining the consistency of details (costumes, actor positions, etc.) from scene to scene.

documentary A nonfiction, journalistic film composed of interviews, historical background, and other factual reports surrounding a specific subject.

focus group A small group of unbiased viewers who preview a film for a production company and offer their opinions.

indie A film produced independently, outside of the major studio system.

matte shot A shot incorporating an artist-created backdrop.

post-production Editing, effects, and other work done on a film after primary filming is completed.

soundstage An area within a studio comprised of large sets.

Steadicam A special camera that allows scenes to be shot smoothly as a Steadicam operator moves across a set or location.

---

glamorous life, with dreams of becoming an actor, screenwriter, or director. What follows are only some of the major developments in the history of this evolving, ever-changing industry.

The desire to create more than static, nonmoving images emerged soon after the development of still photography. If one picture could capture a single moment, inventors realized, then it should be possible to devise a similar technique for capturing a series of moments. Flip cards, the first version of moving pictures, worked on a simple principle. If a series of still pictures can capture the movements of someone running, showing the pictures in rapid succession would give the illusion of the movement of running. In 1877 Eadweard Muybridge successfully captured a horse in motion by using 24 cameras and trip wires that triggered the camera shutters as the horse ran along.

In 1894, using film for the first time instead of plates, the famous inventor Thomas Edison produced a short movie called *The Sneeze*. Georges Melies introduced narrative films in 1899 in France, and in 1903 Edwin Porter filmed *The Great Train Robbery*, the first motion picture that told a story using modern filming techniques. Porter used editing to put together a story that he had filmed out of sequence.

Motion pictures became increasingly popular in the early 1900s, with the advent of the movie house and silent film stars such as Charlie Chaplin and Rudolph Valentino. It was not until 1927, when *The Jazz Singer* with Al Jolson was produced, that talking movies began to be made. In the 1920s the first animated films were released for theater distribution. The 1920s also saw the rise of the studio moguls who built the large production companies such as Paramount and Metro-Goldwyn-Mayer (MGM). These companies dominated the industry for years, with tight control of talent, publicity, and film distribution.

The 1930s is often considered the first golden era of filmmaking. It is estimated that 65 percent of the population went to the movies in 1938, accounting for 80 million tickets sold every week. The studios flooded the theaters with films, both good and bad, to keep the public entertained. Though many silent film stars couldn't find success in the new talkies, others, like Charlie Chaplin and Greta Garbo, thrived. Ernst Lubitsch, Frank Capra, and George Cukor are only a few of the great directors who worked during this period.

During World War II, films provided an escape from hardship and tragedy, as well as an aid to the government to educate people about the war effort. Frank Capra, George Stevens, John Huston, and other great filmmakers of the era dedicated themselves to making documentary films for the government. Many feature films were patriotic in nature, or served as portraits of quality American life being protected by the soldiers overseas. A special war tax attached to each theater ticket allowed moviegoers to make a contribution just by being entertained.

After the war, however, this close relationship between the film industry and the government soured. The government demanded that the big studios give up their theaters, greatly limiting the studios' control over the features shown across the country. The studios were also hurt by the anti-Communism sentiment that swept the nation. The government formed the House Un-American Activities Committee (HUAC) in 1947 to sniff out supposed Communist sympathizers in the film industry. A blacklist of actors, screenwriters, and directors believed to be pro-Communist ended the careers of many filmmakers. Hollywood received a great deal of negative publicity, and a public backlash of films evolved, including a boycott by the American Legion. Today, the scandal still has an impact, demonstrated by the uproar when Elia Kazan, director of such film classics as *A Streetcar Named Desire* and *On the Waterfront*, who cooperated with the HUAC by naming those in the industry he believed to be Communists, was announced as the winner of a special Academy Award in 1999. The Oscars were picketed and Nick Nolte, Ed Harris, and other nominees refused to applaud during Kazan's acceptance.

Also contributing to the demise of the big studios was the rush to the suburbs.

Americans were leaving the big cities and, therefore, their proximity to the grand movie houses. They also began to spend their recreational dollars on records for their new hi-fi's and for tickets for travel on the new airlines. By the late 1940s the studios had to allow contracts with filmmakers and stars to lapse, ending the studios' years of complete power over the industry.

Television changed the film industry in a variety of ways, and it continues to do so. With the popularity of TV growing in the early 1950s, movies had competition like nothing before. In 1946 the film industry made more money domestically than at any other time in its history—a gross of $1.7 billion. The early 1950s saw a large drop-off in movie attendance, and by 1962, domestic gross had been cut nearly in half to $900 million. In the 1950s the movies began to compete by offering elements (and gimmicks) viewers couldn't find elsewhere. Although the Technicolor process of color film had been perfected in 1933, filmmakers still shot primarily in black and white (B&W). Not only were B&W films less expensive to produce than color films, but filmmakers had also honed their skills with B&W, and were more comfortable with it. But B&W TV was growing in popularity and film producers recognized the need to use color more frequently to draw viewers to movie theaters. The industry also tried a few technological stunts, such as 3-D. *House of Wax* and other horror films used 3-D primarily, but other genres dabbled in it as well. The musical *Kiss Me, Kate* was presented in 3-D. This process, however, was short-lived. And though Cinerama, a film industry gimmick that consisted of films presented on a large, wraparound screen, lasted a bit longer than 3-D, it too sizzled out within 10 years, ending with Stanley Kubrick's *2001: A Space Odyssey* in 1968. CinemaScope, another big-screen novelty, proved more successful and inspired other wide-screen processes such as VistaVision and Panavision.

Film producers offered something else TV viewers couldn't get at home: films with controversial subject matter and dialogue. Otto Preminger adapted the play *The Moon Is Blue* in 1953 and released it without the Movie Production Code's seal of approval. The code had been in place since the 1930s to essentially censor films on the basis of morality. Preminger sprinkled his film with a few frank discussions of sex and use of such words as "virgin." Although *The Moon Is Blue* is tame and coy in contrast to later films, its success led other filmmakers to test the boundaries of the code more aggressively. The success of foreign films not subject to the code also proved the public's appreciation of more daring films. By the late 1960s the code had become barely relevant, and it was abandoned in 1967 in favor of the ratings system still used today.

Despite the film industry's early efforts to separate itself entirely from television, TV came to have a large impact on the way films were made. Filmmakers and actors cut their teeth with TV projects; films became smaller in scope with lower budgets; and some television screenplays, such as *Marty* and *A Catered Affair*, were adapted for the big screen.

The film industry's survival in the face of great competition was evidenced in the 1970s. In addition to enjoying greater financial success, films also enjoyed another artistic golden era. The late 1960s and early 1970s brought along pioneering films that explored politics, violence, society, and sexuality. Filmmakers like Robert Altman (*Nashville*), Francis Ford Coppola (*The Godfather*), Arthur Penn (*Bonnie and Clyde*), Martin Scorsese (*Taxi Driver*), Roman Polanski (*Chinatown*), and Woody Allen (*Manhattan*), made films that were both critically and financially successful. Though many of these filmmakers still make quality films today, their earlier work stands out. The film sequel also evolved during this period; film series had long been a tradition, but Coppola was the first to label a film Part II when he released his sequel to *The Godfather*. Horror movies such as *Halloween* and *Friday the 13th* capitalized on their formulas well into the 1980s and 1990s, and other genres, such as action films and comedies, followed suit with their own sequels.

The revolutionary period of the 1970s went unmatched in the 1980s. Whereas the 1970s produced a long list of great directors, the 1980s produced relatively few breakout filmmakers. David Lynch (*Blue Velvet*), Spike Lee (*Do the Right Thing*), Tim Burton (*Beetlejuice*), and Barry Levinson (*Diner*) established careers in the industry, and some female directors, such as Susan Seidelman (*Desperately Seeking Sus*an) and Joan Micklin Silver (*Crossing Delancey*), made films that met with both critical and financial success. But the 1980s are mostly marked by the introduction of VCRs in American homes. By the middle of the decade, even small towns had video rental stores, and filmmakers seemed to make films with an eye toward the video version. Some films even went directly to video, losing little in the translation. But the 1980s also laid the groundwork for the two major developments of the 1990s: the big budget, special effects spectacle, and the independent film. The success of George Lucas (*Star Wars*) and Steven Spielberg (*E.T.*) ushered in a new standard of big-budget filmmaking and experimentation with special effects and computer technology. Lucas and Spielberg helped to establish the tradition of the summer blockbuster, as film studios began to compete for younger, primarily male, audiences. With *Independence Day, Men in Black, Star Wars I–III, Lord of the Rings: Return of the King,* and *Pirates of the Caribbean: Dead Man's Chest*, the top moneymakers of the late 1990s and 2000s, this is a trend that is likely to continue. And industry executives weren't the only ones tracking weekend grosses. The 1990s and 2000s also saw the regular publication of the top 10 films for any given week, and the public became more aware of film successes and failures.

At the other end of the spectrum, the inexpensively produced work of independent filmmakers hearkened back to the glory days of the 1970s. The success of the Sundance Film Festival, and the attention given the films it spotlighted, revealed an audience for more personal, artful films. The independently produced *Pulp Fiction* not only made a lot of money, but also won awards and inspired several imitations. Also, many women, minority, and gay filmmakers found their voices in independent cinema.

Advances in computer technology have created a renaissance in animation that continues today. Some of the most popular movies of recent years, such as *WALL-E, Ratatouille, Shrek,* and *Finding Nemo*, have been animated films. Another major animation trend is the emergence of high-quality animation in a variety of genres that is geared toward adults. Two examples of animated features in this trend include *Persepolis* and *Waltz with Bashir*, which were nominated for Academy Awards in 2007 and 2008, respectively.

One other major trend in recent years is the growth of the global film industry and the popularity of foreign-produced films with American audiences. For example, *Slumdog Millionaire*, which won the Academy Award for Best Picture in 2008, featured a British director, cinematographer, and screenwriter and a cast of professional and amateur actors from India.

Today, producers and directors strive for a union of all the different aspects of great filmmaking. They attempt to create work that is artful, technologically enhanced, and financially rewarding.

STRUCTURE OF THE INDUSTRY

Most movie productions begin with the selection of the story to be told. The movie may be based on a novel, a play, or an original script. With documenta-

Film Industry Facts, 2006

- Forty-two percent of workers in the motion picture and video industry had part-time or variable schedules.

- People in this industry worked an average of 29 hours a week.

- Nearly 60 percent of workers in the industry were under the age of 45.

- Overall employment in the motion picture and video industry is expected to grow by 11 percent through 2016, about as fast as the average rate of growth for all industries.

Source: U.S. Department of Labor

ries, the movie focuses on a nonfiction subject.

The second most important step after developing the story line or subject is to acquire funding. With commercial films, the company sponsoring the production pays the production costs and approves the steps in the process of making the film.

In the days of the studio contracts, the conception, production, and financing of films was all done within one studio. For example, 20th Century Fox would have producers, staff writers, directors, and actors and actresses, from whom they would choose for a particular film.

Today's system is different. Although there are people who will sign contracts to do several films for one studio for a prearranged salary, most people work on a project-by-project basis. Producers now bring a project to a studio with an estimated cost of production and perhaps the main actors and actresses already cast, and a studio may agree to back the production. The studio will pay for the costs of producing the film and for the salaries of the crew and cast in exchange for the film's profits when it is released.

If the movie is successful, it will bring in more money from ticket, DVD, or electronic download sales than it cost to produce. Movies have become very expensive projects, with many films costing millions of dollars to produce. These films require huge sales to make any money for the company sponsoring the film. Small productions need not sell as many tickets, DVDs, or downloads, but frequently the actors and actresses are not well known, and attracting viewers becomes more difficult.

With the increased cost of film production, the independent producer has to be a good salesperson to be able to persuade a studio of the marketability of a film idea. If there are popular actors and actresses involved in the film, or a particular story line has done well before, the producer is more likely to find financing than if a new idea or unknown actors are involved. Some studios are more willing to take the risk of a lesser known cast and story if the cost of production is not too high.

Occasionally, a producer will go to a studio with just the idea for a film. With studio backing, he or she may be able to attract bigger names to work on the film. Studios have developed a "step deal" for this and other arrangements. With a step deal, the studio can withdraw funding from a project if the producer cannot get an adequate script or staff together.

Documentary filmmakers usually have more difficulty securing financing than a mass-market motion picture. If the funding is sought through endowments, government agencies, or broadcasting stations, the producer and director should anticipate putting together a fairly lengthy proposal with extensive research on the selected topic. For example, the length of the documentary needs to be planned out and explained. A timetable for the research, filming, and editing has to be calculated. The potential investors also need biographical information on the more important staff members of the documentary so they know the background of the people with whom they are entrusting their money. The producer may have to provide a shortened version of the film (a pilot) to show what the full-length project will look like. It can take from six months to 10 years to secure financing for a documentary.

Once funding has been found for a project, a payment schedule is worked out with the producer of the documentary. Some funds are usually supplied up front, with various amounts distributed along the way and the remaining money delivered after the completion of the project.

A film crew on a documentary can be as small as four people—a producer-director, a camera operator, a sound technician, and a lighting technician—although some documentaries require a large staff.

As with other forms of film production, the lower the costs, the easier it is to find funding.

After funding has been arranged, the filmmakers prepare to film. Whether you're making a documentary or a feature film, you'll need a script. In the case of a feature film, *screenwriters* write and rewrite the script to develop characters, tighten the plot, and keep within time limitations. The action must be planned carefully. Timing, continuation of narrative, camera angles, and the many other details that go into making a cohesive piece of work need to be worked out as thoroughly as possible before the filming begins. If the producer waits until the actual production to decide on major aspects of the project, the costs increase dramatically.

Decisions about where the filming is to be done, whether in a studio or on location, go into the cost analysis of the project. Casting of the actors, actresses, narrators, and other talent that will be in the project affect the budget. How long the filming will take, the special effects required, and the overall size of the staff and production all determine the final budget for a film. The studio production department needs all this information before final approval of the contract can be made.

Depending on the size of the project, live-action filming can take several days to several months. The picture is normally filmed out of sequence. The film can be shot in a studio on a soundstage, where everything is re-created to look like an actual location. The film can also be produced on location, in the actual setting where the story takes place.

Once the filming is done, the film is reassembled in a studio. Special effects, music tracks, and any conversation that may have been muffled by other noises during the filming are added at this point. This type of work requires both precision and split-second timing to assure that the on-screen action matches the sound heard.

Once the project is completed, the people in charge of the production review the film. If the final product is acceptable, the film is released. This means that the film is distributed to theaters or made available to consumers directly via cable or commercial television stations or DVDs. It can also be made available for download onto computers, MP3 players, or mobile communication devices.

Now it is up to the marketing and distributing staff to build an audience for the film. Their job is to encourage the public to watch the production and to make the public aware of where the film is playing or how to purchase or rent it. Without an audience, even the best motion picture will have little impact.

Most work in the motion picture industry revolves around Hollywood and New York City. Actors, however, can get their start in smaller productions in any number of cities around the country.

CAREERS

There are many career opportunities in the film industry, from becoming an actor or director to working as an editor, animator, or special effects worker. A short sampling of the many career opportunities in film follows in the paragraphs below.

The Best Film Schools

More than 500 colleges and universities offer film studies programs. The following film schools are considered to be the best in the nation:

American Film Institute (Los Angeles, Calif.)
http://www.afi.com
Degrees Awarded: Master's degrees in cinematography, directing, editing, producing, production design, and screenwriting

Columbia University (New York)
http://wwwapp.cc.columbia.edu/art/app/arts/film
Degrees Awarded: Bachelor's degrees in creative writing, film studies, and theatre; Master's degrees in acting, creative writing, directing, dramaturgy, film studies, filmmaking, playwriting, stage management, and theatre management and producing; Doctorate in theatre

University of California—Los Angeles
http://www.tft.ucla.edu/ftv_mfa
Degrees Awarded: Bachelor's degree in film and television; Master's degrees in animation, cinema and media studies, cinematography, moving image archive studies, production, production/directing, and screenwriting; Doctorates in cinema and media studies

University of Southern California (Los Angeles, Calif.)
http://www-cntv.usc.edu/programs
Degrees Awarded: Bachelor's degrees in animation and digital art, business administration-emphasis in cinema-television, cinema television, interactive entertainment, writing for screen and television; Master's degrees in animation and digital arts, cinema-television, interactive media, and motion picture producing; Doctorates in cinema-television and media arts and practice

Actors and actresses have the job of interpreting the roles they read in scripts and bringing the characters to life. They work closely with directors to achieve the best possible performance. They may sing and dance as well as speak in a production, or they may work as extras.

Animators are artists who design the cartoons that appear in movies, television shows, and commercials.

Audio recording engineers oversee the technical end of sound recording during filming. *Recording mixers* combine music and sound effects with a film's action.

Boom operators place and operate microphones to record dialogue and other sounds during filming.

Business managers and executives plan, organize, direct, and coordinate the operations of film-related businesses. They may oversee an entire company, a geographical territory of a company's operations, or a specific department within a company.

Casting directors audition actors and actresses for productions. They observe the person's physical appearance, voice, expressiveness, and experience. They recommend actors to producers and directors. Some casting directors may be involved with arranging contracts for performers.

Choreographers create or develop dance patterns and teach them to performers so that they can be performed in movies.

Cinematographers, or *directors of photography*, work with the director to achieve the best possible framing, lighting, style, continuity, and exposure in a film. They must have a refined aesthetic sensibility as well as strong technical knowledge. They select and oversee the members of the camera crew.

Camera operators use motion picture cameras and equipment to photograph subjects or material for movies. Their instructions usually come from cinematographers or directors of photography. *Key grips* manage the crew and equipment (such as cameras, lights, rigging, etc.) that are used by the director of photography during filming. *Best boys* (of both genders) assist key grips with their duties.

Composers create much of the music heard in films. *Arrangers* take composers' musical compositions and transcribe them for other instruments or voices; work them into scores for film, theater, or television; or adapt them to styles that are different from the one in which the music was written.

Costume designers plan, create, and maintain clothing and accessories for all characters in a stage, film, television, dance, or opera production. They are assisted by *key costumers*. Once costumes have been made for a film or show, *wardrobe supervisors* keep them in good condition by ironing, mending, and cleaning them, and doing any necessary minor alterations.

Dancers perform dances alone or with others that will be filmed for use in motion pictures.

Directors read scripts, help select cast members, direct rehearsals, and oversee the activities of writers and editors. They are responsible for getting the best possible performances from actors. Directors also work with *cinematographers* to determine camera angles, lighting, and the overall way the picture will look on film.

Distribution and marketing staff are responsible for finding theaters to show films and arranging all advertising and promotional activities surrounding a film. A film's success is frequently influenced by its marketing. Bad projects may do somewhat better with good marketing, but good projects can certainly be hurt without strong marketing and distribution.

Entertainment lawyers handle contract negotiations, intellectual-property issues, and a variety of other legal issues for individuals and companies in the film industry.

Extras, also known as *background performers*, have nonspeaking roles in films and TV shows. They work in the background of film scenes, following the orders of directors and crew members. They may work in crowd scenes, or may simply be one of a few people appearing with the principal performers.

Film commissioners work as advocates for a particular city, state, or region to encourage film companies to film in the area.

Film distributors ensure that films are placed into theatrical release in movie theaters and other venues.

Film editors work with producers and directors to create an effective and accurate presentation of a script. They use specialized equipment and computers to edit the film.

Film writers express, edit, promote, and interpret ideas and facts about films and the motion picture industry in written form for newspapers, magazines, books, Web sites, and radio and television broadcasts. *Critics* review movies for print publications, Web sites, and television and radio stations. *Columnists* or *commentators* analyze news and social issues as they relate to the motion picture industry. They write about events from the standpoint of their own experience or opinion. *Staff writers* are employed by magazines and newspapers to write news stories, feature articles, and columns about the film industry.

Foley artists re-create sound effects for a film, matching the sounds with images.

Hairstylists and *makeup artists* use cosmetics, greasepaint, wigs, plastics, latex, and other materials to change the appearance of actors' hair and skin.

Lighting technicians, also known as *gaffers*, set up and control lighting equipment for motion pictures, television broadcasts, taped television shows, and video productions. *Best boys* (of both genders) assist gaffers with their duties.

Location scouts search for locations that will be used in films (such as a gritty bar,

an old farm, or an 18th-century mansion). They secure permission to use these locations from police and fire departments, companies, or private citizens.

Marketing research analysts collect, analyze, and interpret data in order to determine potential demand for films. By examining the buying habits, wants, needs, and preferences of consumers, research analysts are able to recommend ways to improve a film, increase sales, and expand customer bases.

Matte painters are artists who create backgrounds for films via actual painting or computer software.

Model makers design and build scale duplicates of real or imaginary items that are too expensive to purchase or are unavailable.

Music conductors direct large groups of musicians or singers in the performance of a piece of music for a motion picture.

Musicians perform, compose, conduct, and arrange music for films.

Producers plan and coordinate the activities of all employees involved in a production. Most importantly, they are responsible for deciding the size of the production and its budget. Producers coordinate the work of all employees engaged in writing, directing, filming, staging, and editing a movie. They also discuss scripts with a variety of workers, including writers, directors, and editors. In general, producers are responsible for overseeing and making the final decisions on most matters related to a production.

Production assistants help the technical or editorial crew in all types of work, from getting coffee to hauling production equipment.

Production designers and *art directors* are involved with the selection, development, and design of props, scenery, costumes, makeup, and other artistic details.

Property masters oversee the acquisition, usage, and disposal of props used during a film.

Public relations specialists, sometimes known as *publicists*, develop and maintain programs that present a favorable public image for actors/actresses or a film studio.

Screenwriters write scripts for entertainment, education, training, sales, television, and films. They may choose themes themselves, or they may write on a theme assigned by a producer or director, sometimes adapting plays or novels into screenplays.

Script readers are responsible for reading screenplays that are submitted to production companies, film studios, or agents. They provide a brief summary of the screenplay and a recommendation on whether or not it should be considered for development.

Set decorators perform work that is similar to interior designers on movie sets.

Set designers create the blueprints that are used to build film sets.

Sound designers oversee every aspect of the soundtrack of a movie—from music and dialogue to sound effects such as thunderstorms and punches during a fight scene.

Special effects workers make the illusion of movies, theater, and television seem real. They may specialize in a variety of areas, including computer animation, sound effects, pyrotechnics, and makeup. Special effects technicians work with a variety of materials and techniques to produce the fantastic visions and startlingly realistic illusions that add dimension to a film.

Storyboard artists draw illustrations and sketches depicting the details of a script. This artwork helps film professionals (including directors, producers, editors, and production designers) get a feel for the film.

Stunt performers are actors who perform dangerous scenes in motion pictures. They may fall off tall buildings, get knocked from horses and motorcycles, imitate fistfights, and drive in high-speed car chases. They must know how to set up stunts that are both safe to perform and believable to audiences. In these dangerous scenes, stunt performers are often asked to double, or take the place of, a star actor. *Stunt coordinators* supervise stunt workers and the development of stunts that will be used in a movie.

Talent agents represent actors and their business interests. They help secure jobs for the actors they represent and work out the terms of the actors' contracts to get the best deal possible for their clients (and for themselves, since most agents work on commission). Without an agent, it can be very difficult for an actor to find work.

Teachers instruct undergraduate and graduate students about film-related subjects such as acting, screenwriting, directing, and animation at colleges and universities.

The Greatest Movies of All Time

In 2008 the American Film Institute convened a blue-ribbon panel of "leaders from across the film community" to pick the best movies of all time. Here were its selections:

1. *Casablanca* (1942)
2. *Citizen Kane* (1941)
3. *Gone with the Wind* (1939)
4. *Lawrence of Arabia* (1962)
5. *On the Waterfront* (1954)
6. *Schindler's List* (1993)
7. *Singin' in the Rain* (1952)
8. *The Godfather* (1972)
9. *The Graduate* (1967)
10. *The Wizard of Oz* (1939)

EMPLOYMENT OPPORTUNITIES

Approximately 2.5 million people in the United States were affiliated in some manner with the motion picture and television industries in 2007, according to the Motion Picture Association of America (MPAA). More than 115,000 companies in all 50 states contributed to the film and television industries in some way in 2008. California and New York are the leading centers of film production in the United States. The MPAA reports that the top 10 production states outside of California and New York are Illinois, Texas, Florida, Georgia, Pennsylvania, New Jersey, North Carolina, Louisiana, Tennessee, and Massachusetts. States with up-and-coming film industries include Michigan, Arizona, Connecticut, New Mexico, and Utah.

The six major producers and distributors of motion pictures in the United States are Paramount Pictures Corporation, Sony Pictures Entertainment Inc., 20th Century Fox Film Corporation, Universal City Studios LLLP, Walt Disney Studios Motion Pictures, and Warner Bros. Entertainment Inc. In addition to these large media companies, there are hundreds of smaller companies with staffs ranging from one or two people to thousands of workers.

INDUSTRY OUTLOOK

Employment in the motion picture and video industry will grow about as fast as the average for all industries through 2016, according to the U.S. Department of Labor. Despite the economic downturn in recent years, the movie industry continues to grow, with revenue of $9.79 billion in 2008—an increase of nearly 2 percent from 2007, according to the MPAA. Worldwide box office sales reached an all-time high of $28.1 billion in 2008—an increase of 5.2 percent from the previous year.

The film industry is greatly ruled by trends. Though filmmakers and industry executives attempt to carefully analyze the success and failure of films, it is nearly impossible to predict which films will capture the public's imagination and attention. So many different elements play parts in a film's success. How a film is promoted and distributed, the other films out at the time, and societal attitudes toward the subject matter are just a few of the factors that determine success. Studios are constantly on the lookout for the next big picture, but they are also anxious to play it safe and follow the formulas of reliable film product.

Big-budget films will likely continue to rule the industry. Production companies will hire the most popular big-name actors and directors to draw huge profits. Special effects and animation will continue to create new jobs for those talented with computers.

Special effects and popular stars don't guarantee success, however, so film executives will continue to look to independent filmmakers and festivals for original talent. Also, the unexpected success of such small-budget movies as *The Blair Witch Project, You Can Count on Me, Garden State, Requiem for a Dream,* and *Juno* has proven that movies without stars, special effects, and big budgets can sometimes make more money than many high-profile projects.

Another major trend in the film industry is that movies are no longer just watched in movie theatres and rented in video stores. They are now available for delivery by mail; for download onto computers, MP3 players, and mobile devices; and for streaming on the Internet. In fact, the MPAA reports that there are more than 50 Web sites in the United States alone that allow users to view, rent, or download feature films. These new delivery methods have translated into increased demand for movies—which is good news to people in the industry. In fact, 610 feature films were released in 2008, according to the MPAA, an increase of 23 percent from 1999.

The film industry faces a few major challenges over the next decade. Tax breaks from other English-speaking countries (especially Canada) are causing more American productions to move abroad. When production leaves the United States, thousands of jobs and the economic benefits that film production brought to a particular area are lost. To fight this economic loss, several cities and states have begun offering the film industry incentives and tax breaks to encourage filming in the United States. The motion picture industry is also losing billions of dollars as a result of piracy, which occurs when an individual obtains a movie without paying for it or purchases a movie from a company or person who has copied it without permission. The industry is combating piracy by initiating lawsuits against those who violate copyright laws, implementing improved security in movie theaters (to reduce the illegal taping of movies), and lobbying Congress to develop legislation that will reduce piracy.

SECTION 2

Careers

Actors

SUMMARY

Definition
Actors play parts or roles in motion pictures, on stage, or on television or radio.

Alternative Job Titles
Performers
Thespians

Salary Range
$7,500 to $75,000 to $1 million+

Educational Requirements
High school diploma

Certification or Licensing
Required

Employment Outlook
About as fast as the average

High School Subjects
Speech
Theater

Personal Interests
Entertaining/performing
Film and television
Theater

Film and television actor Greg Serano caught the acting bug while in college. "I was hanging out with a friend," he recalls, "who was acting in a production and while backstage one day, there was an actor in his play that kind of resembled me, and I thought he was *terrible*. So I started repeating his lines how I thought they should be said. The next play, I auditioned against him and got the part. I worked on four theater productions over two years. After working on stage, what made me want to work in film and TV was seeing a special on the E! cable network titled "How to Make It in Hollywood." My best friend and I drove to Los Angeles in 1996. I then worked on getting an agent, and within four months started auditioning,

and within two months of auditioning had booked my first role."

WHAT DOES AN ACTOR DO?

Acting seems like a glamorous and fairly easy job. In reality, it is demanding, tiring work that requires a special talent. The hours can be long, there can be significant gaps between employment, and an actor's popularity can be strongly influenced by his or her choice of acting jobs, as well as the whims of the viewing public.

Before they can even begin acting, actors must find a part in an upcoming production. This may be in a comedy, drama, musical, or opera. Established actors often have an *agent* who helps them locate parts, but inexperienced actors without a proven track record often must find roles on their own. Then, having read and studied the part, the actor must audition before the director, casting director, and other people who have control of the production. This requirement is often waived for established artists. In film and television, actors must also complete screen tests, which are scenes recorded on film, at times performed with other actors, which are later viewed by the director and producer of the film.

If selected for the part, the actor then spends hundreds of hours in rehearsal and must memorize many lines and cues. This is especially true in live theater; in film and television, actors may spend less time in rehearsal and sometimes improvise their lines before the camera, often performing several attempts, or "takes," before the director is satisfied. Television actors often take advantage of teleprompters, which scroll their lines on a screen in front of them while performing. Radio actors generally read from a script, and therefore rehearsal times are usually shorter.

In addition to such mechanical duties, the actor must determine the essence of the character being portrayed and the relation of that character to the overall scheme of the work. For some film roles, actors must also sing and dance and spend additional time rehearsing songs and perfecting the choreography. Some roles require actors to perform various stunts, which can be quite dangerous. Most often, these stunts are performed by specially trained *stunt performers.* Others work as *stand-ins* or *body doubles.* These actors are chosen for specific features and appear on film in place of the lead actor; this is often the case in films requiring nude or seminude scenes.

Actors in films may spend several weeks involved in a production, which often takes place on location; that is, in different parts of the world. Actors in the theater may perform the same part many times a week for weeks, months, and sometimes years. This allows them to develop the role, but it can also become tedious. Television actors involved in a series, such as a soap opera or a situation comedy, also may play the same role for years, generally in 13-week cycles. For these actors, however, their lines change from week to week and even from day to day, and much time is spent rehearsing their new lines.

While studying and perfecting their craft, many actors work as *extras*, the nonspeaking characters who appear in the background on screen or stage. Many actors also continue their training. A great deal of an actor's time is spent attending auditions.

Actors work under a wide variety of conditions. For example, those employed in motion pictures may work in air-conditioned studios one week and be on location in a hot desert or on a snow-covered mountain the next. Once they are done filming, some actors—especially top stars—are required to promote their movies or shows by appearing as guests on television and radio shows or participating in interviews for magazines and newspapers.

To Be a Successful Actor, You Should...

- be committed to developing your acting skills
- have a strong speaking voice
- be an excellent communicator
- have confidence
- be able to accept constant rejection as you break into the field
- be willing to work long hours
- be able to memorize a large number of lines

The world of acting is very uncertain. Aspirants never know whether they will be able to get into the profession, and, once in, there are uncertainties about whether their work will be well received and, if not, whether they can survive a bad production.

WHAT IS IT LIKE TO BE AN ACTOR?

Greg Serano is a film and television actor with 11 years as a Screen Actors Guild (SAG) actor who is now based in New Mexico after living in Los Angeles during his early acting career. He also teaches acting to children, teens, and adults at the STUDIO: an actor's space in Albuquerque, New Mexico. (Visit http://www.imdb.com/name/nm0784833 to learn more about his career.) Since 1996, Greg

has had the opportunity to work on more than 40 films, pilots, TV shows, miniseries and movies of the week including *Legally Blonde, C.S.I., E.R., In the Valley of Elah, Beer for My Horses, Terminator 4,* and as a series regular for four seasons on ABC Family's *Wildfire.* Greg says that the best part of being an actor is the good pay and the fact that the work can be a lot of fun. He cites "having to wait long periods of time between work/auditions" as the major drawback to a career in the field.

Greg says there are really no typical days for actors. "It all depends," he explains, "on how many scenes you're in. How many lines? Are there stunts? Elaborate sets/lighting? The only typical part of my work would be the hours—generally 12 hours 'on set' is the average. Prepping for scenes normally includes sitting in front of the mirror in my trailer repeating lines over and over and over and over until I've memorized them. It also involves finding the other actors in the scene and 'running it' till we're up. When not in a scene, I like to watch the director work with the actors and watch the monitors. Some days, there is lots of 'downtime,' so to fill time there are books, PlayStation, movies, talking with other actors and the crew, and eating!"

Robert Parnell has been an actor for five decades. Some of his film and TV credits include *The Magic Boat, Palooka, Made in America, Heart and Souls, Presque Isle, Two Mothers, Midnight Caller, Dr. Quinn Medicine Woman, Nash Bridges, America's Most Wanted*, and *Back to the Streets of San Francisco*. He has won several awards for his work, including the San Francisco Bay Area Critics' Award, the Florida Critics' Award, and the Dramalogue Outstanding Performance Award. Robert is a member of SAG, Actors' Equity Association, and the American Federation of Television and Radio Artists.

"A typical day on the set depends on the shoot schedule for that particular day," Robert says. "Generally, start times are early in the morning. If the location of the shoot is some miles distant, you need to get up early because if you are in a metropolitan area you will hit rush-hour traffic. They don't like you to be late for your call time. It takes a lot of coordination to set up a shot and reorganizing could effect the entire day of shooting. Usually you will find that you will still wait around to begin, but they will hustle you into wardrobe and makeup anyway. Craft-services will provide meals. A large trailer will have individual rooms where you can hang out. During this time, you should study your lines. Rehearsal time on the set is very brief and they expect you to be ready with your lines. Depending on the schedule you may have just one scene or several in a day. When you are between scenes or setups, you shouldn't wander too far. The producers may decide they suddenly need you. Always keep in mind that moviemaking is a costly business for the producers, and they expect professionalism. Between scenes I find that I am constantly going over my lines for the next scene. Usually it is an eight-hour day for actors, but you will never know for sure until you are informed by a production assistant that you are released."

Good Advice

Actor Robert Parnell offers the following advice to aspiring actors:

- Be a voracious reader. Educate yourself—not just about acting, but about everything. Study people. A good actor is a good listener on and off the stage.

- Act, act, act. Before even thinking about turning professional, get into community theater productions or student films.

- Take classes in improvisation, voice, and dance.

- Be positive. Rejection happens.

- Think about the other important matters in life: marriage, children, financial needs. The percentage of actors making big incomes is very low. Don't do it for fame and fortune; do it because you love and need it. My greatest reward has been the applause of an appreciative audience.

DO I HAVE WHAT IT TAKES TO BE AN ACTOR?

To be a successful actor, you need to not only have a great talent for acting, but also a great determination to succeed. You must be able to memorize hundreds of lines and should have a good speaking voice. The ability to sing and dance will help you stand out during casting calls and auditions. Almost all actors, except the biggest stars, are required to audition for a part before they receive the role. In film and television, you will generally complete screen tests to see how you will appear on film. In all fields of acting, a love for acting is a must. It might take many years for an actor to achieve any success.

While union membership may not always be required, many actors find it advantageous to belong to a union that covers their particular field of performing arts. These organizations include the Actors' Equity Association (stage), Screen Actors Guild (motion pictures and television films), or American Federation of Television and Radio Artists (TV, recording, and radio). In addition, some actors may benefit from membership in the American Guild of Variety Artists (nightclubs, and so on), American Guild of Musical Artists (opera and ballet), or organizations such as the Guild of Italian American Actors for productions in a specific language.

HOW DO I BECOME AN ACTOR?

Education

High School

There are no minimum educational requirements to become an actor. However, a minimum of a high school diploma is recommended.

Greg Serano offers the following advice to high school students who are interested in becoming actors: "First, ask questions of working actors before you do anything. Watch out for scams—there are a lot out there! Second, train, train, train. Like anything else, you've got to work at it and do it in the space/realm that you'll be in (a real acting workshop with real scenes from TV/movies or stage plays). Find a reputable acting coach and get to work!"

Postsecondary Training

It is a good idea to earn at least a bachelor's degree in a program in theater or the dramatic arts to prepare for this career. In addition, graduate degrees in the fine arts or in drama are nearly always required should you decide to teach dramatic arts.

College can also provide you with acting experience. More than 500 colleges and universities throughout the country offer dramatic arts programs and present theatrical performances. Actors and directors recommend that those interested in acting gain as much experience as possible through acting in plays in high school and college or in those offered by community groups. Training beyond college is recommended, especially for actors interested in entering the theater. Joining acting workshops, such as The Actors Studio (http://www.theactorsstudio.org), can often be highly rewarding.

Certification or Licensing

There is no certification available, but actors working in film and television must belong to SAG. Many actors also belong to the American Federation of Television and Radio Artists and the Actors' Equity Association. As a member of a union, you'll receive special benefits, such as better pay and compensation for overtime and holidays.

Internships and Volunteerships

The best way to explore this career is to participate in school or local theater productions. Even working on the props or lighting crew will provide insight into the field. You can also volunteer with local film commissions or independent film-makers to get more experience. Working as an extra is another good way to get exposure to the field.

Breaking Into the Business: A Story from Actor Robert Parnell

I suppose I was lightly bit by the acting bug when I attended Pasadena City College in California. I ran into a classmate who was standing in a hallway and mumbling things to himself. He explained that he was going to audition for a play. He suggested that I do the same, since they were looking for someone older to play the father. [Robert had served in the Navy for four years and was older than many of the students.] With the exception of doing a school play in the seventh grade, I had not acted. When my friend went in for his audition, I slipped into a seat in the back and watched him and others doing a scene from the play. At the end, the director asked if there was anyone else who wanted to audition. I rose apprehensively and read some "father" lines. I felt that I did okay, and I got the part. The director was the school's drama teacher and happened to be the best teacher I had ever had.

I did a number of plays there, but after two years I felt I was ready for the big time and stuck out my thumb to hitchhike to New York. I studied a bit and saw many Off Broadway shows. To augment my small GI Bill, I worked two different jobs, at a shoe store during the day and a bakery at night. After only nine months, my mother's illness required me to return to California. I then enrolled at Los Angeles State College and majored in drama, again appearing in most of the school's plays. Two years later I married and had two children in rapid succession. Theater was put on hold while I struggled to make a living driving cabs in Los Angeles, reading gas meters, etc.

Finally, in 1966 I heard about an audition at the professional theater, The Ivar, in Hollywood. This was the West Coast premier of *Who's Afraid of Virginia Woolf?* I got the part and the producer paid my initiation fee to join the Actors' Equity Association, an essential union to appear in professional theater. Finally, I was being paid to do what I loved. However, when the show eventually closed, I still had mouths to feed and found a job as a private investigator with a large company in Los Angeles. I soon became a supervisor and in 1977 was transferred to the home office in San Francisco as a vice president. Money was good, but I found the Bay Area had a vibrant theatrical community and working all day and acting at night was more than I wanted to handle. I decided to quit the firm and started my own. Thus I could control my hours.

While doing a play in 1985, I was seen by a film and television agent who offered to represent me. I had never really considered this, thinking that I was an artist and needn't pursue the commercial aspect. How wrong I was. I soon found that acting in front of a camera required a disciplined skill and was exciting in its own way and, incidentally, did occasionally pay quite well. At this stage of my life, early 70s, I still do theater, film, and TV and hope to continue as long as there are roles.

WHO WILL HIRE ME?

Approximately 70,000 actors are employed in the United States. Motion pictures, television, and the stage are the largest fields of employment for actors, with television commercials representing as much as 60 percent of all acting jobs. Most of the opportunities for employment in these fields are either in Los Angeles or in New York.

As cable television networks continue to produce more and more of their own programs and films, they will become a major provider of employment for actors. Home entertainment options (DVDs, video, Internet, cell phones, etc.) will also continue to create new acting jobs, as will the music-video business.

The lowest numbers of actors are employed for stage work. In addition to Broadway shows and regional theater, there are employment opportunities for stage actors in summer stock, at resorts, and on cruise ships.

The best way to enter acting is to start with high school, local, or college productions and to gain as much experience as possible on that level. Very rarely is an inexperienced actor given an opportunity to perform on stage or in film in New York or Hollywood. The field is extremely difficult to enter; the more experience and ability beginners have, the greater the possibilities for entrance.

Those venturing to New York or Hollywood are encouraged first to have enough money to support themselves during the long waiting and searching period normally required before a job is found. Most will list themselves with a casting agency that will help them find a part as an extra or a bit player, either in theater or film. These agencies keep names on file along with photographs and descriptions of the actors' features and experience, and if a part comes along that may be suitable, they contact the appropriate person. Very often, however, names are added to their lists only when the number of people in a particular physical category is low. For instance, the agency may not have enough athletic young women on their roster, and if the applicant happens to fit this description, her name is added.

To learn more about breaking into this career, you might also consider visiting the SAG Web site (http://www.sag.org/content/getting-started-actor-faq) to read the online publication *Getting Started as an Actor*.

WHERE CAN I GO FROM HERE?

Many film and television actors get their start in commercials or by appearing in government and commercially sponsored public service announcements, films, and programs. Other actors join the afternoon soap operas and continue on to evening programs.

New actors normally start in bit parts and have only a few lines to speak, if any. Actors advance by being cast in larger supporting roles and then, perhaps, a starring role in an independent movie, with advancement to the ranks of leading actor or actress an option for some professionals. Only a very small number of actors ever reach that pinnacle, however.

Screen Actors Guild Membership by Category, June 2008

Television actors: 49,889

Theatrical/motion picture actors: 48,835

Voice-over actors: 25,796

Commercial actors: 24,259

Background actors: 22,990

Dancers: 12,556

Singers: 10,306

Stunt professionals: 7,745

Young performers (minors): 5,362

Puppeteers: 1,047

Source: Screen Actors Guild

Some actors eventually go into related occupations and become drama coaches, drama teachers, producers, stage directors, motion picture directors, television directors, radio directors, stage managers, casting directors, or artist and repertoire managers. Others may combine one or more of these functions while continuing their career as an actor.

WHAT ARE THE SALARY RANGES?

The wage scale for actors is largely controlled through bargaining agreements reached by various unions in negotiations with producers. These agreements normally control the minimum salaries, hours of work permitted per week, and other conditions of employment. In addition, each artist enters into a separate contract that may provide for higher salaries.

In 2008 the minimum daily salary of any member of SAG in a speaking role was $759 (or $2,634 for a five-day workweek). Motion picture actors may also receive additional payments known as residuals as part of their guaranteed salary. Many motion picture actors receive residuals whenever films, TV shows, and TV commercials in which they appear are rerun, sold for TV exhibition, or put on DVD. Residuals often exceed the actors' original salary and account for about one-third of all actors' income.

According to the U.S. Department of Labor, actors employed in the motion picture and video industries had mean hourly earnings of $29.05 in 2008. The department also reported the lowest paid 10 percent earned less than $7.99 an hour, while the highest paid 10 percent made more than $80.00.

The annual earnings of film and television actors are affected by frequent periods of unemployment. According to SAG, most of its members earn less than $7,500 a year from acting jobs. Unions offer health, welfare, and pension funds for members working over a set number of weeks per year. Some actors are eligible for paid vacation and sick time, depending on the work contract.

In all fields, well-known actors have salary rates above the minimums, and the salaries of the few top stars are many times higher. Actors in television series may earn tens of thousands of dollars per week, while a few may earn as much as $1 million or more per week. Salaries for these actors vary considerably and are negotiated individually. In film, top stars may earn as much as $20 million per film, and, after receiving a percentage of the gross earned by the film, these stars can earn far, far more.

Until recent years, female film stars tended to earn lower salaries than their male counterparts; the emergence of stars such as Julia Roberts, Jodie Foster, Nicole Kidman, Angelina Jolie, Reese Witherspoon, and others has started to reverse that trend. The average annual earnings for all motion picture actors, however, are usually low for all but the best-known performers because of the periods of unemployment.

WHAT IS THE JOB OUTLOOK?

Employment for actors is expected to grow about as fast as the average for all careers through 2016, according to the U.S. Department of Labor. There are a number of reasons for this. The growth of satellite and cable television in the past decade has created a demand for more actors, especially as cable networks produce more and more of their own programs and films. The rise of home entertainment options (such as direct-for-Web movies, mobile content produced for cell phones or other portable electronic devices, and DVD and online rentals) has also created new acting jobs, as more and more films are made strictly for the home market.

Despite the growth in opportunities, there are many more actors than there are roles, and this is likely to remain true for years to come. This is the case in all areas of the arts, and even those who are employed are normally employed during only a small portion of the year. Many actors must supplement their income by working other jobs as secretaries, waiters, or taxi drivers, for example. Almost all performers are members of more than one union in order to take advantage of various opportunities as they become available.

It should be recognized that of the 70,000 or so actors in the United States today, an average of only about 10,500 are employed at any one time. Of these, few are able to support themselves on their earnings from acting, and fewer still will ever achieve stardom. Most actors work for many years before becoming known, and most of these do not rise above supporting roles. The vast majority of actors, meanwhile, are still looking for the right break. There are many more applicants in all areas than there are positions. As with most careers in the arts, people enter this career out of a love and desire for acting.

Animators

SUMMARY

Definition
Animators are artists who design the cartoons that appear in movies, television shows, and commercials.

Alternative Job Titles
Motion cartoonists, multimedia artists

Salary Range
$31,570 to $56,330 to $100,390+

Educational Requirements
High school diploma; some postsecondary training highly recommended

Certification or Licensing
None available

Employment Outlook
Much faster than the average

High School Subjects
Art
Computer science

Personal Interests
Computers
Drawing
Entertaining/performing
Film and television

Sometimes it takes an extraordinary effort to break into the animation industry, especially with top employers. But the extra effort can pay off. And if you don't believe it, just listen to animator Michel Gagné's story of how he broke into the business. "I was interested in animation at an early age," he recalls. "I started doing my own animated experiments at the age of 14 or so, using a Super-8 camera. As I finished high school, I saw *The Secret of Nimh* and made my mind up that I was going to work for Don Bluth, the director of the film" [and a pioneer in the animation industry].

"I applied to the classical animation program at Sheridan College in Canada and was accepted. After my second year there, I got my first industry job at a studio in Ottawa called Atkinson Film Arts. I was an animator on a TV special called *For Better or for Worse: The Bestest Present.*

"Following that project, I returned to Sheridan College for a third year and made a short film called *A Touch of Deceit.* As soon as the film was completed, I flew to California and showed up at the doorstep of Don Bluth Studios. When I asked to meet Don in person, I was told 'No' and asked to leave the premise. I begged the secretary to take the videocassette of my film and show it to Don. After several minutes of begging, she took the video and told me that she'd see what she could do but to not expect anything. Disappointed, but not beaten, I flew back to Toronto where I immediately got a job at a small commercial studio called Light Box. Two weeks later, I received a phone call from John Pomeroy, the animation director at Bluth Studios. He asked me if I could start the following Monday."

WHAT DOES AN ANIMATOR DO?

Animators design the cartoons that appear in films and television shows. They also create the digital effects for many films and commercials. Making a big-budget animated film, such as *WALL-E*, *Ratatouille*, *A Bug's Life*, or *Shrek*, requires a team of many creative people. Each animator on the team works on one small part of the film. On a small production, animators may be involved in many different aspects of the project's development.

An animated film begins with a script. *Screenwriters* plan the story line, or plot, and write it with dialogue and narration. *Designers* read the script and decide how the film should look—should it be realistic, futuristic, or humorous? They then draw some of the characters and backgrounds. These designs are then passed on to a *storyboard artist* who illustrates the whole film in a series of frames, similar to a very long comic strip. Based on this storyboard, an artist can then create a detailed layout.

The most common form of animation is cell animation, but this method has changed greatly as a result of the emergence of computers. Animators examine the script, the storyboard, and the layout,

To Be a Successful Animator, You Should...

- be extremely creative
- be skilled at using animation software
- have a good sense of humor
- be observant
- be able to work well with others
- have excellent communication skills
- have flexibility in order to accommodate your employers' vision
- have a thick skin in order to accept occasional criticism
- be willing to continue to learn throughout your career
- be able to market your skills to potential employers

and begin to prepare the finished artwork frame by frame, or cell by cell. Some animators create the "key" drawings. These are the drawings that capture the characters' main expressions and gestures at important parts in the plot. Other animators called *inbetweeners* create the "in between" drawings—the drawings that fill in the spaces between one key drawing and the next. The thousands of final black-and-white cells are then scanned into a computer. Some animators forego creating on paper altogether and instead use computer software to draw directly into a computer system. In computer or digital animation, the animator creates all

All About
Queen's Counsel

In addition to working as an animator, Alex Williams also draws *Queen's Counsel*, a cartoon strip in *The (London) Times*. He details the genesis of the strip below.

Queen's Counsel began life as a cartoon strip about politicians (for a short while I had a job working for a Member of Parliament at Westminster [where the Parliament of the United Kingdom of Great Britain and Northern Ireland meets]). But I couldn't sell the strip. I think it was too similar to some TV material out there, and I didn't really understand my target audience well enough. When I became a law student I put wigs on the characters and turned them into lawyers. And because I was a student lawyer myself, this was obviously an area where I could write material that felt truthful—even autobiographical. In the early 1990s there was a fashion for lawyer jokes—mostly hate jokes really—and I found that I had tapped into a kind of a zeitgeist. In 1993 I sent the strip to three publications, and I got two offers. Since I was broke at the time, I picked the publication that paid the most—*The Times*. They publish a section about law every week, so it seemed like a good long-term fit. I've been there ever since, and I still love doing it. I also have a new collection of law cartoons that came out recently. It's titled *101 Ways to Leave the Law*, and is published by JR Books.

Visit http://www.alex-williams.com and http://www.qccartoon.com to learn more about Alex Williams and *Queen's Counsel*.

solves. Animators are relying increasingly on computers in various areas of production. Computers are used to color animation art, whereas formerly every frame was painted by hand. Computers also help animators create special effects and even entire films. (One program, Macromedia's Flash, has given rise to an entire Internet cartoon subculture.)

In stop-motion animation, an object, such as a clay creature or doll, is photographed, moved slightly, and photographed again. The process is repeated hundreds of thousands of times. Movies, such as *Chicken Run*, were animated this way.

Other people who work in animation are *prop designers*, who create objects used in animated films, and *layout artists*, who visualize and create the world that cartoon characters inhabit.

Most animators work in large cities where movie and television studios are located. They generally work in well-lit, comfortable environments. Staff animators work a standard 40-hour workweek but may occasionally be expected to work evenings and weekends to meet deadlines. Freelance animators have erratic schedules, and the number of hours they work may depend on how much money they want to earn or how much work they can find. They often work evenings and weekends but are not required to be at work during regular office hours.

Animators can be frustrated by employers who curtail their creativity, asking them to follow instructions that are contrary to what they would most like to do. Many freelance animators spend a lot of time working alone at home, but animators have more opportunities to interact with other people than most working artists.

the images directly on the computer screen. Computer programs can create effects like shadows, reflections, distortions, and dis-

WHAT IS IT LIKE TO BE AN ANIMATOR?

Michel Gagné is a four-time Annie-nominated (*Osmosis Jones*, *The Iron Giant*, *Quest for Camelot*, and *Prelude to Eden)* animator who is based in Bellingham, Washington. "I studied animation at Sheridan College School of Visual Arts in Ontario, Canada, and began my professional animation career in 1985. Through the years I've worked for Don Bluth Studios, Warner Bros., Disney, Pixar, Cartoon Network, and Nickelodeon on more than 20 feature films, including *The Iron Giant*, *Osmosis Jones*, and *Ratatouille*. I continue to be involved in the animation industry in various capacities, including character design, special effects animation, production design, and conceptual art. I also have an active independent career creating short films, books, comics, and various other projects.

"As an animator," he continues, "I love the fact that I can utilize my creativity and talent on a daily basis. I love seeing my creations materialize on the screen. I love the friendships I've made and continue to make on all the various projects I'm involved with. Working in a community of amazing artists is challenging and inspiring at the same time. Making a living at something you love is a true blessing." Michel says that there are a few drawbacks to working as an animator. "It's hard to keep making a steady paycheck as the work is usually on a per project basis," he explains. "Deadlines can often mean long hours of intense work. I should also mention that it's easy to get out of shape working at a desk all day."

One of Michel's most memorable moments as an animator came when he worked on the movie *Osmosis Jones*. "I came up with an idea for the opening titles. I pitched the idea to the directors and producer but was told that, most likely, the Farrelly brothers (who were directing the live-action sequences in the movie) would have their own team handling that part of the movie. Undeterred, I decided to go ahead and produce the sequence on my own time and without permission. When the executives at Warner Bros. saw what I had done, they applauded and quickly integrated my sequence in the final movie."

"I grew up with animation," says Alex Williams, an animator and cartoonist based in London and Los Angeles. "The main influence on my career has always been my father, animator Richard Williams [a legendary animator who has won two Oscars]. Dad is something of a workaholic and many of my earliest memories were of him drawing scenes from his film *The Thief and the Cobbler*. I continue to be inspired by his work. But for him, I doubt I would even be in this business. As well as animation I also do a cartoon strip (*Queen's Counsel*) in *The* (London) *Times,* which is pretty heavily influenced by cartoonists like Garry Trudeau and Jules Feiffer. I also hugely admire Posy Simmonds's work; her graphic novels are wonderful. Other than that, I did briefly become a lawyer in my mid 20s, but it didn't stick, and I soon went back to animation.

"The best thing about the business," he elaborates, "is forging relationships with really creative and interesting people. I loved working for Brad Bird [a winner of two Oscars for animation] on *The Iron Giant*. He is such a talented director and made me look at the medium in a whole new way. He has a huge enthusiasm for animation and forces you to look very carefully at your work and the kind of choices you make. There are also a couple of story artists I love to work with—people I can call up and spitball ideas. Actually, I have a whole network of people I bounce ideas off. It's a great medium with so many smart people working in it."

Alex says that another exciting aspect of his work is getting the opportunity to work on great projects. "I am very proud to have worked on *The Lion King*, *Who Framed Roger Rabbit?*, *The Iron Giant,* and *Harry Potter*. On the down side, I travel more than I would like to. I have worked in the United States, Canada, London, Germany, Denmark, and Japan. There is also a level of insecurity in the business that never really goes away, since so much of it is project based. You can feel it at the award ceremonies. Whenever anyone picks up an award and makes a speech, what they really want to say is 'thank God I'll be working for the next five years.'"

DO I HAVE WHAT IT TAKES TO BE AN ANIMATOR?

You must be very creative to be successful as an animator. In addition to having artistic talent, you must be able to generate ideas, although it is not unusual for animators to collaborate with writers for ideas. You must have a good sense of humor (or a good dramatic sense) and an observant eye to detect people's distinguishing characteristics and society's interesting attributes or incongruities.

You also need to be flexible. Because your art is commercial, you must be willing to accommodate your employers' desires if you are to build a broad clientele and earn

---

Take a Visit to the *Insanely Twisted Shadow Planet*

● ● ● ● ● ● ●

In addition to working as an animator, Michel Gagné also creates computer games. He is currently working on one called *Insanely Twisted Shadow Planet (ITSP)*. Below, he tells readers a little more about the game.

ITSP is an epic side-scroller I'm producing with my partners at Fuelcell studios. The initial inspiration for *ITSP* was a series of interstitials called *Insanely Twisted Shadow Puppets* I created back in 2005. That was the starting point, but the game has evolved way beyond that. Some of the best games of all time strike an excellent balance between action and problem solving, and *ITSP* aims to bring those elements together with very unique art style combined with feature-film quality animation.

Visit http://www.gagneint.com and http://www.insanelytwisted.com to learn more about Michel Gagné and *ITSP*.

---

a decent living. You must be able to take suggestions and rejections gracefully.

You should also have extensive knowledge of animation software and be willing to continue to learn throughout your career since animation and computer technology change almost constantly. "Employment in animation can be difficult if your skills are not up to par," says Michel Gagné. "It's important to be versatile and familiar with a variety of computer software. The field is quite competitive, and you have to be very good in order to make a living at it."

HOW DO I BECOME AN ANIMATOR?

Education

High School

In high school, take art, of course, as well as computer classes. Math classes, such as algebra and geometry, will also be helpful. If your school offers animation and graphic design classes, be sure to take those.

Postsecondary Training

You do not need a college degree to become an animator, but there are a number of animation programs offered at universities and art institutes across the country. You may choose to pursue an associate's, bachelor's, a master's of fine art, or a Ph.D. in computer animation, digital art, graphic design, or art. Some of today's top computer animators are self-taught or have learned their skills on the job.

"Obviously a good general training in art and design is essential," says Alex Williams. "I would also advise any student to learn as many different software packages as possible. The business is almost wholly digital now, and it's not likely to go back. You need to know Maya and PhotoShop at a minimum. Final Cut, Premiere, and After Effects are all very useful. The more different software packages you can handle, the more useful you are to any company, especially if you can get under the hood and fix technical problems. Couple that with a great artistic training and you will never be out of work."

Certification or Licensing

No certification or licensing is available for this profession.

Internships and Volunteerships

Larger employers, such as Pixar, offer apprenticeships or internships. To enter these programs, applicants must be attending a college animation program. Interns at Pixar must have completed their junior year of college, be a current graduate student, or have graduated during the year the internship begins. Program participants might work as camera and staging-artist interns, who "create sequences of shots that convey the story through the application of traditional filmmaking principles in a 3-D computer graphics environment." Other internship options at Pixar are available in technical direction, production management, story, marketing, engineering, and editorial.

Volunteering with a local animation or film production company is the next best thing to landing an internship. This experience will give you a great introduction to the field and help you make valuable contacts in the field.

WHO WILL HIRE ME?

"My first paid work was as an inbetweener on the 1988 feature film *Who Framed Roger Rabbit?*," recalls Alex Williams. "I did inbetweens for a few months until I got promoted to assistant animator. It was a wonderful project because we could all see what a huge breakthrough it was going to be, a genuinely innovative film. [My] dad was directing the animation so I had an inside track. One of the best ways to break into the business is to try to find a large project that is rapidly crewing up. Studios get less fussy about portfolios when they have to hire 150

And the Oscar Goes to . . .

The following animated feature films have won Oscars in recent years:

2008: *WALL-E* (Andrew Stanton)

2007: *Ratatouille* (Brad Bird)

2006: *Happy Feet* (George Miller)

2005: *Wallace & Gromit in The Curse of the Were-Rabbit* (Nick Park and Steve Box)

2004: *The Incredibles* (Brad Bird)

2003: *Finding Nemo* (Andrew Stanton)

2002: *Spirited Away* (Hayao Miyazaki)

2001: *Shrek* (Aron Warner)

For more information on animated feature films that have been nominated for or won Academy Awards, visit http://www.oscars.org/awardsdatabase.

One new way up-and-coming animators have made themselves known to the animating community is by attracting an audience on the World Wide Web. A portfolio of well-executed Web cartoons can help an animator build his reputation and acquire jobs. Some animators, such as the Brothers Chaps (creators of http://homestarrunner.com), have even been able to turn their creations into a profitable business.

WHERE CAN I GO FROM HERE?

Animators' success, like that of other artists, depends on how much the public likes their work. Very successful animators work for well-known film companies and other employers at the best wages; some become well known to the public.

WHAT ARE THE SALARY RANGES?

Multimedia artists and animators who were employed in the motion picture and video industry earned annual mean salaries of $56,330 in 2008, according to the U.S. Department of Labor. Salaries for all multimedia artists and animators ranged from less than $31,570 to more than $100,390.

Self-employed artists do not receive fringe benefits such as paid vacations, sick leave, health insurance, or pension benefits. Those who are salaried employees of companies do typically receive such benefits.

people in a couple of months. Nowadays there is almost always a big project crewing up somewhere around the world."

Approximately 87,000 animators and multimedia artists are employed in the United States. Employers of animators include producers, movie studios, and television networks. In addition, a number of these artists are self-employed, working on a freelance basis. Some do animation on the Web as a part-time business or a hobby. Others work for computer game companies.

WHAT IS THE JOB OUTLOOK?

Employment for animators and multimedia artists is expected to grow much faster than the average for all careers through 2016, according to the U.S. Department of Labor. The growing trend of sophisticated special effects in motion pictures should create opportunities at industry effects houses such as Sony Pictures Imageworks, DreamQuest Software, Industrial Light & Magic, and DreamWorks SKG. Furthermore, growing processor and Internet connection speeds are creating a Web animation renaissance. Demand is also increasing as animation is increasingly growing in mobile technologies and in non-entertainment–based fields such as scientific research or design services. Because so many creative and talented people are drawn to this field, however, competition for jobs will be strong.

Animated features are not just for children anymore. Much of the animation today is geared toward an adult audience. Interactive computer games, animated films, network and cable television, and the Internet are among the many employment sources for talented animators. More than 60 percent of all visual artists are self-employed, but freelance work can be hard to come by, and many freelancers earn little until they acquire experience and establish a good reputation. Competition for work will be keen; those with an undergraduate or advanced degree in art or film will be in demand. Experience in action drawing and computers is a must.

And the Annie Goes to . . .

The Annie Awards are the animation industry's highest honor. They are presented by the International Animated Film Society, ASIFA-Hollywood. The following animated feature films have won Annies in recent years:

2008: *King Fu Panda*

2007: *Ratatouille*

2006: *Cars*

2005: *Wallace & Gromit in The Curse of the Were-Rabbit*

2004: *The Incredibles*

2003: *Finding Nemo*

2002: *Spirited Away*

2001: *Shrek*

2000: *Toy Story 2*

For more information on animated feature films that have been nominated for or won Annie Awards, visit http://annieawards.org.

Film Directors

SUMMARY

Definition
The director coordinates the elements of a film and is responsible for its overall style and quality.

Alternative Job Titles
Filmmakers

Salary Range
$30,250 to $64,430 to $500,000+

Educational Requirements
High school diploma; bachelor's degree highly recommended

Certification or Licensing
None available

Employment Outlook
About as fast as the average

High School Subjects
Art
English
Theater

Personal Interests
Entertaining/performing
Film and television
Theater

"Hands down, the favorite movies I've directed have been the cheapest," says John Putch, an independent filmmaker. *"Mojave Phone Booth* (http://www.mojavephonebooth.net) and *Route 30* (http://www.route30movie.com) cost around $60,000 each. They remain my most creative and rewarding experiences ever. Not unlike the freedom I had making Super-8s when I was a kid, these movies left the expense and ego at the door and were a pure creative pleasure. The only obstacle to making garage films is you have to do 50 things at once. You have no help so you have to be very organized and clever in your approach to telling the story."

WHAT DOES A FILM DIRECTOR DO?

"A director is the author of the motion picture," says John. "He or she takes the script and is responsible for interpreting it and telling the story in the correct tone and style set forth in the screenplay. Putting the cast and creative crew together in order to focus the point of view is a very important part of this job."

Film directors have the ultimate responsibility for the tone and quality of the films they direct. They interpret the stories and narratives presented in scripts and coordinate the filming of their interpretations. They are involved in preproduction,

production, and postproduction. They audition, select, and rehearse the acting crew; they work on matters regarding set designs, musical scores, and costumes; and they decide on details such as where scenes should be shot (on a soundstage, on location in a rain forest, etc.), what backgrounds might be needed, and how special effects (such as computer-generated imagery, car crashes, or explosions) could be employed.

Film directors are often assisted by *casting directors*, who are in charge of auditioning performers. The casting director pays close attention to attributes of the performers such as quality of voice, physical appearance, and acting ability and experience, and then presents to the director a list of suitable candidates for each role.

One of the most important aspects of the film director's job is working with the performers. Directors have their own styles of extracting accurate emotion and performance from cast members, but they must be dedicated to this goal.

Two common techniques that categorize directors' styles are montage and mise-en-scene. *Montage directors* are concerned with using editing techniques to produce desired results; they consider it important to focus on how individual shots will work when pieced together with others. Consider Alfred Hitchcock, who directed the production of one scene in *Psycho*, for example, by filming discrete shots in a bathroom and then editing in dialogue, sound effects, and music to create tremendous suspense. *Mise-en-scene*

directors are more concerned with the pre-editing phase, focusing on the elements of angles, movement, and design one shot at a time, as Orson Welles did in many of his movies. Many directors combine elements of both techniques in their work.

The film's *production designer* creates set design concepts and chooses shoot locations. He or she meets with the filmmaker and producer to set budgets and schedules and then accordingly coordinates the construction of sets. Research is done on the period in which the film is to take place (for example, Elizabethan England, pre-Columbian South America, or New York City in the year 2500), and experts are consulted to help create appropriate architectural and environmental styles. The production designer also is often involved in design ideas for costumes, makeup and hairstyles, photographic effects, and other elements of the film's production. Production designers are assisted in this work by *art directors*. Low-budget films may just have an art director who handles the tasks of production designers.

The *director of photography*, or *cinematographer*, organizes and implements the actual camera work. Together with the filmmaker, he or she interprets scenes and decides on appropriate camera motion to achieve desired results. The director of photography determines the amounts of natural and artificial lighting required for each shot and such technical factors as the type of film to be used, camera angles and distance, depth of field, and focus.

To Be a Successful Film Director, You Should...

- be able to handle stress and meet deadlines
- be a leader and be able to make intelligent snap decisions
- be organized
- have excellent communication skills
- be able to handle occasional criticism and second-guessing from coworkers
- be ambitious and willing to work very hard to attain success

Motion pictures are usually filmed out of sequence, meaning that the ending might be shot first and scenes from the middle of the story might not be filmed until the end of production. Directors are responsible for scheduling each day's sequence of scenes; they coordinate filming so that scenes using the same set and performers will be filmed together. In addition to conferring with the production designer and the director of photography, filmmakers meet with technicians and crew members to advise on and approve final scenery, lighting, props, and other necessary equipment. They are also involved with final approval of costumes, choreography, and music.

After all the scenes have been shot, postproduction begins. The director works with *picture and sound editors* to cut apart and piece together the final reels. The *film editor* shares the director's vision about the picture and assembles shots according to that overall idea, synchronizing film with voice and sound tracks produced by the sound editor and music editor.

While the director supervises all major aspects of film production, various assistants help throughout the process. In a less creative position than the filmmaker's, the *first assistant director* organizes various practical matters involved during the shooting of each scene. The *second assistant director* is a coordinator who works as a liaison among the production office, the first assistant director, and the performers. The *second unit director* coordinates sequences such as scenic inserts and action shots that do not involve the main acting crew.

The work of the director is considered glamorous and prestigious, and of course directors have been known to become quite famous. But directors work under great stress, meeting deadlines, staying within budgets, and resolving problems among staff. "Nine-to-five" definitely does not describe a day in the life of a director; 16-hour days (and more) are not uncommon. "When you are directing, the hours are extremely long," says film director Laurie Agard. "There are often 20-hour days where you have to be very monofocused, and your friends and family have to be very forgiving!" Because directors are ultimately responsible for so much, schedules often dictate that they become immersed in their work around the clock, from preproduction to final cut. Nonetheless, those able to make it in the industry find their work to be extremely enjoyable and satisfying.

WHAT IS IT LIKE TO BE A FILM DIRECTOR?

John Putch is an independent film director who is best known for indie favorites *Valerie Flake, Bachelorman, Mojave Phone Booth*, and *Route 30*. John has also directed television shows such as *Scrubs, My Name Is Earl, Ugly Betty*, and *Grounded for Life*, as well as multiple television movies and miniseries. (Visit his Web site, http://www.putchfilms.com, to learn more about his career and films.) "I grew up in a show business family," John says. "My father had his own summer stock theater in Pennsylvania, and my family all worked there from birth until my father's death in 1983. When I was a kid, he put a Super-8 movie camera in my hands and encouraged me to make films. I was hooked. I spent my weekends and free time making films with my friends, rather than skateboarding at the mall. And because all my folks' friends were professional actors, I was able to convince them to be in my little films. I had great casts even in my Super-8s."

After a successful career as an actor in the 1970s and '80s, John started making short films with a 16mm camera using money he earned as an actor. "I was very interested in TV and film directing as a career," he recalls. "I shopped and self-promoted my shorts to anyone who would listen. Then I got a break from low-budget producer Andrew Stevens, who hired me to direct a family comedy. He was only concerned with one thing: could I shoot it in 12 days. Naturally I said yes. That movie led to five more for Andrew over the next three years. I built my reel and kept trying to get work making films for other people. In 1998, my wife and I mortgaged our house and made a film of our own called *Valerie Flake*. The film successfully premiered at the Sundance Film Festival in 1999 and helped start me off as a legitimate director. I've been building on that professional foundation ever since."

Laurie Agard is an award-winning independent director, writer, and producer. (Visit http://www.laurieagard.com to learn more about her work.) Laurie says she became a director because working as a writer was too solitary of an endeavor. "I craved the camaraderie of a larger creative community," she recalls. "My scripts were optioned by larger studios and then never made. So I formed my own production company and wrote, produced, and directed my first film, a children's comedy, *Frog and Wombat*, which has thus far been my favorite film project. A large part of a small community all came together to create this indie film and a wonderful, almost palpable, creative energy was generated. Nothing beats that. The film was edited on an ancient 35mm flatbed in a supply closet in the Saul Zaentz Film Center while *The English Patient* was being edited on the other four floors of the building,

And the Oscar Goes to . . .

The following directors have won the Oscar for best director in recent years:

2008: Danny Boyle (*Slumdog Million-aire*)

2007: Joel Coen and Ethan Coen (*No Country for Old Men*)

2006: Martin Scorsese (*The Departed*)

2005: Ang Lee (*Brokeback Mountain*)

2004: Clint Eastwood (*Million Dollar Baby*)

2003: Peter Jackson (*The Lord of the Rings: The Return of the King*)

2002: Roman Polanski (*The Pianist*)

2001: Ron Howard (*A Beautiful Mind*)

2000: Steven Soderbergh (*Traffic*)

For more information on Academy Award-winning directors, visit http://www.oscars.org/awardsdatabase.

vision that allows you to inspire others to help you create a successful and entertaining film. John Putch says that the most successful directors "have an opinion and a point of view and confidence when making creative decisions."

"Successful directors have to be persistent, persistent, and more persistent," says Laurie Agard. "You have to remember that every moment is about 'telling a story' and nothing else. You have to know the big picture, and you have to know how the story with each character and each scene serves the bigger story. You have to be able to understand the story not only emotionally, but also visually, musically, etc., and be able to communicate what you want in a way that other people will understand. And hopefully you inspire them to give you something even greater than you initially wanted."

HOW DO I BECOME A FILM DIRECTOR?
Education
High School

At the very least, a high school diploma, while not technically required if you wish to become a director, will still probably be indispensable to you in terms of the background and education it signifies. As is true of all artists, especially those in a medium as widely disseminated as film, you will need to have rich and varied experience in order to create works that are intelligently crafted and speak to people of many different backgrounds. In

and later my film sold in 45 territories around the world. It made its television premiere on HBO."

DO I HAVE WHAT IT TAKES TO BE A FILM DIRECTOR?

To be a successful film director, you should have strong communication and organization skills. You should also have a passion for filmmaking and a creative

high school, courses in English, art, theater, and history will give you a good foundation. Further, a high school diploma will be necessary if you decide to go on to film school. Be active in school and community drama productions, whether as a performer, set designer, or cue-card holder.

Postsecondary Training

In college and afterward, take film classes and volunteer to work on other students' films. Dedication, talent, and experience have always been indispensable to a director. No doubt it is beneficial to become aware of one's passion for film as early as possible. Woody Allen, for example, recognized early in his life the importance motion pictures held for him, but he worked as a magician, jazz clarinet player, joke writer, and stand-up comic before ever directing films. Allen took few film courses in his life.

On the other hand, many successful directors, such as Francis Ford Coppola and Martha Coolidge, have taken the formal film school route. There are more than 500 film studies programs offered by schools of higher education throughout the United States. According to the American Film Institute, the most reputable are: Columbia University in New York City, New York University, the University of California at Los Angeles (UCLA), and the University of Southern California. These schools have film professionals on their faculties and provide a very visible stage for student talent because they are located in the two film-business hot spots, California and New York. (The tuition for film programs offered elsewhere, however, tends to be much less expensive than at these schools.)

Film school offers overall formal training, providing an education in fundamental directing skills by working with student productions. Such education is rigorous, but in addition to teaching skills it provides aspiring directors with peer groups and a network of contacts with students, faculty, and guest speakers that can be of help after graduation.

The debate continues on what is more influential in a directing career: film school or personal experience. Some say that it is possible for creative people to land directing jobs without having gone through a formal program. Competition is so pervasive in the industry that even film school graduates find jobs scarce (only 5 to 10 percent of students who graduate from film schools each year find jobs in the industry).

Certification or Licensing

No certification or licensing is available for this profession.

Internships and Volunteerships

Look for any opportunity to work around film professionals—be it via a formal internship organized by your college film department or a volunteer opportunity obtained through cold-calling film production companies, independent filmmakers, or film commissions. The key is to make as many contacts as possible so you will have some job leads when it comes time to break into the industry.

Facts About the Academy Awards and Film Directors

- The first Academy Awards were held on May 16, 1929.

- The Academy Awards, often known as Oscars, are made of gold-plated britannium, a metal alloy. Each award is 13 and a half inches tall and weighs 8 and a half pounds.

- It takes approximately three to four weeks to manufacture 50 statuettes.

- Oscars were made of painted plaster for three years during World War II because of metal shortages. After the war, Oscar-winners were allowed to redeem their plaster statuettes for metal ones.

- More than 2,700 Oscars have been presented.

- John Ford, director of classic movies such as *Stagecoach*, *The Quiet Man*, and *Mister Roberts*, won four Oscars for directing—the most of any director in the history of the Academy Awards. William Wyler (*Roman Holiday*, *Ben Hur*, *Mrs. Miniver*, and *The Best Years of Our Lives*) places second with three best director Oscars.

- The oldest person awarded an Academy Award in direction was Clint Eastwood for *Million Dollar Baby* (2004). His age: 74 years, 272 days. The youngest? Norman Taurog (32 years, 260 days) for *Skippy* (1930/31).

Source: Academy of Motion Picture Arts and Sciences

WHO WILL HIRE ME?

Approximately 93,000 directors and producers are employed in the United States. Film directors are usually employed on a freelance or contractual basis. Directors find work, for example, with film studios (both major and independent), at television stations and cable networks, with record companies, through advertising agencies, and, like John Putch and Laurie Agard, through the creation of their own independent film projects.

"It's tough to go out and just get hired as a director," Laurie Agard says. "That's why I formed my own production company. I think if you love directing and want to pursue it as a career, then you have to try and get there in any way possible. Directing is not like a lot of jobs where there is a clear entry path. Nothing really leads to directing—you just have to convince someone that your vision is worth spending money on and that you can pull off creating a film based on your vision. I believe that less than 10 percent of all features are directed by women, and less than 20 percent of television is directed by women, so there are hurdles to jump, but people are jumping them! Last June, the Directors Guild of America had its first-ever event honoring its female members, and I co-directed the evening's tribute film, *A Celebration of Women Directors*. This involved three months of volunteer work, but on that project I met fellow director Betty Thomas, whom I'm currently assisting on *Alvin and The Chipmunks: The Squeakuel* for Fox 2000. Because of this I'm meeting a lot of people I normally wouldn't meet working as an independent filmmaker. I think (or hope) that if you love film and you're persistent, you just keep doing what you love and doors will open."

It is considered difficult to begin as a motion picture director. With nontraditional steps to professional status, the occupation poses challenges for those seeking employment. However, there is somewhat solid advice for those who wish to direct motion pictures.

Many current directors began their careers in other film industry professions, such as acting or writing. Consider Jodie Foster, who appeared in 30 films and dozens of television productions before she went on to direct her first motion picture at the age of 28. Obviously it helps to grow up near the heart of "Tinseltown" and to have the influence of one's family spurring you on. The support of family and friends is often cited as an essential element in shaping the confidence you need to succeed in the industry.

As mentioned earlier, film school is a breeding ground for making contacts in the industry. Often, contacts are the essential factor in getting a job; many Hollywood insiders agree that it's not what you know but who you know that will get you in. Networking often leads to good opportunities at various types of jobs in the industry. Many professionals recommend that those who want to become directors should go to Los Angeles or New York, find any industry-related job, continue to take classes, and keep their eyes and ears open for news of job openings, especially with those professionals who are admired for their talent.

A program to be aware of is the Assistant Directors Training Program of the Directors Guild of America (see "Look to the Pros" for contact information). This program provides an excellent opportunity to those without industry connections to work on film and television productions. The program is based at two locations, New York City for the East Coast Program and Sherman Oaks, California, for the West Coast Program. Trainees receive hands-on experience through placement with major studios or on television movies and series, and education through mandatory seminars. The East Coast Program requires trainees to complete at least 350 days of on-set production work over a two-year period; the West Coast Program requires 400 days over the same time span. While they are working, trainees are paid, beginning with a weekly salary of $651 in the East and $628 in the West. Once trainees have completed their program, they become freelance second assistant directors and can join the guild. The competition is extremely stiff for these positions.

Keep in mind that Hollywood is not everything. Directors work on documentaries, on television productions, and with various types of video presentations, from music to business. Many create their own independent films and distribute them on their own.

WHERE CAN I GO FROM HERE?

Advancement for film directors often comes in the form of recognition from their peers, professional film organizations, and the media. Directors who work on well-received movies receive awards

Related Jobs

• art directors

• artist-and-repertoire managers

• casting directors

• directors of photography

• film editors

• producers

• radio directors

• screenwriters

• sound editors

• stage managers

as well as further job offers. Probably the most glamorized trophy is the Academy Award: the Oscar. Oscars are awarded in more than 20 categories, including one for best achievement in directing, and are given annually at a gala to recognize the outstanding accomplishments of those in the field. (See the sidebar, "And the Oscar Goes to . . ." for a list of recent award-winning directors.) Candidates for Oscars are usually judged by their peers. Directors who have not worked on films popular enough to have made it in Hollywood should nevertheless seek recognition from reputable organizations. One such group is the National Endowment for the Arts, an independent agency of the U.S. government that supports and awards artists, including those who work in film. The endowment provides financial assistance in the form of fellowships and grants to those seen as contributing

to the excellence of arts in the country. Directors also receive awards by submitting their films to festivals, such as the Sundance Film Festival, the Cannes Film Festival, or the Chicago International Film Festival.

WHAT ARE THE SALARY RANGES?

Earnings for directors vary greatly. Most Hollywood film directors are members of the Directors Guild of America (DGA), and salaries (as well as hours of work and other employment conditions) are usually negotiated by this union. Generally, contracts provide for minimum weekly salaries. The minimum weekly salary for directors was $4,726 in 2009. This figure increases based on the cost of the picture being made. Keep in mind that because directors are freelancers, they may have no income for many weeks out of the year.

Although contracts usually provide only for the minimum rate of pay, most directors earn more, and they often negotiate extra conditions.

The U.S. Department of Labor reports that the median annual salary of film, stage, and radio directors and producers was $64,430 in 2008. Among this group, the lowest paid 10 percent earned less than $30,250, and the highest paid 25 percent earned more than $166,400.

Directors working under DGA contracts also receive paid vacation days, lodging and meals while filming, and access to pension and health insurance plans.

WHAT IS THE JOB OUTLOOK?

Employment for film directors is expected to grow about as fast as the average for all occupations through 2016, according to the U.S. Department of Labor. This optimistic forecast is based on the increasing global demand for films made in the United States, continuing U.S. demand for home video and DVD rentals, and growth in demand for content for the Internet and cell phones or other portable electronic devices. However, this field is highly competitive and turnover is high. Most positions in the motion picture industry are held on a freelance basis. As is the case with most film industry workers, directors are usually hired to work on one film at a time. After a film is completed, they must seek out new assignments.

Television offers directors a wider variety of employment opportunities, including directing sitcoms, made-for-television movies, newscasts, commercials, and music videos. The number of cable television networks is growing, and directors are needed to help create original programming to fill this void. Half of all television directors work as freelancers. This number is predicted to rise as more cable networks and production companies attempt to cut costs by hiring directors on a project-to-project basis.

Film Editors

SUMMARY

Definition
Film editors use specialized equipment and technology to turn an unedited draft of a film into a finished product.

Alternative Job Titles
Sound editors
Special-effects editors
Video editors

Salary Range
$24,640 to $50,560 to $112,410+

Educational Requirements
Some postsecondary training

Certification or Licensing
None available

Employment Outlook
About as fast as the average

High School Subjects
Art
Computer science
Theater

Personal Interests
Computers
Film and television
Theater

Film editor Patrick McMahon says that one of the most interesting and rewarding experiences of his career occurred when he edited the HBO documentary film *Baghdad ER*. "At the time, I was working on a series for Showtime called *Masters of Horror* with John Carpenter when my friend Jon Alpert called me from Baghdad, Iraq. He is a documentary filmmaker, and he just wanted to talk. He was seeing things that he was having trouble handling. When he came back to New York with the footage he asked me to come to work on the film. I was in the middle of a job, but after talking to my wife I agreed to go for two weeks. After two weeks we took what I had edited up to Sheila Nevins, who runs HBO's documentary division. After the screening we all sat around unable to speak because we were all crying. We had just watched a young soldier die. I ended up staying in New York working on the film for five more months. I did the job at a loss of pay (which was tough because I had two kids in college), but it felt like the right thing to do. I ended up being nominated for an Emmy for that film even though I went into it for non-career motives."

WHAT DOES A FILM EDITOR DO?

Film editors work closely with producers and directors throughout an entire project. They assist in the earliest phase, called preproduction, and during the production phase, when actual filming occurs. Their skills are in the greatest demand during postproduction, the completion of primary filming. During preproduction, in meetings with producers, editors learn about the objectives of the film or video. If the project is a feature-length motion picture, the editor must understand the story line. The producer may explain the larger scope of the project so that the editor knows the best way to approach the work when it is time to edit the film. In consultation with the director, editors may discuss the best way to accurately present the screenplay or script. They may discuss different settings, scenes, or camera angles even before filming or taping begins. With this kind of preparation, film editors are ready to practice their craft as soon as the production phase is complete.

Feature-length films, of course, take much more time to edit than television commercials. Therefore, some editors may spend months on one project, while others may work on several shorter projects simultaneously.

Film editors are usually the initial decision makers when it comes to choosing which segments will stay in as they are, which segments will be cut, or which may need to be redone. Editors look at the quality of the segment, its dramatic value, and its relationship to other segments. They then arrange the segments in an order that creates the most effective finished product. They rely on the script and notes from the director, along with their natural sense of how a scene should progress, in putting together the film, commercial, or show. They look for the best shots, camera angles, line deliveries, and continuity.

Some editors specialize in certain areas of film. *Sound editors* work on the soundtracks of television programs or motion pictures. They often keep libraries of sounds that they reuse for various projects. These include natural sounds, such as thunder or raindrops, animal noises (such as the roar of a lion or birds singing), motor sounds, or musical interludes. Some sound editors specialize in music and may have training in music theory or performance. Others work with sound effects. They may use unusual objects, machines, or computer-generated noise-makers to create a desired sound for a film.

Film editors do most of their work in film studios or at postproduction companies using editing equipment. They typically work in a small, cramped studio office or editing room. Working hours vary widely depending on the film. During the filming of a commercial, for instance, film editors may be required to work overtime, at night, or on weekends to meet a project deadline. Many feature-length films are kept on tight production schedules that allow for steady work unless filming gets behind.

During filming, film editors may be asked to be on hand at the filming location. Locations may be outdoors or in other cities, and travel is occasionally required. More often, however, the film editor works in the studio.

To Be a Successful Film Editor, You Should...

- be creative
- be able to work well with others
- have strong communication skills
- have comprehensive knowledge of editing techniques
- have a feel for the narrative form
- have good computer skills
- be highly organized
- have good time-management skills and be able to work under deadline pressure
- be willing to continue to learn throughout your career

WHAT IS IT LIKE TO BE A FILM EDITOR?

Patrick McMahon began his career in 1972 as an apprentice film editor on a Woody Allen film. He advanced to assistant a year later and became a full-time editor in the late 1970s. He spent 23 years working mostly in New York and has spent the last 15 years in Los Angeles. Patrick has edited television series, miniseries, movies, feature films, and documentaries. (You can learn more about his career by visiting http://www.imdb.com/name/nm0573073.) "I grew up in a working class family in British Columbia and thought I might be a professional hockey player," he says. "I had no inclination toward the film business, but when I met and married an American girl she introduced me to a friend of hers who was a film editor. I thought he was a cool guy, and he seemed happy with his work. When I moved to New York I started looking for work as an apprentice editor, hoping someday to become an assistant, but not really thinking about graduating to editor. A few years later I knew I had found my calling.

"The responsibilities of an editor vary from show to show or film to film," he continues, "but there are two main ones. The editor is the creative supervisor of postproduction. The director is the boss, but in most cases he or she relies heavily on the editor. The other is to put the film together. I take the dailies (what has been shot the day before) and cut them as precisely as I can from the moment I get them. I try for the final cut on the first pass, because I know there will be several more passes and the further along the assembly is in the beginning, the further you and the director can take it before you start burning out on the footage and getting too used to things as they are. I also do as much as I can to clean up sound and put music to the assembled cut. I carry a drive filled with scores from other films that I have used for temp music in the past, so when my cut is presented it feels like a movie, not a work in progress. In today's computerized world, that is expected of the editor."

Vanick Moradian has been a film editor for more than 20 years, and has edited many films and television shows including *Who's Your Caddy?*, *Tortilla Heaven*, *Half Past Dead*, and *The Pursuit of Hap-*

pyness. (Visit http://www.imdb.com/ name/nm0602395 to learn more about his career.) "The idea of becoming a filmmaker first entered my mind when I was 14 and saw *Close Encounters of the Third Kind*," he recalls. "I saw it three times in theaters, and I was thoroughly fascinated by it. But I didn't get serious about a career in film until my second year in junior college. Once I made the decision, I knew exactly what I had to do. I attended the University of Southern California's School of Cinematic Arts. During my first semester, I was quickly exposed to all facets of filmmaking. Cinematography and editing were the classes that grabbed my attention right away. There was a technical aspect to both that I found very engaging. Being technical comes naturally to me. But after I edited my first film, I realized that editing was more than just cutting out the bad parts and leaving the good ones in. An entire world opened up to me that I hadn't noticed before. It was as if I had just learned a new language. Ultimately, what tipped the scale for me in choosing between editing and cinematography was the fact that I found editing to be more suited to my personality. It is more solitary, and I do my best work when I'm alone. I could still express myself and be creative without dealing with all the madness of production."

Randy Carter has been a film editor for more than 15 years. He is currently a freelance editor, and he mainly works on cable TV movies and television shows and direct-to-DVD features. Randy's work can be seen on the SyFy Channel, Lifetime, and other cable channels. Some of his editing credits include *An Acciden-*

tal Christmas, *Bachelorman*, and the TV series *Dante's Cove*. (You can learn more about his career by visiting http://www. imdb.com/name/nm0003739.) "I always knew that I wanted to be in the film business," he says, "but like everyone else, I assumed that I wanted to direct. When I was an undergraduate, I completed a thesis project where I wore every hat imaginable (writer, director, producer, editor, director of photography, etc.). The most fun I had was working in the editing room, putting all of the pieces together. When I showed the completed project to my film professor, he was pretty brutal in his criticisms of most aspects of my show, but said that he thought it was one of the best-edited projects he had seen in his 20 years as a film professor. It didn't take a rocket scientist to figure out that if I enjoyed this aspect of the filmmaking process the most, and apparently had some skills in this area, that this is the job I should pursue. When I went to film school I had the opportunity to direct a short, as well as edit a different short. These experiences sealed the deal for me in terms of what I wanted to do—edit."

Randy says that the most rewarding part of his job is seeing someone's vision come to life on the screen. "As film editors, we are basically storytellers," he says, "and it's my job to make sure that the story is told clearly and as interestingly as possible. When everything comes together correctly, there's nothing better. It really is a dream job for me, and I wouldn't prefer doing anything else in the world."

Randy says that being an editor can be very challenging at times. "Oftentimes," he explains, "things are not shot as you would like them, or performances are not as you would prefer. Editing is like putting together a jigsaw puzzle, but sometimes

not all the pieces are there, and you still have to make the picture make sense. It's at these times—when you're able to devise a way around a missing piece of the puzzle and still tell the story that's trying to be told—that I feel the most satisfied with my work."

DO I HAVE WHAT IT TAKES TO BE A FILM EDITOR?

Editors must be able to work coopera-tively with other creative people when editing a film. They should remain open to suggestions and guidance while also maintaining their confidence in the pres-ence of other professionals. "One of the most important components of the job is handling people," says Patrick McMahon. "The editing room is a very small and intense place and the editor must work with sound editors, composers, directors, producers, and studio and network exec-utives in that cramped space. Often they are at odds, and how you handle the dif-ferences between parties can determine the degree of your success."

There are also times when editors work alone in the editing room for hours without interacting with others. "Edit-ing is often solitary work," says Vanick Moradian. "You're in a room all day in front of the computer. If that doesn't match your personality, then it's prob-ably not the right line of work for you. But if you love being creative, then as an editor you will have plenty of opportu-nities to manipulate images and sound in a creative manner. And with today's sophisticated tools you can really push the boundaries."

Advice from a Pro
● ● ● ● ● ● ● ● ● ● ●

Patrick McMahon offers the following advice for aspiring film editors:

The advice that I would give to high school students interested in the editing field comes from my own experience. When I started as a working-class, 22-year-old with two years of junior college to my credit, all I wanted to do was to keep the people I was working for happy. I was thrilled to get coffee and lunch for everyone. I arrived to work every morn-ing a half hour before everyone else so I could clean and prepare the room. I wasn't thinking, like people who have been to film school often do, that I was already an editor and that menial chores were beneath me. This endeared me to the editors and directors that I worked for. I didn't do it for that reason, I was just happy to be there, but hindsight tells me that moviemaking is a team job and there is a food chain that goes way up. You always have someone that you are serving, and you can't lose track of that. People will appreciate your efforts and move you up just to keep you around if you make their job easier. If you act impa-tient and ask for advancement, you won't be around long.

The other advice I would offer is that everyone wants to be in the film busi-ness, so you have to be persistent. You might get rejected a lot, but if you keep on going you can succeed. When I was looking for my first job, I had an editor tell me, "Don't worry. A thousand people can say no, but only one has to say yes."

A successful editor has an understanding of the history of film and television and a feel for the narrative form in general. "The film editor at the most basic level," says Randy Carter, "is responsible for taking all of the material that is shot for a project and assembling it in the proper order, picking from the various takes and angles that have been photographed. In addition, and far more complex, the film editor is responsible, working in conjunction with the director and/or producers, for setting the pace of the storytelling that is at the heart of filmmaking. Knowing *when* to cut is just as important, if not more important, then knowing *what* to cut to."

Computer skills are also important and will help you to learn new technology in the field. You may be required to join a union to do this work, depending on the studio.

HOW DO I BECOME A FILM EDITOR?
Education
High School
Take broadcast journalism and other media and communications courses to gain some practical experience in video editing. Because film editing requires a creative perspective along with technical skills, you should take English, speech, theater, and other courses that will allow you to develop your writing skills. Art and photography classes will involve you with visual media. Because of the technical nature of film editing, take computer classes to become com-

fortable and confident using basic computer programs.

Postsecondary Training
Some film studios require editors to have a bachelor's degree. Yet actual on-the-job experience is the best guarantee of securing lasting employment. Degrees in liberal arts fields are preferred, but courses in cinematography and audiovisual techniques help film editors get started in their work. You may choose to pursue a degree in such subjects as English, journalism, theater, or film. Community and two-year colleges often offer courses in the study of film as literature. Some of these colleges also teach film editing. Universities with departments of broadcast journalism offer courses in broadcast editing and also may have contacts at local television stations. The American Film Institute's Web site (http://www.afi.edu) offers listings of high schools with film courses and other resources for teachers and students.

"Many people will tell you that film school is no longer a necessity to work in the film business, and I suppose there is some truth to that," says Randy Carter. "The tools (Final Cut Pro, Adobe Premiere, etc.) of an editor have become much more readily available. But just because someone knows how to use a hammer doesn't mean he can build a house. I personally feel that a film school can be extremely important for an editor, both in terms of learning editing techniques in a larger context, but also to learn other aspects of filmmaking. Knowing what a director of photographer or a sound mixer does can be very helpful in the process."

Training in film editing is also available in the military, including the Air Force, Marine Corps, Coast Guard, and Navy.

Certification or Licensing

No certification or licensing is available for this profession.

Internships and Volunteerships

Larger studios may offer apprenticeships for film editors. Apprentices have the opportunity to see the work of the film editor up close. The film editor may eventually assign some of his or her minor duties to the apprentice, while the film editor makes the larger decisions. After a few years, the apprentice may be promoted to film editor or may apply for a position as a film editor at other studios.

Large television stations and film companies occasionally offer students volunteer positions or internships. Most people in the film industry start out doing minor tasks helping with production. These production assistants get the opportunity to observe the film professionals at work. By working closely with a film editor, a production assistant can learn television or film operations as well as specific film editing techniques.

WHO WILL HIRE ME?

"Editing is still one of the jobs in the movie business where people do really work their way up," says Randy Carter. "Most people will start as an apprentice or assistant editor and, over time, gain the experience and contacts to ultimately work as a film editor. I can't stress enough

how important networking is. No one is going to hire an editor sight unseen from a resume and reel. Most people like to work with someone they've worked with before and can trust. If they haven't worked with someone before, they usually ask people they respect to recommend someone. Virtually every job I've ever had can be traced back through recommendations of four people I met while working at my first staff job as an assistant editor."

Some film editors work primarily with news programs, documentaries, or special features. They may develop ongoing working relationships with directors or producers who hire them from one project to another. Many film editors who have worked for a studio or postproduction company for several years often become independent contractors. They offer their services on a per job basis to producers of films and advertisements, negotiate their own fees, and typically have purchased or leased their own editing equipment.

With a minimum of a high school diploma or a degree from a two-year college, you can apply for entry-level jobs in many film or television studios. Most studios, however, will not consider people for film editor positions without a bachelor's degree or several years of on-the-job experience. "As soon as I graduated," recalls Vanick Moradian, "my first priority was to get a job—any job—in postproduction. I knew that was what I wanted to do. Remarkably, after only two months, a friend from film school called me and told me there was an opening for an assistant editor on a low-budget, independent action movie that he had interviewed for. But he had the opportunity to work on a bigger movie, so he recommended me. After I interviewed with the editor, he hired me right away. I think my film school experience and my sheer desire for the job convinced him that I was the right person. The skills I had acquired in film school enabled me to communicate with him at a very professional level. That and the fact that I was willing to do the job for the paltry salary they were offering sealed the deal! During my six years as an assistant editor, I constantly sought opportunities to edit whatever I could. In addition to the projects that I had done in film school, I also edited a couple of short films for others for free just so I could have a reasonable reel to show to people. Then, in 1994, I finally got a chance to edit three episodes of a live-action Japanese comic book TV series (which never aired in the United States). I had finally broken through as an editor and was able to get more work. I have been working consistently ever since."

Those who have completed bachelor's or master's degrees have typically gained hands-on experience through school projects. Another benefit of going to school is that contacts that you make while in school, both through your school's career services office and alumni, can be a valuable resource when you look for your first job. Your school's career services office may also have listings of job openings. Some studio work is union regulated. Therefore you may also want to contact union locals to find out about job requirements and openings.

Professional associations also provide their members with job assistance.

And the Oscar Goes to . . .

The following editors have won the Oscar for best film editing in recent years:

2008: Chris Dickens (*Slumdog Millionaire*)

2007: Christopher Rouse (*The Bourne Ultimatum*)

2006: Thelma Schoonmaker (*The Departed*)

2005: Hughes Winborne (*Crash*)

2004: Thelma Schoonmaker (*The Aviator*)

2003: Jamie Selkirk (*The Lord of the Rings: The Return of the King*)

2002: Martin Walsh (*Chicago*)

2001: Pietro Scalia (*Black Hawk Down*)

2000: Stephen Mirrione (*Traffic*)

For more information on Academy Award-winning film editors, visit http://www.oscars.org/awardsdatabase.

For example, American Cinema Editors allows its members to post their resumes at its Web site.

WHERE CAN I GO FROM HERE?

Advancement for film editors comes with further experience and greater recognition. Some film editors develop good working relationships with directors or producers. These film editors may be willing to leave the security of a studio job for the possibility of working one-on-one with the director or producer on a project. These opportunities often provide film editors with the autonomy they may not have in their regular jobs. Some are willing to take a pay cut to work on a project they feel is important.

Some film editors choose to stay at their studios and advance through seniority to editing positions with higher salaries. They may be able to negotiate better benefits packages or to choose the films they will work on. They may also choose which directors they wish to work with. In larger studios, they may train and supervise staffs of less experienced or apprentice film editors.

WHAT ARE THE SALARY RANGES?

Film and television editors are not as highly paid as others working in their industries. They have less clout than directors or producers, but they have more authority in the production of a project than many other film professionals. According to the U.S. Department of Labor, the median annual wage for film and television editors was $50,560 in 2008. A small percentage of film editors earned less than $24,640 a year, while some earned more than $112,410. The most experienced and sought-after film editors can command much higher salaries.

Benefits for full-time workers include vacation and sick time, health, and sometimes dental, insurance, and pension or 401(k) plans. Self-employed editors must provide their own benefits.

WHAT IS THE JOB OUTLOOK?

The U.S. Department of Labor predicts that employment for film and television editors will grow about as fast as the average for all occupations through 2016. The growth of cable television and an increase in the number of independent film studios will translate into greater demand for editors. This will also force the largest studios to offer more competitive salaries in order to attract the best film and television editors. The digital revolution will greatly affect the editing process. Editors will work much more closely with special-effects houses in putting together projects. When using more visual and sound effects, film and television editors will have to edit scenes with an eye toward the special effects that will be added.

"I think the employment outlook for feature-film editors hasn't really changed in the last 20 years," says Vanick Moradian. "The opportunities are still there, and the challenges of breaking in are still the same. But there is more need for visual content nowadays, and therefore, one could argue that there is more need for editors. It's just that it may not necessarily be in theatrical motion pictures. There is a great demand for content on the Internet, and even for use on cell phones. These are short-form projects that may not have the glamour of Hollywood, but the creative satisfaction and the financial rewards are still pretty good. The bottom line is you're still telling stories with pictures and sound. Unfortunately, the one area where the field has changed negatively is that a lot more is expected of editors, but a lot less time is given. When I first started out, I was just a picture editor. Nowadays, I'm also expected to be a sound designer, a music editor, a visual effects compositor, and more. These are all immensely enjoyable in their own right, but deadlines are shrinking every day, which sometimes results in very long hours at the office."

Producers

SUMMARY

Definition
Producers are responsible for the overall operation of a film, including organizing and securing the financial backing; deciding which scripts will be used or which books will be adapted for film; hiring the director, screenwriter, and cast; overseeing the budget and production schedule; overseeing post-production; and monitoring the distribution of the film.

Alternative Job Titles
Executive producers
Line producers
Producer/directors
Writer/producers

Salary Range
$30,250 to $92,920 to $500,000+

Educational Requirements
High school diploma; bachelor's degree highly recommended

Certification or Licensing
None available

Employment Outlook
About as fast as the average

High School Subjects
Business
English (writing/literature)
Speech
Theater

Personal Interests
Business
Film and television
Reading/books
Selling/making a deal
Theater

"While each production is rewarding in its own way and provides lessons to apply to future work," says producer Brent Morris, "I would have to say producing the film *American Gun*, by writer/director Alan Jacobs, was the most challenging and required the most varied set of producorial skills. On that film I worked with the director from very early on in the process through the distribution stage. It was an ambitious schedule of 40 shooting days in six different states (Vermont, New York, New Hampshire, Florida, Nevada, California). We did not have very much money, so planning and extensive location scouting were important to find the right places to shoot and the right crew to execute the vision. Casting was also challenging as the agent for our lead actor tried to break the contract the week before we started. I worked very hard through the three months of shooting, and post-production took another year. I learned many valuable lessons about working on limited budgets, shooting in mixed formats (35mm, digital video), negotiating under difficult terms, and keeping the faith to overcome what seemed at the time impossible obstacles. I also feel the film stands on its own as a dramatic piece and is a moving testament to the struggles that gave it birth."

WHAT DOES A PRODUCER DO?

Historically, the primary role of a *producer* is to organize and secure the financial backing necessary to undertake a motion picture project. These days, due to the size of some films, there may be many producers on a film—some of whom are hired or brought on to do specific jobs other than financing. The *director*, by contrast, creates the film from the screenplay. Despite this general distinction, the producer often takes part in creative decisions, and occasionally one person is both the producer and director. On some small projects, such as a nature or historical documentary for a public television broadcast, the producer might also be the writer and cameraman.

The job of a producer generally begins in the preproduction stage of filmmaking with the selection of a movie idea from a script or other material. Some films are made from original screenplays, while others are adapted from books. If a book is selected, the producer must first purchase the rights from the author or his or her publishing company, and a writer must be hired to adapt the book into a screenplay format. Producers are usually inundated with scripts from writers and others who have ideas for a movie.

To Be a Successful Producer, You Should…

- be organized and detail-oriented
- have business training so you can deal with budgets and other financial concerns
- have strong people skills
- be a good judge of talent
- be willing to travel and work long hours
- be able to handle stress and meet deadlines

Producers may have their own ideas for a motion picture and will hire a writer to write the screenplay. Occasionally a studio will approach a producer, typically a producer who has had many commercially or artistically successful films in the past, with a project.

After selecting a project, the producer will find a director, the technical staff, and the star actor or actors to participate in the film. Along with the script and screenwriter, these essential people are referred to as the package. Packaging is sometimes arranged with the help of talent agencies. It is the package that the producer tries to sell to an investor to obtain the necessary funds to finance the salaries and cost of the film.

There are three common sources for financing a film: major studios, production companies, and individual investors. A small number of producers have enough money to pay for their own projects. Major studios are the largest source of money, and finance most of the big-budget films. Although some studios have full-time producers on staff, they hire self-employed, or independent, producers for many projects. Large production companies often have the capital resources to fund projects that they feel will be commercially successful. On the smaller end of the scale, producers of documentary films commonly approach individual donors; foundations; art agencies of federal, state, and local governments; and even family members and churches. The National Endowment for the Humanities and the National Endowment for the Arts are major federal benefactors of cinema.

Raising money from individual investors can occupy much of the producer's time. Fund-raising may be done on the telephone as well as in conferences, business lunches, and even cocktail parties. The producer may also look for a distributor for the film even before the production begins.

Obtaining the necessary financing does not guarantee a film will be made. After raising the money, the producer takes the basic plan of the package and tries to work it into a developed project. The script may be rewritten several times, the full cast of actors is hired, salaries are negotiated, and logistical problems, such as the location of the filming, are worked out; on some projects it might be the director who handles these tasks, or the director may work with the producer.

During the production phase, the producer tries to keep the project on schedule and the spending within the established budget. Other production tasks include the review of dailies, which are prints of the day's filming. As the head of the project, the producer is ultimately responsible for resolving all problems, including personal conflicts such as those between the director and an actor and the director and the studio. If the film is successfully completed, the producer monitors its distribution and may participate in the publicity and advertising of the film.

To accomplish the many and varied tasks that the position requires, there are several types of producers, such as *associate producers*, sometimes called *coproducers*, and *line producers*. Job titles and responsibilities, however, vary from project to project. In general, associate producers work directly under the producer and oversee the major areas of the project, such as the budget. Line producers handle the day-to-day operations of the project. Another title, *executive producer*, often may refer to the person who puts up the money, such as a *studio executive*, but it is sometimes an honorary title with no functional relevance to the project. (It is almost impossible to know what the executive producer's actual duties are unless you know the players and the movie.) In the past 10 years, many producers who handle the day-to-day duties of producing have negotiated for executive producer credits. This is because only three producers can take home an Academy Award, according to rules established by the Academy of Motion Picture Arts and Sciences. Therefore, when a picture seems as though it might have a chance for a best picture award, those three credits are highly sought after.

The job of *production assistant* is typically an entry-level position. Some may perform substantive tasks, such as reviewing scripts, while others are hired to run errands.

Producers have greater control over their working conditions than most other people working in the motion picture industry. They may have the autonomy of choosing their own projects, setting their own hours, and delegating duties to others as necessary. The work often brings considerable personal satisfaction, but it is not without constraints. Producers must work within a stressful schedule complicated by competing work pressures and sometimes daily crises. Each project brings a significant financial and professional risk. Long hours and weekend work are common. "This is a very, very demanding business," says Doug Claybourne, who has worked as a producer on more than 20 feature films, including *Nights in Rodanthe, North Country, The Fast and the Furious, Mr. Baseball, The Mask of Zorro, Jack, The War of the Roses, Light of Day*, and *Rumble Fish*. "It takes all of your energy to succeed; however, if you are fortunate, you are working on something you can care dearly about—which is so rare."

WHAT IS IT LIKE TO BE A PRODUCER?

Brent Morris has worked as a producer and production manager in the entertainment industry since the late 1980s. During his career, he has worked on more than 30 feature films, including *Mon-*

Related Jobs

- art directors
- artist-and-repertoire managers
- assignment editors
- assistant directors
- casting directors
- directors of photography
- film directors
- film editors
- news anchors
- online producers
- production managers
- radio directors
- radio producers
- reporters
- screenwriters
- sound editors
- stage managers
- television directors

---

ster, American Gun, Smoke Signals, The Grand, Unknown, The Devil's Rejects, and *Beer for My Horses*. He also teaches production workshops at the Maine Media Workshops in Rockport, Maine. (Visit his Web site, http://www.indieproduction.com, to learn more about his career.) "I was a theater major at the University of California at Los Angeles in the early 1980s, intending to pursue a career in live theater as an actor and director," he recalls. "I quickly found that the opportunities for meaningful employment in that arena were fairly limited, at least in

Great Movie Memories

● ● ● ● ● ● ● ● ● ● ● ● ●

The editors of *What Can I Do Now? Film* asked Doug Claybourne, a producer for more than 30 years, to detail his most personally rewarding film projects.

Rumble Fish has a special place in my heart. It was filmed in my hometown of Tulsa, Oklahoma, and it was the first film I produced for Francis Ford Coppola as a director. It was very artistically made and about "something"—about brothers, family, coming of age, and the bonds of family. It used music and sound, stop-motion photography, and color and black-and-white film in a unique way. *Rumble Fish* starred Matt Dillon and featured Laurence Fishburne, who I worked with on *Apocalypse Now*. It was the first film for Nicholas Cage and also featured Dennis Hopper, Sophia Coppola, and Diane Lane. I've done three films with Diane. It had all the elements of a great picture—it just did not find an audience.

Next, I would think *Hearts of Darkness: The Making of Apocalypse Now*, which was an idea I had when I was producing *The War of the Roses*. I thought, "Wouldn't it be cool to make a documentary about a film that was made 13 years ago (at that time)." I knew Eleanor Coppola [the wife of Francis Ford Coppola] had shot 50 hours of footage, but no one had ever done anything with it. We took that footage and shot interviews and made these amazing discoveries and made something really beautiful with it. That was special. That film is about every artist going into his work with the same fears—the fear of failure, an empty page, not knowing if you are going to succeed or fail—just looking to your instinct to guide you. That's what it's about—having the guts to do that.

Los Angeles. I had always enjoyed movies, and my father and sister were professional actors, so the entertainment field came naturally, I suppose. I answered a job posting for interns at a production company and started reading screenplays for film producers, which led to a paying job six months later as an office and producer's assistant. I ran around town with scripts, typed up letters, filed, and wrote story analysis. For the most part I found the work interesting and pursued the opportunities that opened to me from that time, including associate producing and later line producing and production managing feature films.

"I am mainly a line producer charged with executing a budget and schedule for creative and executive producers who have raised financing. I initially create a shooting schedule and budget; consult with producers and directors on overall aims of the production (i.e., format, scope, distribution plans); then set up an office, hire crew, negotiate deals with crew, vendors, locations, and unions, and generally supervise the entire production, process. I approve call sheets for daily work, payments to cast/crew/vendors, and sign off on cost reports to the financiers. At the end of physical production, I wrap the files and office and send anything required to postproduction facilities and the offices of the producers."

Brent says that some of the best aspects of being a producer are the creative stimulation he gets from working in the industry, having the opportunity to work with a wide range of subject matter, the sense of belonging one gets in a group/

team setting, the good pay (when working), the opportunity to meet interesting people, and traveling and working in different locations (he has worked in Romania, Canada, Mexico, and other locales). Asked to list the negatives of work in the field, Brent cites uncertain employment, the ups and downs in financial status, the long hours while working, and the fact that this career is hard on family life.

DO I HAVE WHAT IT TAKES TO BE A PRODUCER?

"It is important for producers to have tenacity, a great deal of organizational skill, motivation to carry through when times are difficult, and the ability to clearly articulate ideas and concerns to others," says Brent Morris. "A producer must make sure things happen in a timely manner and find creative solutions to a myriad of logistical and financial problems. A willingness to work very hard and long hours and keep a schedule in an unstructured environment is critical. Ultimately a producer must be willing to take a stand on hard issues when conflicting ideas are at odds with the goals of the overall production, and he or she must be willing to fight for the creative needs of the production when necessary."

Producers come from a wide variety of backgrounds. Some start out as magazine editors, business school graduates, actors, or secretaries, messengers, and production assistants for a film studio. Many have never formally studied film. Most producers, however, get their position through several years of experience in the industry, perseverance, and a keen

sense for what projects will be artistically and commercially successful.

Producers must be highly organized. They are often responsible for budgeting and other financial concerns, so a good sense for business can be beneficial as well. Producers work with teams of professionals and must be able to bring people together to work on the single goal of completing a project. "Good producers recognize talents in others and motivate their teams to do their best work for the sake of the overall project and future relationships," says Brent.

Doug Claybourne says that successful producers have a good balance between their professional and personal lives. "If you put the business first all the time, then you sacrifice a great deal in your life," he says. "I think you have to find a balance if you want a well-rounded life. One has to have a sense of knowing what 'you need' for your own well-being. What kind of producer do I want to be? I have to be honest with myself and others—fair and truthful with the material I want to do. And I have to work on what I care about—not just commercial junk. I have always been in it for the art, not simply for the money, but don't tell anyone."

HOW DO I BECOME A PRODUCER?

There is no minimum educational requirement for becoming a producer. Many producers, however, are college graduates, and many also have a business degree or other previous business experience.

Advice from an Expert

Doug Claybourne, a producer of more than 20 feature films, offers the following advice to aspiring producers:

Be very sure that becoming a producer is what you want to do. The film industry is a very challenging business, and it can be cutthroat. You can enjoy your work, but don't kid yourself; you have to be very good at what you do to work as a producer. It is a real challenge in this market to make films. They are very expensive. There are not a lot of them being made. The industry is very competitive, and it's all about relationships. Don't get me wrong. I love making films, but one should know going in that a career in the film industry is serious business. If you know this going in, and you say, "Okay, I get it," then just dive in and do it. The most important things to do are to write, write, and write, and get to know your audience, marketing and distribution, and the digital side. In short, learning about not just the making of the film, but who you are making it for. Do what you love doing and follow your heart to your career.

Education

High School

Useful high school classes for aspiring producers include speech, mathematics, business, psychology, and English. Joining your school's drama department will provide you with valuable experience; most theatrical productions require people working behind the scenes to organize, promote, and seek funding. Such experience can give you a sense of a producer's responsibilities.

Postsecondary Training

Formal study of film, television, communications, theater, writing, literature, or art is helpful, as the producer must have the background to know whether an idea or script is worth pursuing. Many entry-level positions in the film industry are given to people who have studied liberal arts, cinema, or both.

In the United States there are more than 1,000 colleges, universities, and trade schools that offer classes in film or television studies; more than 120 of these offer undergraduate programs, and more than 50 grant master's degrees. A small number of Ph.D. programs also exist.

Graduation from a film or television program does not guarantee that you will get a job in the industry. Some programs are quite expensive, costing more than $90,000 in tuition alone for three years of study. Others do not have the resources to allow all students to make their own films.

Programs in Los Angeles and New York City, the major centers of the entertainment industry, may provide the best opportunities for making contacts that can be of use when seeking employment.

Certification or Licensing

No certification or licensing is available for this profession.

Internships and Volunteerships

You will most likely participate in an internship while in college. Depending on your major, you might work at a film production company, a Fortune 500 company, or another business setting. An internship will help you to get hands-on experience in the field and allow you to make valuable industry contacts.

Another good way to get experience is to volunteer for a student or low-budget film project; positions on such projects are often advertised in local trade publications. Community cable stations also hire volunteers and may even offer internships.

WHO WILL HIRE ME?

Many producers in the film industry are self-employed. Others are salaried employees of film companies, television networks, and television stations. Approximately 1,700 motion picture, television, and new-media producers are members of the Producers Guild of America. The greatest concentration of motion picture producers is in Hollywood and New York City.

Becoming a producer is similar to becoming president of a company. Unless a person is independently wealthy and can finance whichever projects he or she chooses, prior experience in the field is necessary. Because there are so few positions, even with experience it is extremely difficult to become a successful producer.

Most motion picture producers have attained their position only after years of moving up the industry ladder. Thus, it is important to concentrate on immediate goals, such as getting an entry-level position in a film company. Some enter the field by getting a job as a production assistant. An entry-level production assistant

may make copies of the scripts for actors to use, assist in setting up equipment, or may perform other menial tasks, often for very little or even no pay. While a production assistant's work is often tedious and of little seeming reward, it nevertheless does expose one to the intricacies of filmmaking and, more importantly, creates an opportunity to make contacts with others in the industry.

Those interested in the field should approach film companies, television stations, or television networks about employment opportunities as a production assistant. Small television stations often provide the best opportunity for those who are interested in television producing. Positions may also be listed in trade publications.

WHERE CAN I GO FROM HERE?

There is little room for advancement because producers are at the top of their profession. Advancement for producers is generally measured by the types of projects they do, increased earnings, and respect in the field. At television stations, a producer can advance to program director. Some producers become directors or make enough money to finance their own projects.

WHAT ARE THE SALARY RANGES?

Producers are generally paid a percentage of the project's profits or a fee negotiated between the producer and

Breaking Into the Business:
A Story from Producer Doug Claybourne

I was an art major at the University of Tulsa. Then I pursued graduate studies at the Art Center College of Design [an arts college in Pasadena, California]. I founded the Art Directors Club for Students, a branch of the ADLA in Los Angeles. It was a way for students to get to know the pros before we got out of school. I met some amazing designers—Saul Bass, Mike Salisbury, and David Willardson. Then one day I realized that the professors at the Art Center really did not know what made a piece of art "work"—there was just no definition. That was deflating, so I said to one of those great designers, David Willardson, I think, "I want to do something important."

Next thing I knew I received a call from Mike Salisbury. I was hired to be his assistant art director at *City Magazine*, a weekly publication in San Francisco owned by Francis Ford Coppola. I met Francis and his wife Ellie. I worked 100 hours a week for six months. I was very proud of the work. It was amazing. I realized during that six months that my skills were working with larger groups of people. I was motivating six people in an art department, but I was also a former quarterback and a catcher. I was an all-star athlete in high school, but an art student in college. So if you put two and two together, you can find film in there. During this time, I also met George Lucas, Steven Spielberg, and all these great people at Francis's home. But, the topper was one day on the way to work I saw this beautiful magazine I had spent 100 hours a week working on to complete laying in a gutter. It was so sad. That was it. I wanted out.

So I quit the magazine and told Francis I was going back to film school. I left in December 1975 just before he started *Apocalypse Now* in March 1976. The next month, he let everyone go at the magazine or sold it to get ready for the movie—he was downsizing.

Mike Salisbury started a company in Los Angeles. I worked for him and lived above the office while I was waiting to go back to film school at the Art Center. We were doing movie ads in the form of posters. I actually worked on the first poster for *Apocalypse Now* with Mike Salisbury. Its tagline was "Apocalypse Now—has begun." About that time, I read in a book something Coppola said: "The problem with film students is they are not willing to take risks."

I took that to heart. He had just started shooting *Apocalypse Now*. I had just started classes in film school. I sent him a telex saying, "I'll work for nothing just to see if the movie business is something I'm really interested in." I hated the idea that I was perhaps going to go to school for another three years, and then I might not like the movie business. I got a telex back that said, "We'll give you $400 getting-out-of town money . . . come on over," and that was it. I left Los Angeles thinking I was going to the Philippines for eight weeks; the movie ended up taking a year in production. We finished in May 1977 after 238 days of shooting.

I went to work as a production assistant on my first film. I came back as the first assistant director and with a deal with Francis Ford Coppola to work for him for four years. If I did this, he would get me into the Directors Guild of America, which he did in the second year while working on *The Black Stallion*. I took over that movie as the assistant director in Canada for another 24 weeks of shooting then I returned to be the postproduction coordinator on *Apocalypse Now* for two and a half years. It was released in August 1979.

a studio. Producers and directors who were employed in the motion picture and video industries had mean annual earnings of $98,903 in 2008, according the U.S. Department of Labor. Producers just starting out in the field earned less than $30,250. Producers of highly successful films can earn $500,000 a year or more, while those who make low-budget, documentary films might earn considerably less than the average. In general, producers in the film industry earn more than television producers. Most producers must provide their own health insurance and other benefits.

WHAT IS THE JOB OUTLOOK?

Employment for producers is expected to grow about as fast as the average for all careers through 2016, according to the U.S. Department of Labor. Though opportunities may increase with the expansion of cable and satellite television, news programs, video and DVD rentals, and an increased overseas demand for American-made films, competition for jobs will be high. Live theater and entertainment will also provide job openings. Some positions will be available as current producers leave the workforce.

Production Designers and Art Directors

SUMMARY

Definition
In films, videos, and television commercials, production designers are responsible for the overall look of the visual elements. They approve the props, costumes, and locations. Art directors are the top assistants of production designers; they ensure that the production designer's vision is implemented. In the past, the art director title was used to denote the head of the art department (hence the Academy Award for best art direction).

Alternative Job Titles
Production artists

Salary Range
$40,730 to $150,000 to $250,000+

Educational Requirements
Bachelor's degree

Certification or Licensing
None available

Employment Outlook
Faster than the average

High School Subjects
Art
Computer science
Speech
Theater

Personal Interests
Entertaining/performing
Film and television
Theater

In 1976 art director Jack Fisk began working with legendary director Terrence Malick on *Days of Heaven*. It was their second film together. "We were looking for wheat fields for a story that took place in 1916 in Texas," Jack recalls. "By the time we had a budget and could search for a location to shoot the movie, all the wheat in Texas had already been harvested. I traveled north looking for the expansive fields we needed and soon I was driving through farmland in Canada. After extensive searching by car and airplane for a couple of weeks, we settled on some farmland in southern Alberta about 30 miles north of Montana. The wheat belonged to the Hutterites, a sect much like the Amish. They agreed to rent us use of their land, but told us they would be harvesting the beautiful wheat in six weeks.

"The director, Terry, told me he needed to shoot the fields full of wheat for about two weeks before they harvested them. He also said that he would need to see the house and barns in the background and shoot from inside the house looking out onto the wheat fields. That meant I would only have four weeks to complete all construction on the house, the barn, and the barracks. I went back to Los Angeles and packed up my clothes and supplies and got on a plane the next day for Lethbridge, Canada. I brought up some friends that were carpenters and hired the local Hutterite kids to help out on Sundays after church. Their sect would never formally allow this, but I noticed that on Sunday afternoon no elders ever visited the set, so I believe they knew what I was doing and avoided a confrontation where they would have to reprimand the kids.

"The carpenter friends that came up from California and the Hutterites were passionate about the challenge and worked in difficult weather to try and finish the sets on time. There was no real road to the location where we were building the house, and the truck bringing our first load of lumber turned over rounding a small hill near the pond. During the week the Hutterite elders often came by the set and too often told me that it would be impossible to finish the house in four weeks.

"I called another friend, also an art director, and hired him to find some artists that could silkscreen wallpaper for the interior of the house from some old period patterns. He did that and organized the rental of some great period dressing and drove it up to Canada in a rented truck. I was able to divide up the work and find enough energetic and talented artisans to work on the separate tasks independent of each other. Everything we did was unorthodox and not by the book. Without a lot of luck and cre-

> ## To Be a Successful Production Designer or Art Director, You Should...
>
> - have a positive attitude
> - be able to work well under deadline pressure
> - enjoy finding solutions to problems
> - be creative
> - be able to work with both hand tools and software programs
> - enjoy conducting research
> - have good interpersonal skills
> - be willing to travel
> - have good communication skills

ative thinking there was no way we could complete the sets in time.

"The sets were completed moments before principal photography began and my career as an art director was safe for a while longer. That was the most difficult job I ever attempted and to this day whenever I am working on a film and someone says, 'we only have four weeks,' I relax and smile."

WHAT DOES A PRODUCTION DESIGNER OR ART DIRECTOR DO?

Production designers are responsible for all visual aspects of on-screen productions. In film and video and broadcast advertising, the production designer has a wide variety of responsibilities and often interacts with an enormous number of creative professionals. Working with directors, producers, and other professionals, production designers interpret scripts and create or select settings in order to visually convey the story or the message. The production designer oversees and channels the talents of set decorators and designers, model makers, location managers, propmasters, construction coordinators, and special-effects people. In addition, production designers work with writers, unit production managers, cinematographers, costume designers, and postproduction staff, including editors and employees responsible for scoring and titles. The production designer is ultimately responsible for all visual aspects of the finished product.

"When designing the look of a motion picture or a television show, the production designer works with the script, the director's ideas, and the budget to conceive a look for the film that incorporates all three," says Jack Fisk. "If the film is to be shot on location, the production designer works with location scouts to find settings that work best for the film and meet the infrastructure needs of the production company. Some great locations cannot be used because they are too difficult to reach by car or truck or there is no housing for the crew nearby. Then the production designer—using the facts about the chosen locations, the script, research, and the budget—designs and creates concept sketches or models to illustrate his ideas to the director, the producer, and other departments. Sometimes an illustrator or concept artist is hired to complete these presentations.

"During this early preproduction time," Jack continues, "the production designer and art director work closely with the production manager and line producer to finalize a budget for the art department so that set construction can begin, and the art director works with the set designer (draftsman) to make working drawings for the construction coordinator based on the designs of the production designer and research."

The director may hire a *storyboard artist* to illustrate his or her ideas for camera moves and editing of complicated scenes or sometimes the entire film. A few directors will draw a storyboard themselves or use a software program such as Frame Forge 3D.

Preproduction on a film is designed to be the most efficient use of time and money. The time budgeted for set design and construction is tight and with a set deadline there is constant revision and planning to complete the sets on time for the scenic painters and decorators to complete their contributions and have them ready for shooting.

Because each film is different, and often it has a group of filmmakers that have not worked together before, things do not always work out as planned. It is to the credit of film professionals that they are able to adapt and compensate to make the impossible possible.

Breaking Into the Business: A Story from Production Designer Jack Fisk

I majored in fine arts at the Pennsylvania Academy of Fine Arts in Philadelphia. When I was going to school, there were no film schools. I learned about films by watching them, but I never thought about working on films for a living. I saw *Jules and Jim* while at school and was fascinated by the period look of the film. I also remember a wonderful movie, *Lawrence of Arabia*, that blew me away in terms of its scope and visual storytelling.

My best friend was making short animated films in art school and was accepted into the American Film Institute's first class in Beverly Hills, California. I decided to move out to California with him. We drove out to together from Philadelphia, with all of our possessions in a U-Haul truck. It was an exciting beginning for me because I had never been to California and didn't know what to expect. Before leaving the East Coast I had seen a wonderful art exhibit at the Metropolitan Museum of Art in New York City by the artist James Rosenquist. His paintings, up to 80-feet wide, were of jets, spaghetti, babies, and other Americana influenced by his work painting billboards. I thought that when I arrived in Los Angeles I would look for a job painting billboards. When I started looking for work at outdoor advertising companies, I discovered that the scenic artists from the movie studios had taken all the painting jobs as it was a slow time for studio movies in California.

We rented a small place near Whiskey A Go Go [a world-famous music club] and soon I found a job working on a small nonunion film about motorcycle gangs and hippies. [On the] first day, I was holding traffic during shots and was about a quarter of a mile from the set, so I didn't learn much about filmmaking. As the days progressed I found more things I could do to be helpful on the film. Soon I imagined that they would have trouble getting their work done on the film if I wasn't there. I would do anything—move lights, cable, get coffee, change film, and I even wrangled chickens—to keep me near the set so I could see what was going on and learn more about filmmaking.

I loved the group effort it took to create something and the pressure of completing a day's work before it got too dark to shoot. I met a lot of people working on the set and before the film was completed they told me of other films coming up. Through this network of film workers I was able to continue working on low-budget, nonunion films in Los Angeles. I soon thought of myself as a filmmaker and couldn't imagine doing anything else, even though I was only making $100 a week.

After working on small films for a few months I ended up working in the art department. I felt comfortable there because of my art training, and I loved the idea of creating sets, aging them, and dressing them to look real. Sometimes in the art department you are given menial tasks that could last most of the film. For *In Pursuit of Treasure*, an American Film Institute (AFI) film, I was hired to make gold bricks (the treasure). I spent my days in the basement of a motel in Kanab, Utah, casting plaster bricks and painting them gold.

(continued on next page)

(continued from previous page)

I slept in the editing room. I got that job when my friend David Lynch gave it up to go back to Los Angeles to work on his own film *Eraserhead* at AFI. He loved the job, or so he told me, and he had developed a way to cast the bricks efficiently. By the time I took over he had already made hundreds of gold bricks.

I became friends with the production manager on *In Pursuit of Treasure*. When he started his next film, *Angels Hard as They Come* (another low-budget bikers vs. hippies movie that Jonathan Demme had cowritten and was producing for Roger Corman), he suggested me to be the art director. I was up against the art director of *In Pursuit of Treasure* whom I had just worked for.

When I met the producer and director I talked about the script, the sets, and other films, but forgot to mention that I had never art directed a movie. I mean, they never asked. After our second meeting Jonathan told me that they would like me to art direct their movie, but they could only pay me $375 a week. I acknowledged that $375 was not a lot of money, but I told them that I loved the script and would do it anyway. I did not tell them that I had just been offered 300 percent more than my last job.

Roger Corman is famous for making low-budget exploitation movies. In the early 1970s he employed many young filmmakers that went on to be famous in their own right—Jonathan Demme, Jack Nicholson, and Ron Howard, to name a few. Anyway, by this time I only wanted to make more films, and I felt I was being paid to learn!

Production designers supervise the project from preproduction through production with the assistance of *art directors*. Art directors are the top assistants of production designers. They must have both creative and management skills to ensure that the production designer's vision is being implemented. They are responsible for the entire operation of the production division or just particular departments such as construction, props, locations, special effects, and set dressing.

Production designers and art directors often work under pressure of a deadline and yet must remain calm and pleasant when dealing with coworkers. They must work as many hours as required—usually many more than 40 per week—in order to finish projects in accordance with predetermined schedules.

WHAT IS IT LIKE TO BE A PRODUCTION DESIGNER OR ART DIRECTOR?

Some of Jack Fisk's many film credits as a production designer/art director include *The Invasion, The New World, Mulholland Drive, The Straight Story, The Thin Red Line, Days of Heaven, Carrie,* and *Badlands.* "The challenges of doing something I've never done before excite me most about working on films," he says. "I also love the travel, and when you shoot in a location for several months, you get to know the people and so much more about a place than you would on a casual visit. I have made films in Canada, Australia, England, Italy, the Solomon Islands, and all over the United States. I have searched for locations in many more countries around the world, and I can't wait to see where the next film leads me.

"As an art director or now production designer on a film," he continues, "you are responsible for providing all the backgrounds for a movie. It may be locations or constructed sets, but most times it is both. The most important part of film design is to make all the physical elements work together in a unified visual idea that helps tell the story. My crew usually consists of myself, an art director, an assistant art director, an art department coordinator, a set decorator and his assistants, a property master and his assistants, a construction coordinator and carpenters and metal workers, a scenic artist and his crew, and a special-effects crew. I haven't worked on any big visual effects films, but look forward to at least one. Having worked on films for about 40 years I can say that I have met some wonderful people, and I still look forward to going to work. Of course, there were difficult moments, but I can't remember what they were."

Lori Agostino is an art director, production designer, and visual artist in Los Angeles, California. Some of her film and television credits include *Get Him to the Greek*, *Still Waiting*, *Sons of Anarchy*, and *The Travels of Shakamuni*. (Visit http://www.loriagostino. com and http://www.imdb.com/name/nm1322086 to learn more about her career.) "I studied architecture, but out of school I went in a completely different direction and started painting and showing my work," she says. "At a certain point I really missed architecture and decided to start working with those skills again. I have always enjoyed doing architectural models, and an opportunity arose to actually start doing miniatures for visual effects (VFX). This is where I started my film career, building models for films that are blown up! (A very Dadaist process!) Because of my love of making architectural models, I pursued this direction first, but soon realized that I was a designer at heart, and while I enjoyed the craft, I really missed doing the design. So I went back to school and studied production design and art direction for film at the University of California at Los Angeles. I love what I do. Period. Every facet of the process is interesting to me, so I love my job.

"My main duty as an art director is to facilitate the production designer's designs," she continues. "This means that I make sure that every component of the process is done correctly. I oversee the placement of sets on stages and the construction of the sets (the construction coordinator runs the crews, but it's my responsibility to make sure that it is all completed on time, on budget, and most importantly, true to the design). I do material gathering, hardware, oversee graphics for signage and picture cars, location surveys, opening and closing sets—I am responsible for basically anything to do with the sets. The skills required are drafting, graphics, construction knowledge, breaking down the script (understanding what a set needs to be built for the camera and the action of the film), among others."

DO I HAVE WHAT IT TAKES TO BE A PRODUCTION DESIGNER OR ART DIRECTOR?

"I think the most important quality an art director/production designer can have is a positive attitude," says Jack Fisk, "and I look for that in all the people I hire to work with me. Our work is high pressure and a lot of money is at stake. If a set is not ready on time it can cost a film company hundreds of thousands of dollars for every day shooting is delayed. Changes in the shooting schedule because of weather or an actor's availability may move a set up by days or weeks, adding to the pressure to get it completed in time for shooting. So you can see the advantage of having positive people around you."

Deadlines are a constant part of the work, and an ability to handle stress and pressure well is key. "To be able to keep calm in chaos is a beneficial quality to have if you are going to work on films," Jack says. "I try to never say something is impossible, and usually it isn't. I love the challenge of figuring out a way to give the director everything he needs to tell the story. Passion and a love for

your work is another important element in being able to withstand the challenges of making a film."

The work of production designers and art directors requires creativity, imagination, curiosity, and a sense of adventure. They must be able to work with all sorts of tools and building materials; use specialized equipment and computer software, such as graphic design programs; and be able to communicate the ideas behind their work. "If you want to be a production designer, I would recommend learning a few software programs like Sketchup, Photoshop, and a CAD drawing program," says Jack. "You will need to be able to read working drawings to communicate with the set designers and even be able to draw some of your own. You will need a basic understanding of construction, architecture, lighting, and composition, along with a desire to research. Research is an ongoing and important part of film design. An innate design sense will be a big help, as will getting along with people."

Other requirements for production designers and art directors include time management, communication, and organization skills, as well an ability see the "big picture." "As an art director/production designer you need to be able to keep an overview of the film and not get lost in specific detail," Jack says. "It is with your guidance that the sets, props, locations, costumes and special effects all work together visually in the movie."

Since the film industry is located primarily in Los Angeles and New York City,

Rewarding Experiences

Production designer Jack Fisk details some of the most rewarding experiences of his career:

- While I was working on *The Thin Red Line* in Guadalcanal I spent a lot of time with the natives of the island. I built a period village with the women while the men watched and chewed beetle nut. Men in Guadalcanal plan and women work. The oldest people on the island would bring their grandchildren to the village we were building to show them what their villages used to look like.

- In creating the look for *The New World* I got to work with Dr. William Kelso, the archeologist who discovered where the original Jamestown fort was in 1994. He shared his latest discoveries with us so that we could incorporate them into the set of the Jamestown fort. Later he would bring students and young archeologists to see how the fort might have been. His enthusiasm for our work was rewarding. One day while he was visiting the set he asked why I had located a saw pit near the front of the fort by the water. I told him I was thinking that it would be more pleasant to work near the water sawing and that logs could be sent down the river to the saw pit easily. A few days later he contacted me to tell me that he had just found evidence of a saw pit outside the real fort in almost the exact location that I had chosen for our set piece. Some design, some history, and some common sense.

- I love to create a set and be in it a few moments alone and imagine how it might have been to live in the period of the film before the film crew comes in and takes it over for shooting; it is never so complete again once the filming begins.

you may need to relocate to find a position in these fields. "If you're interested in working in film you're going to have to live in a city where films are made," says Lori Agostino. "That is a very important component to working in film!" Lori says that the most important skills for art directors include "design skills, a good eye, being able to visualize scenes, the ability to work with people (as film is a *very* collaborative process), being a good leader, and being able to think on your feet." She also says that it is important to not take design changes personally.

"In film, things change daily; it's what happens when hundreds of people collaborate on a creative project. Learn to work within this structure. If you take it personally, you'll never survive." Also, know that thousands of people are vying for your job. Stay focused and be the best you can be at it. This goes a long way in terms of getting your next production, which is another thing to understand; every four to six months you're looking for a new production to work on. You must have nerves of steel to get through to the next job!"

HOW DO I BECOME A PRODUCTION DESIGNER OR ART DIRECTOR?

Education

High School

There are a variety of high school courses that will provide both a taste of college-level offerings and an idea of the skills necessary for success on the job. These courses include art, drawing, art history, graphic design, illustration, photography, advertising, shop, and desktop publishing.

Other useful courses that you should take in high school include business, computing, drama, English, technical drawing, cultural studies, psychology, and social science.

Postsecondary Training

A college degree is usually a requirement for production designers and art directors; however, in some instances, it is not absolutely necessary. Courses in art direction, production design, photography, filmmaking, set direction, advertising, marketing, layout, desktop publishing, and fashion are also important for those interested in entering this field.

Because of the rapidly increasing use of computers in design work, it is essential to have a thorough understanding of how computer art and layout programs work. For smaller productions, the production designer or art director may be responsible for using these software programs; for larger films, a staff person, under the direction of the designer or director, may use these programs.

Certification or Licensing

No certification or licensing is available for this profession.

Internships and Volunteerships

Many universities and professional art schools offer graduates or students in their final year a variety of workshop projects and internships. These programs provide students with opportunities to develop their personal design styles as well as their portfolios. They also help them make valuable contacts in the industry. Volunteering with a local production company will also give you a good introduction to job options in the field.

WHO WILL HIRE ME?

Typical employers include film and television production houses, movie studios, Web designers, multimedia developers, computer game developers, or television stations. Other employers include advertising agencies, publishing houses, museums, packaging firms, photography studios, marketing and public relations firms, desktop publishing outfits, digital prepress houses, or printing companies.

The positions of production designer and art director are not entry level. Typically, a person on a career track toward the position of production designer or art director is hired as an assistant to an established professional.

Serving as an intern is a good way to get experience and develop skills. Graduates should also consider taking an entry-level job at a film or television studio, production company, or in a publisher's

Production Designer Spotlight: Robb Wilson King

Robb Wilson King has been a production designer for more than 25 years. He has worked on dozens of films and television shows, including *Breaking Bad*, *Hostel: Part II*, *Just Friends*, *Paparazzi*, *Barbershop 2: Back in Business*, *Scary Movie*, *Price of Glory*, *Rush Hour*, *Rudy*, *Marked for Death*, and *Iron Eagle*. (Visit http://www.imdb.com/name/nm0455204 to learn more about his career.) Rob discussed his career with the editors of *What Can I Do Now? Film*.

Q. What made you want to enter the film industry?

A. My advantage began with being born in Hollywood to a jazz pianist mother and a theme park iconic designer father. In my early childhood, I had an actual boat bed my father built that I sailed for the first seven years of my life in the center of my room. My "fort" was on the back lot of Disney on the *Zorro* set. My awareness of film sets, architecture, and the culture of film was ingrained early.

However, I felt that I could learn more studying elsewhere. I went to San Francisco and studied at the San Francisco Art Institute. From there, wanderlust took me to New York City, where I studied with the legendary Stella Adler. It was in New York that I absorbed stage design, script breakdown, and the complex art of method interpretation. I then went back to Los Angeles to study architecture at the Southern California Institute of Architecture, which completed my unorthodox approach to my newfound career.

My hunger for changing landscapes, exotic interpretation, visual challenge, and a certain personal poetry all existed in film design. Once this passion was determined, moving into this new field was made easier.

I must admit that not a single thing has changed to this day. My eagerness for the challenge remains unabated.

Q. What are your primary and secondary duties when you work on a film?

A. The first challenge is the interview and capturing the job. Your basic instinct comes into play after fully reading the script. Once the script is absorbed, you have to ask yourself, "How can my brand of production design serve this narrative, this director, and my own artistic aesthetic?" It is the culmination of your ideas, your valued instinct, your passions that should be present at that meeting. It is at that meeting that you establish the depth of your participation.

If successful, the project is yours. It becomes time to morph the director's vision with your own knowledgeable sense of just where and how to achieve it.

The search for locations to fulfill the variety of scenes is the next step. It is the discovery of just what's out there that can accommodate the script and/or change it to conform to something more intriguing. This is one of my favorite elements of the process.

Once the locations are understood and approved, it's off to the races with the beginning of the set design portion. All your "wizards" are involved here—creating the most interesting, detailed, and ambitious designs that

(continued on next page)

(continued from previous page)

you can both afford and achieve in your timeframe.

All departments are now armed with the meat of the project. They are always ready for this phase of the project, where everyone has the exuberance to deliver. The production designer has become a conductor of a vast orchestra. He or she seductively creates a safe path—with remarkable clarity—to the final vision (that vision shared in that first meeting with the director). There is no more satisfying endeavor than to get to that finish line as heroes.

Q. What do you like most and least about working in the field?

A. The infinite variety of subjects still holds me captive. For example, in any given year three different stories may come your way. Each story will need to be researched, completely understood, and methodically visualized into your own aesthetic.

What a gift to learn, to create, to achieve unparalleled satisfaction when the project is delivered. The absolute thrill of getting there—the process—holds sway over any experience that might be gained after the project has been distributed or aired. One should not focus on what the result might be, but rather the intense desire to hit all the marks while making the product.

The process that sweeps you and your fellow wizards into a focused sense of urgency deals with the vision, the budget, the general fears, the pressures of limited time, and continual outside influences. But at the end of the day, nothing can be more fulfilling than watching the rise of your conceptual drawings into living, breathing realities.

My least favorite moments in my life in film are the occasional downtimes—the time that you find yourself free-falling from the energy-packed reality of creation to the quiet of a mission completed. The good news—as you go along—is that you do get better at replacing this rush with a more personal one. For instance, you learn to regard your down time as a brief, but important, time to focus and learn cultures, travel, languages, new computer techniques, and maybe take an occasional nap.

Q. What is the employment outlook for production designers and the motion picture industry?

A. With the constant changing of the financial landscape these days, studios, indie filmmakers, and documentarians all are feeling the pinch. As a consequence of reduced funding, loss of hedge funds, and slowing of the credit reserves, production has been severely cut—sometimes drastically.

Because of this reduction in available financing, the state of pictures has been reduced, causing A-category production designers to take on projects with smaller budgets, different

art department to gain initial experience. Either way, aspiring production designers and art directors must be willing to acquire their credentials by working on various projects. "Look for other young people who want to make films and be prepared to do any type of work just to get your foot in the door," advises Jack

pay scales, and less grand ambitions. Those projects are followed by other cuts, where the wait for available projects trickling down to you is longer. And so it goes. Where you are on that scale will dictate your consideration on both feature and television projects.

Not to despair, however. I have lived through countless speed bumps, downturns, strikes, etc. This industry is very resilient and is always keeping an eye out for new talent that has exciting ideas, fresh viewpoints, and abundant energy. We might be entering a new era of self-generated projects that do not rely on the traditional studio system.

It is important to keep your antenna high, passions intact, your beliefs healthy. Try to experience all aspects of the work. Starting on the lowest tier is always the best because you can learn everyone's job. You can begin a more organic, richer development, which will answer questions and allow you to learn techniques that have been the staples of our work for years.

You can learn important things on just about any film you work on—both good or bad. Just try to bring excellence and intelligence to every project. Attitude is everything. Try not to limit your capacity by being arrogant. The realm of possibility surrounds you; be sure to partner up with it every day. You will learn and celebrate your newfound art.

Q. What are some of the most interesting or rewarding things that have happened to you while working in this field?

A. The world of film moves so quickly. New ideas and techniques are available to the filmmaker like never before. It is our job as production designers to try to keep up with the evolution of these amazing tools. We should not be afraid to grow with the industry, but not afraid to keep alive the historically proven methods, as well.

The esteem I have for every visual partner I have had in my career is very important to me. This legion of wizards have taught me, left me in awe. Their contributions are etched in my memory.

The magic is still in the process, the nurturing of an idea, the consummate energy and focus, the completion of the quest.

Q. What advice would you give to those just entering the field of production design?

A. You as a new player now have everything at your fingertips. That, coupled with your instincts and vision, means you can become a most valued partner to any director, producer, and writer. There is not a single story out there that you cannot enhance and bring to life. Keep your ambitions attainable. Keep your star rising by avoiding the pitfalls of indulgence. Grow slowly and then soar. And maybe someday I might get a chance to work for you.

Fisk. "If they don't pay much, be thankful they aren't charging you. You will find others as serious as you and by networking you will learn of new films that you might be able to work on. The more you know about all positions on a film crew the easier it is for you to communicate your ideas to them."

WHERE CAN I GO FROM HERE?

While some may be content upon reaching the position of production designer, many production designers take on even more responsibility within their organizations, become film or television directors, start their own design agencies, or pursue production design opportunities outside the motion picture industry. Many people who get to the position of production designer do not advance beyond the title but move on to work on more prestigious films or at better-known production companies. Competition for top positions continues to be strong because of the large number of talented people interested in entering these careers.

Art directors advance by becoming production designers, by working on more prestigious film projects, and by working for larger companies.

WHAT ARE THE SALARY RANGES?

The weekly base pay for a motion picture art director who is a member of the International Alliance of Theatrical Stage Employees is approximately $3,000, but top production designers can negotiate higher salaries of more than $10,000 per week. Production designers who work on nonunion productions typically have lower earnings.

Art directors employed in all industries had median annual earnings of $76,980 in 2008, according to the U.S. Department of Labor. Top art directors earned $154,840 or more. Mean annual earnings for art directors employed in the motion picture and video industries were $101,780 in 2008.

Film companies employing production designers and art directors pay into the Art Directors Guild's Health & Pension Fund. Production designers and art directors who are members of the International Alliance of Theatrical Stage Employees or National Association of Broadcast Employees and Technicians receive health insurance and a pension as part of their membership benefits. Freelance nonunion production designers and art directors employed in the motion picture and television industries are usually responsible for providing their own health insurance and other benefits.

WHAT IS THE JOB OUTLOOK?

The U.S. Department of Labor predicts that employment for production designers and art directors who work in the motion picture industry will grow faster than the average for all careers through 2016. These professionals play a major role in the look of a film and, as a result, will continue to be in steady demand in coming years. However, it is important to note that there are more production designers and art directors than the number of available job openings. As a result, those wishing to enter the field will encounter keen competition for salaried staff positions as well as for freelance work.

Screenwriters

SUMMARY

Definition
Using dialogue, images, and narration, screenwriters write scripts for dramas, comedies, documentaries, adaptations, and educational programs. They may write complete original scripts, or work on assignment by a producer or director. Screenwriters either work freelance or as part of a staff of writers.

Alternative Job Titles
Scriptwriters
Staff writers
Story editors

Salary Range
$15,000 to $95,250 to $500,000+

Educational Requirements
High school diploma; some postsecondary training recommended

Certification or Licensing
None available

Employment Outlook
About as fast as the average

High School Subjects
English (writing/literature)
History
Journalism
Theater

Personal Interests
Entertaining/performing
Film and television
Reading/books
Selling/making a deal
Theater
Writing

Screenwriters write scripts for entertainment, education, training, sales, television, and films. They may choose themes themselves, or they may write on a theme assigned by a producer or director, sometimes adapting plays or novels into screenplays. Screenwriting is an art, a craft, and a business. It is a career that requires imagination and creativity, the ability to tell a story using both dialogue and pictures, and the ability to negotiate with producers and studio executives.

WHAT DOES A SCREENWRITER DO?

Suppose you have an idea for a science fiction TV movie—your movie, set in the not-so-distant future, concerns green Martians. With a powerful telescope, the U.S. government has been watching these green Martians plowing the red dust of their planet for several years; then one day, without warning, the green Martians turn a shade of purple, a kind of pale fuchsia, and the world panics. You tell your friends about your brilliant idea for a movie—they all think it's stupid, but you don't care. You think it's brilliant. This confidence and love for your work, and your fearlessness in the face of rejection, are possibly your most important assets in your career as a *screenwriter*.

Your idea for a movie will, if you're lucky, be the first step in a long trek to seeing the show in theaters. Because not only must you be good at characterization, plot, writing dialogue, and the many other techniques of storytelling, you must also be a good salesperson—you'll be expected to represent your work, defend, and promote it. And although the idea formed in the privacy of your own head, you'll be collaborating on the movie with many professionals. Depending on your involvement with the project, you may be working directly with producers, directors, editors, and other writers. You may be required to be on the set during filming, and you may be expected to make revisions at the drop of a hat. And if a small production team films the movie, you may be involved in casting, finding locations, and even promoting the film.

So, you have your purple Martian idea. What's next? There are various ways that writers get their work produced. Some writers compose entire scripts, sitting alone in their homes with their computers. They pay close attention to the elements of the story, developing interesting characters and situations. They come up with the lines the characters will say to each other. All of this requires not just talent, but an understanding of how a story moves forward. Writers gain this understanding by watching movies and TV shows, and read-

ing short stories and novels. They also read published scripts of well-written films. In composing your Martian script, you must also format it properly, with spacing for cues, directions, and spoken lines.

Then comes the next step: selling the script. This can be the most frustrating and difficult aspect of being a screenwriter. Thousands of people are trying to sell their scripts to TV and the movies. Selling your script requires a contact within the industry. Some writers have many connections with producers and directors; they've gained these connections by living in Los Angeles, the base for film and television production. These writers promote themselves and their work. They may take entry-level jobs with production companies and get to know the people who make decisions on scripts. Many writers also have *agents*; for a percentage of the money you make from the script, an agent will use his or her connections in the industry to get the script read and considered for production. But the services of an agent can be as difficult to obtain as a reading by a producer. And even if you do sell your Martian script, there's no guarantee that the script will ever be produced. Some writers have made whole careers from selling their ideas and treatments for films that ultimately are never made.

The motion picture industry isn't the only outlet for screenwriters. Practically everything that airs on network TV or cable starts with a written script. Documentaries, sitcoms, newscasts, and educational programs are just some of the television projects that require the work of writers. And not all writers work in Los Angeles; freelance screenwriters can be found all across the country. TV series are frequently filmed outside of L.A., so even series staff writers are finding themselves in New York, Canada, and even Baltimore. And with the number of new cable channels developing with headquarters in various cities across the country, writers can make successful careers outside of L.A. and apart from the networks.

WHAT IS IT LIKE TO BE A SCREENWRITER?

Greg Marcks is a writer/director in Hollywood, California. He has written 16 screenplays, and his directing credits include *11:14* and *Echelon Conspiracy*. "I grew up in Chelmsford, Massachusetts, and attended public high school," he says. "No one in my family worked in the arts or entertainment fields, but from a young age I often wrote stories and drew cartoons. I was fortunate to have access to the public access television station (which was situated in my high school), which my friends and I used to create a sketch comedy show that aired locally. I chose to major in creative writing at Carnegie Mellon University, and it was while I was there that I fell in love with writing feature scripts and directing short 16mm films. I became obsessed with filmmaking and I still am today, which is a practical necessity given how difficult entry into and remaining in the film business can be."

Greg says that the most important thing to know when planning a screen-

> ### To Be a Successful Screenwriter, You Should...
>
> - be very creative
> - be able to work on a deadline
> - know how to create vivid characters, scenes, and storylines
> - have strong communication skills
> - have good research skills
> - be committed to constantly search for your next job

play is that "a story and a screenplay are two different things. Ideally you want to know your story inside and out before you start writing your screenplay. Think of the story as the plan and the screenplay as the execution. A screenplay is a story told in scenes, with each scene necessary to tell the story, but how can you determine if each scene is necessary if you don't already know your story? When I plan a screenplay, I write the story in prose first, without dialog, with each scene represented by either a sentence or a paragraph. Then I let others read it and I revise the condensed story in prose, omitting the parts of the story that are unnecessary until I am ready to begin. This blueprint, a script 'treatment,' can vary from one to 40 pages and helps keep you on track during the actual screenwriting. In preparing to write my film *11:14*, I spent several months outlining the story,

Lingo to Learn

agent A person with connections in the industry; for a percentage of the final sale of a script, an agent will represent a writer, showing the script to producers and directors.

draft A complete written script, either revised or unrevised. A "rough" draft is an initial version of a script; a "final" draft is a script ready for production.

pitch A description of an idea, usually verbal, presented to a producer or director. A writer pitches screenplay ideas hoping to be hired to write the entire script.

reader An entry-level position in a production company; a reader reads scripts submitted to the company, analyzes them, and determines which are worthy of being passed on to producers.

treatment A written proposal for a script; between one and 40 pages. A treatment offers a plot summary.

and as a result it only took one month for me to write the screenplay."

Greg says that one of the best parts of his job is the fact that he is "always working on something new and collaborating with a variety of interesting, creative people. I consider myself very lucky in that I am able to make a living doing what I actually want to do. Many of my friends do not, however, and you have to be prepared for years of working other kinds of jobs to support your creative ambitions. The cons are an unstable and unpredictable lifestyle, as well as the rigorous demands on one's time and personal life.

As a matter of necessity most people in this field are based in either New York or Los Angeles, primarily Los Angeles, and these cities are not for everyone. While there are occasionally glamorous moments in the film business, most of it is long, hard work. But if you love movies like I do, it is also very rewarding."

Chris Wehner has worked as a screenwriter for more than 10 years. His screenplay, *El Camino*, is currently in development with Golden Light Films. Chris also served as editor in chief and publisher of *Screenwriter's Monthly* magazine and is the author of *Screenwriting on the Internet: Researching, Writing & Selling Your Script on the Web*. He has presented countless seminars on screenwriting at such conferences as Selling to Hollywood and The Las Vegas Screenwriter's Conference, and is the founder of screenwritersutopia.com, one of the most popular Web sites for writers on the Internet. "I started Screenwriter's Utopia in order to network with others and help aspiring writers reach their goals," he says. "Some of the pros of being a screenwriter are that I can work from home and set my own hours. I can also work in my pajamas if I want! It's also just being able to do what you love; that is the greatest reward." Chris says that one of the major cons of this career is not being produced. "I have been published many times," he says, "have had scripts optioned, one in development, and yet I wait to see something I have written make it to the big screen. There are tens of thousands of optioned and sold screenplays that never make it and become a movie. They're kind of like 'bills' that never become 'laws.'" Chris offers the following advice to aspiring screenwriters: "Write, write, write. Also, read and watch a lot of movies. Live life, learn about life, and then write about it!"

DO I HAVE WHAT IT TAKES TO BE A SCREENWRITER?

"Screenwriters have to be good critics of their own work and also be patient with themselves," says Greg Marcks. "It takes a long time to develop the craft, as well as a personal voice and style. Ideally you should be able to know yourself objectively. And you have to be happy spending the majority of your time alone in front of a computer. Screenwriting can be a very lonely endeavor, and you have to be prepared to write many drafts of the same project before a script is finally ready for professionals to read and evaluate. On the business side, however, it also helps if you are personable and can sell yourself and your talents."

Chris Wehner says that the most important skills for screenwriters are "creativity, perseverance, and talent. You have to have that ability to create something magical from 100 empty, blank, and dead pages of paper. You have to bring them to life."

As a screenwriter, you must be able to create believable characters and develop a story. You must also be proficient in such skills as dialogue writing, creating plots, and doing research. In addition to creativity and originality, you need an understanding of the marketplace for your work. You should be aware of what kinds

of scripts are in demand by producers. Word processing skills are also helpful.

Varied interests and curiosity are also important for screenwriters. One day you might be researching the slang used in Tombstone, Arizona, in the 1880s and the next social customs of Confucian China.

In addition to the stress caused by the instability of working on a freelance basis, there's a lot of stress in the work itself. Screenwriters must meet constant deadlines. And because the process requires a great deal of collaboration, they must be ready to throw away something they have just spent a great deal of time writ-

Related Jobs

- agents
- columnists/commentators
- copywriters
- critics
- directors
- editorial writers
- fiction and poetry writers
- humorists
- lyricists
- news writers
- playwrights
- producers
- reporters
- script readers
- technical writers
- theatrical writers

ing if others on their team have a different approach.

HOW DO I BECOME A SCREENWRITER?

Education

High School

Though talent plays a big part in a writer's success, technical skill is also important. Take English courses that will introduce you to both classic and contemporary works of fiction. From these novels and plays, you can pick up the techniques of storytelling. In drama and theater courses, as well as drama clubs, you'll learn about dialogue and scenes; you may even have the opportunity to direct a production or to play a role.

Additionally, many schools also have speech and debate teams, as well as journalism departments, which train students in news writing, editorials, research, and writing yearbook copy.

Postsecondary Training

Producers aren't generally interested in a writer's educational background—you'll be judged on your writing and ideas. But film schools will help you develop your writing skills and your understanding of filmmaking. These schools will also help you make some connections in the industry and inform you of internships, competitions, and conferences.

Many colleges and universities have film departments, but some of the most respected film schools are the University of California—Los Angeles (http://www.tft.ucla.edu/ftv_mfa), the University of Southern California (http://www-cntv.usc.edu/programs/writing), the American Film Institute (http://www.afi.com), and Columbia University (http://wwwapp.cc.columbia.edu/art/app/arts/film/index.jsp). Contact these schools or visit their Web pages for information about course work and faculty.

Most college theater departments offer courses in playwriting, and many English

Thoughts on Moviemaking

Greg Marcks offers the following advice to young people who are interested in entering the film industry:

Get as much experience as you can while you and your friends still have the time, money, and inclination to practice and make mistakes. Once other people are paying for your films, they don't want to see mistakes. But everyone makes mistakes, which is how we learn and grow. So take risks and make as many short films as you can. Learn by doing, and if you don't know how to do something, make it up. That way when it comes time to enter the industry as a professional you will already know to some extent what works and what doesn't, and you can inspire with confidence. Also, watch every movie ever made. Learn as much as you can from the masters. If you love a particular film, study it over and over again to see how it is put together. Watching movies is still the most effective film school.

departments are developing undergraduate creative writing programs. In writing workshops, you can develop skills in dramatic and narrative structure. There are also many master of fine arts programs in film, theater, and creative writing.

Certification or Licensing

No certification or licensing is available for this profession.

Internships and Volunteerships

If you attend film school, you will probably be required to participate in an internship. This will allow you the chance to work closely with screenwriters and other television and film professionals. You might get the chance to work as a screenwriter assistant, a script reader, or perhaps perform clerical duties for a production company, independent screenwriter, or other employer. These employers may also offer volunteer opportunities.

WHO WILL HIRE ME?

Jobs as a screenwriter can be extremely hard to come by. Most established screenwriters credit their own persistence and assertiveness—you should be prepared to work for a while at entry-level jobs with production companies and TV series in order to get to know the people who make decisions on scripts. Only about half of the members of the Writers Guild of America (WGA) are actually employed, and that's an improvement over previous years. Though we occasionally hear about very young writers and filmmakers, most screenwriters have had to work for years and years in the industry before establishing themselves.

WHERE CAN I GO FROM HERE?

Competition is stiff among screenwriters, and a beginner will find it difficult to break into the field. More opportunities become available as a screenwriter gains experience and a reputation, but that is a process that can take many years. Rejection is a common occurrence in the field of screenwriting. Most successful screenwriters have had to submit their screenplays to numerous production companies before they find one who likes their work.

Once they have sold some scripts, screenwriters may be able to join the WGA. Membership with the WGA guarantees the screenwriter a minimum wage for a production and other benefits such as arbitration. Some screenwriters, however, writing for minor productions, can have regular work and successful careers without WGA membership.

Those screenwriters who manage to break into the business can benefit greatly from recognition in the industry. In addition to creating their own scripts, some writers are also hired to "doctor" the scripts of others, using their expertise to revise scripts for production. If a film proves very successful, a screenwriter will be able to command higher payment, and will be able to work on high-profile productions. Some of the most talented screenwriters receive awards from the industry, most notably the Academy Award for best original or adapted screenplay.

And the Oscar Goes to . . .

The following screenwriters have won the Oscar for best original screenplay in recent years:

2008: Dustin Lance Black (*Milk*)

2007: Diablo Cody (*Juno*)

2006: Michael Arndt (*Little Miss Sunshine*)

2005: Paul Haggis and Bobby Moresco (*Crash*)

2004: Charlie Kaufman, Pierre Bismuth, and Michel Gondry (*Eternal Sunshine of the Spotless Mind*)

2003: Sofia Coppola (*Lost in Translation*)

2002: Pedro Almodóvar (*Talk to Her*)

2001: Julian Fellowes (*Gosford Park*)

2000: Cameron Crowe (*Almost Famous*)

For more information on Academy Award-winning screenwriters, visit http://www.oscars.org/awards database.

WHAT ARE THE SALARY RANGES?

With some film stars making more than a million dollars a movie, many aspiring writers are under the misconception that the film industry holds big paychecks for them, as well. But film writers get paid a mere fraction of the salaries of on-screen talent. According to the WGA 2008 Theatrical and Television Basic Agreement, earnings for writers of an original screenplay ranged from $62,642 to $117,602 during the 2010–2011 segment of the contract. The U.S. Department of Labor reports that writers employed in the motion picture and video industries had mean annual earnings of $98,820 in 2008.

Although these figures sound high, it is important to remember that work for screenwriters is very cyclical. There will be times when screenwriters will be steadily busy, and others where they will be out of work for months at a time. And since many writers work as freelancers, they generally can't predict how much money they'll make from one year to the next.

Screenwriters who are members of the WGA are eligible to receive health benefits.

WHAT IS THE JOB OUTLOOK?

There is intense competition in the motion picture and television industries. As cable television expands and digital technology allows for more programming, new opportunities may emerge. Studios are always looking for new angles on action, adventure, horror, and comedy, especially romantic comedy stories. The demand for new screenplays should increase in the next decade, but the number of screenwriters is growing at a faster rate. Writers will continue to find opportunities in advertising agencies and educational and training video production houses.

Sound Workers

SUMMARY

Definition
Sound workers help create the audio aspects of a motion picture, from incidental music and sound effects, to its final score.

Alternative Job Titles
Varies by specialty

Salary Range
$16,750 to $60,000 to $1 million+

Educational Requirements
High school diploma; post-secondary training highly recommended

Certification or Licensing
None available

Employment Outlook
About as fast as the average

High School Subjects
Music
Theater

Personal Interests
Entertaining/performing
Film and television
Music
Theater

"I was asked to write additional music for two summer blockbusters, *Wanted* (starring Angelina Jolie, James McAvoy, and Morgan Freeman) and *Get Smart* (starring Steve Carell and Anne Hathaway)," says David Reynolds, a film composer. "Danny Elfman was the composer for *Wanted* and Trevor Rabin was the composer for *Get Smart*, two of my film scoring heroes! Having their trust and confidence in my abilities was truly an honor. Working with them and a huge orchestra to record several slamming chase cues that I wrote was exhilarating. And, going to the movie theater with my family and friends to watch the films and hear music I wrote, knowing that audiences all over the world were watching and listening, was an incredible experience!"

WHAT DOES A SOUND WORKER DO?

The job title "sound worker" covers a wide variety of workers in the film industry who are responsible for creating sound for a film. Sound workers are involved in all steps of the film production process. The following paragraphs detail some of the most popular career options for those interested in working with sound in the film industry. Most of these workers can find employment in other industries, including television, computer and video

> ## To Be a Successful Composer, Arranger, Conductor, or Musician You Should...
>
> - be highly creative
> - have excellent musical ability
> - be proficient in at least one instrument
> - be able to work well with others
> - have an inquisitive nature
> - be able to work under deadline pressure

games, and the performing arts, among other fields.

Composers write original scores and thematic music for films. A score is the music that plays throughout the film apart from any songs that may also be in the film. All composers use the same basic musical elements, including harmony, melody, counterpoint, and rhythm, but each composer applies these elements in a unique way. There is no prescribed way for a composer to go about composing. All composers work in a somewhat different way, but generally speaking they pursue their work in some kind of regular, patterned way, in much the same fashion of a novelist or a painter.

Songwriters write the words and music for songs that will appear in a film and/or on its soundtrack.

Arrangers take composers' musical compositions and transcribe them for other instruments or voices, work them into a score for a film, or adapt them to styles that are different from the one in which the music was written.

Music conductors direct large groups of musicians or singers in the performance of a piece of music that has been composed for a motion picture.

Musicians perform, compose, conduct, and arrange music for films.

Audio recording engineers and *sound engineering technicians* oversee the technical end of sound recording during filming or during the recording of a musical performance that will be used in a film.

Sound mixers combine music and sound effects with a film's action. *Boom operators* work with sound mixers. They place and operate microphones to record dialogue and other sounds during filming.

Sound designers oversee every aspect of the soundtrack of a movie. Some sound designers specialize in music and may have training in music theory or performance. Others work with sound effects. They may use unusual objects, machines, or computer-generated noisemakers to create a desired sound for a film. Sound designers often keep libraries of sounds that they reuse for various projects. These include natural sounds, such as thunder or raindrops, animal noises, motor sounds, or musical interludes.

Foley artists re-create and improve sound effects for a film during postproduction, matching the sounds with images.

Sound editors also work during the postproduction stage of a film. They edit recorded sound and dialogue to create the final soundtrack. They supervise foley artists.

Music licensors negotiate with music labels and up-and-coming bands for the rights to use music in motion pictures. On larger films, a *music supervisor* may handle these licensing duties, as well as hire composers or songwriters to create music or songs for the film.

Sound professionals work in a wide variety of settings. For example, composers and arrangers work in expensive, state-of-the-art home studios or in a bare room with an electronic keyboard or a guitar, depending on their preferences. Music conductors and musicians work in recording studios and concert halls. Sound designers, boom operators, mixers, and related workers work on film sets and on location throughout the world. Music licensors work in typical office settings.

WHAT IS IT LIKE TO BE A SOUND WORKER?

Marco Beltrami is an Academy Award-nominated (*3:10 to Yuma*) film composer who is best known for creating scores for horror and suspense movies. He has composed music for many films, including *Knowing, Live Free or Die Hard, In the Electric Mist, The Omen, Three Burials of Melquiades Estrada, Red Eye, Hellboy, Scary Movie 2, Mimic, Joy Ride, The Dangerous Lives of Altar Boys, Terminator 3, Scream,* and *I, Robot*. (Visit http://www.marcobeltrami.com to learn more about his career.) "Much to the initial regret of my parents, I knew rather early on that I wanted to be a composer," Marco recalls. "I took piano lessons starting in elemen-

tary school, but I always seemed to be more interested in reworking the simple pieces than practicing scales. After high school I decided to get a liberal arts degree in urban studies from Brown University rather than attend music school. But my heart wasn't really in it so I then went to Yale School of Music to get a master of music in composition. During the end of my two years there, I realized I would either have to teach or find commercial employment. I knew little of film scoring, but decided to move to Los Angeles and learn as I went. The more I learned, the more I realized I was well-suited to putting music to moving pictures.

"The first step in creating a film score," he continues, "is the 'spotting,' where you sit with the director and talk about where the music should go. I usually like to watch the picture through and form very general ideas about motives, themes, instrumentation, and colors and from there work on more specific scenes. Directors are accustomed to hearing mock-ups of the score ideas before you actually record with an orchestra, so for this I use a Mac-based program called Digital Performer that runs a variety of sampled instrument libraries, as well as creates a template of original sounds via electronic manipulation."

Marco says that there are many plusses to working as a film composer. "Not only do you get to hear your music performed very soon after you write it," he says, "but the music you write will likely be received by a captive audience watching the film and affect them in lasting ways they might not experience if there were no accompanying picture. In the best case scenario,

To Be a Successful Technical Sound Worker, You Should…

- be proficient using the latest recording technologies and techniques
- have good troubleshooting skills
- be attentive to detail
- have excellent communication skills
- be willing to work long hours to meet production deadlines

the film is a collaborative work of art that allows music and image to play off one another."

David Reynolds is a composer, arranger, conductor, and producer for film and television music. Some of his more than 20 film credits include *Get Smart, Wanted, Cruel Intentions 3, George B., Almost Salinas,* and *Love Happens.* (Visit http://www.davidreynolds.net to learn more about his career.) "I started composing at the age of nine because I didn't like some of the music assigned for my piano lessons," he recalls. "I had some musical ideas bouncing around in my head and wanted to play those instead of my lesson. Instead of making me play only my assigned lesson, my piano teacher encouraged me to supplement my lessons by writing my own pieces. I learned that the best way to remember all my ideas was to write them down, and I became a composer."

David says that one of the pros of writing music for films and television is that he gets to write in a wide variety of styles and genres. "Often I'm asked and/or inspired to try new and interesting ideas like melding electronica with orchestra or exploring unique combinations of ethnic instruments, percussion, and vocals," he explains. "Deadlines are usually tight, so there's not a lot of time to over-think things. I have to rely on my training and good instincts to write quickly and effectively and move on. Everything I write gets demoed and/or recorded, so I get immediate feedback on what's working and what's not working. I'm able to learn very quickly what's effective and what's not."

According to David, some of the challenges of being a film composer include meeting deadlines and creating a score that satisfies the various goals and tastes of directors, producers, and film executives. "Film music can be very powerful in terms of mood-setting and storytelling," he explains. "Yet despite its power, good film music is often very subtle, striking a delicate balance between making itself an integral part of the setting, the characters, and the story without calling too much attention to itself and distracting the audience from the moment. Because deadlines and budgets are usually tight, there is a lot pressure to deliver a score that everyone loves, on time and on budget.

"Film scores exists to serve the needs of the film as defined by filmmakers (the director, producers, and often studio executives)," David continues. "Typically the filmmakers, not the composer, are the decision makers in terms of what music is working and what music is not. Since the score is typically the last creative element that goes into making a film, and because it has tremendous power to influence the audience's experience, there are often many different opinions among the filmmakers about what the music should be and how it should function. Understanding and interpreting the filmmaker's vision and desires for the score, melding seemingly disparate opinions about what the music should be, and delivering a score that the filmmakers love can often be very challenging."

DO I HAVE WHAT IT TAKES TO BE A SOUND WORKER?

David Reynolds says that successful film composers know how to work well with others. "You need to be a team player, a collaborator, and a friend," he says. "Writing film music is a collaborative art. Often, giving a composer the freedom to write great music requires a tremendous amount of trust on the part of the filmmakers. Knowing how to work effectively with many different personalities is essential. You can be a brilliant musician, but if you can't communicate and work with other (often nonmusical) people, you will fail. Your job as a film composer is to be the musical hands of the filmmakers, to create music that delivers on their vision. Listen to what they ask for. Ask questions and learn to meld their vision of the film and its music with your own musical instincts."

All sound workers should have strong communication skills to be able to work with a diverse group of industry professionals, and flexibility to work with a vari-

Good Advice

David Reynolds offers the following advice to high school students who are interested in becoming composers:

First, watch movies and study the scores. A great way to learn what the filmmakers intended is to watch (and listen to) the commentary special feature included on many DVD releases. In the commentary the filmmakers will talk through the whole film, telling stories about the filmmaking process. It's a great way to learn what they were thinking about and what they intended when making their film. Some of the DVDs even have an additional composer commentary track, where the composer talks about his or her experience writing music for the film. Two specific examples of composer commentaries are *Pleasantville* (commentary by composer Randy Newman) and *The Matrix* (commentary by composer Don Davis).

Second, find filmmakers (probably making student films) and get them to let you write a score for their film. There is no greater learning experience than to jump in and actually do it!

ety of musical genres. They should also have good organization skills.

HOW DO I BECOME A SOUND WORKER?
Education
High School

There is no specific course of training that will help you to become a composer. Many composers begin composing from

Composer Spotlight: Donald Rubinstein

Donald Rubinstein is a composer, singer, songwriter, and multimedia artist. He has released nearly 20 CDs and scored several feature films and television shows. His score for the film *Martin* was named "One of the Top 100 Coolest Soundtracks of All Time" by *MOJO* in 2002. (Visit http://www.donaldrubinstein.com to learn more about his work.) Donald discussed his career with the editors of *What Can I Do Now? Film.*

Q. What made you want to become a composer?

A. Music was for me the highest form of expression. I grew up listening to it, though not playing or writing it. I was a poet from a young age. I began to play my first year of college and found I had an aptitude for this highest possible "calling." Once I knew that, my commitment was clear and unfaltering. I transferred into a con- servatory one year later and never looked back.

Q. What are some of the pros and cons of work in the field?

A. The pros are the opportunity to work with others who share a similar passion for creation. The cons are sometimes working with people who do not have that same level of commitment and passion. The very best situation is to be working with creative compatriots. A great director will make you look and sound better as much as you hopefully return the favor. The pay is good and the level of satisfaction from working on a project that can take up to a year to find fruition is significant.

Q. What are the most important personal and professional qualities for composers?

a very early age and receive tutoring and training to encourage their talent. Musically inclined students should continue their private studies and take advantage of everything musical their high school offers. If you are interested in creating music for motion pictures and television, you should listen to as many scores from these sources as possible. Specially gifted students usually find their way to schools or academies that specialize in music or the arts. These students may begin learning composition in this special environment, and some might begin to create original compositions. Marco Beltrami offers the following advice to aspiring composers: "Get strong musical, computer, and business (or social) skills because there is a lot of competition and composers have to first make their own opportunity, and then have the chops to produce when the moment arrives. Also, don't try to copy other composers, but rather hone your own individual talent."

If you are interested in becoming an audio recording engineer or technician, sound mixer, or other type of technical sound worker, you should take computer science, electronics (if offered), and math, including algebra and geometry.

All sound workers should learn as much as possible about music—especially

A. Both personally and professionally for me, the highest level of dedication and commitment is most important. You are there to serve the film in both its realization and greatest achievement. It also helps to be able to navigate what are sometimes very dense interpersonal and political landscapes. There are a lot of people involved in film, and not everyone is there to make the best creative film possible. Many people are there to make money first, and those two components, the creative and bottom line, don't always go hand in hand. You have to learn to stand up for your point of view and to present the vision you believe in to give it the best opportunity to succeed.

Q. **What film have you most enjoyed working on as a composer, and why?**

A. I enjoyed my very first film, *Martin*, with director George Romero because there was so much freedom. George and I had a creative confluence that was unusual. He trusted me, as I did him, and so I was left to dig as deep as I could, knowing that what I did would likely serve his vision as well. I was given the opportunity to follow my creative muse to its end and was lucky that it met with the ends of the director.

Q. **What is your favorite film score, and why?**

A. That is an almost impossible question to answer. There is not one, though I will narrow it down to five knowing there are many more: Bernard Herrmann, *Psycho*; Nino Rota, *8½*; John Williams, *Star Wars*; Gabriel Yared, *Betty Blue*; and Leonard Bernstein, *On the Waterfront*. What links all of these scores is an original point of view—a creative concept that both starts in tradition and moves beyond it. They all succeed in framing and moving the movies forward in unique and wildly successful ways. They each give us both incredible music statements on their own, along with support for the film in inimitably effective ways.

as it relates to its use in motion pictures. Take as many music classes as possible and learn how to play one or more musical instruments, especially the piano, synthesizer, and keyboard. High school orchestras and bands are an excellent source for both practicing and studying music performance.

Postsecondary Training

If you are interested in becoming a composer or musician, you can continue your education in any of numerous colleges and universities or special music schools or conservatories that offer bachelor's and higher degrees. Your course of study will include music history, music criticism, music theory, harmony, counterpoint, rhythm, melody, and ear training. In most major music schools, courses in composition are offered along with orchestration and arranging. Courses are also taught covering voice and the major musical instruments, including keyboard, guitar, and, more recently, synthesizer. Most schools now cover computer techniques as applied to music as well. Some schools offer concentrations or certificates in film and television scoring. One such program is the Scoring for Motion Pictures and Television Program at the University of Southern California. Visit http://www.usc.edu/schools/music/programs/smptv for more information on this interesting program.

In the past, most sound designers learned their trade through on-the-job training. Today, many sound designers earn bachelor's degrees in music, sound design, or audio engineering, and this will probably become more necessary as technologies become more complex. Typical programs focus on computer and music studies, including music history, music theory, composition, sound design, and audio engineering.

Audio recording engineers, technicians, and mixers can prepare for the field by taking seminars and workshops and by pursuing degrees in music engineering and technology at technical schools or community colleges.

Certification or Licensing

No certification or licensing is available for this profession.

Internships and Volunteerships

Aspiring composers, arrangers, musicians, songwriters, and conductors do not generally participate in internships in the same manner as other students. Instead, at a very young age, they begin taking music and voice lessons; participating in school bands and choirs; and learning as much as they can about music by visiting Web sites, listening to music, and talking with their teachers about the field. Many high school students form their own bands, begin composing their own songs, and even direct local youth music groups. In college, musicians and related workers will continue these activities and

perhaps intern or volunteer at a film studio or other employer to get a general feel for the industry.

Recording engineers and other technical workers can participate in internships or apprenticeships in audio at a university or college or trade school. Most university and college programs offer semester-long internship programs at professional recording studios as a way of earning credit.

WHO WILL HIRE ME?

"I will always remember my first big break," says Marco Beltrami. "I had met one of Wes Craven's assistants and gave him a tape of my music while they were in the midst of editing the movie *Scream*. Wes liked the tape, but since I had no real credits to speak of, he asked if I would mind writing a scene on spec. I said sure, so he gave me the entire 13-minute opening sequence and asked me to bring it back two days later. Although I felt panicked, I knew I couldn't blow the opportunity, so I asked a friend if I could use his studio (I didn't have one yet) and completed the task. When Wes heard it, he loved it. The movie was then tested in New York and did well, and I got the job. This began a string of seven or eight further pictures for Miramax."

Many sound professionals, especially composers and musicians, work on a freelance or project basis. Composers are self-employed. They complete their work in their own studios and then try to sell their pieces to music publishers, film and television production companies, or recording companies. Once their work becomes well known, clients, such as film and television producers, dance companies, or musical theater producers, may commission original pieces from composers. In this case, the client provides a story line, time period, mood, and other specifications the composer must honor in the creation of a musical score.

Some sound workers are lucky enough to learn the ins and outs of the field by working with well-known professionals in their field. "My first job in Hollywood was working for legendary film composer Elmer Bernstein," says David Reynolds. "I didn't write any music, but I got to see firsthand, up close and personal, how one of the best in the business did it. It was an amazing learning experience!"

Sound workers should also consider joining music-related societies and associations such as the American Federation of Musicians; Meet the Composer; the American Composers Alliance; Broadcast Music, Inc.; the Society of Composers; American Society of Composers, Authors, and Publishers (ASCAP); Society of Professional Audio Recording Services; and Audio Engineering Society. These organizations provide job leads, professional support, and training opportunities.

WHERE CAN I GO FROM HERE?

Advancement for composers, arrangers, musicians, songwriters, and musical directors often takes place on a highly personal level. Composers, for example, may progress through their career to write or transcribe music of greater complexity and in

The Greatest Film Scores of All Time

1. *Star Wars* (1977, John Williams)
2. *Gone with the Wind* (1939, Max Steiner)
3. *Lawrence of Arabia* (1962, Maurice Jarre)
4. *Psycho* (1960, Bernard Herrmann)
5. *The Godfather* (1972, Nino Rota)
6. *Jaws* (1975, John Williams)
7. *Laura* (1944, David Raksin)
8. *The Magnificent Seven* (1960, Elmer Bernstein)
9. *Chinatown* (1974, Jerry Goldsmith)
10. *High Noon* (1952, Dimitri Tiomkin)

Source: American Film Institute

more challenging structures. They may develop a unique style and even develop new forms and traditions of music. One day, their names might be added to the list of the great composers and arrangers. Some composers become well known for their work with film scores; John Williams, of *Star Wars* fame, is one.

Other types of sound workers advance by working on more prestigious films or working for larger companies. Some go on to write textbooks about their craft or teach at colleges and universities.

WHAT ARE THE SALARY RANGES?

Salaries for music directors, composers, arrangers, and orchestrators employed in all industries ranged from less than

$16,750 to more than $107,280. Median annual earnings for these workers were $41,270. Well-known composers and arrangers can earn salaries that exceed $150,000 a year.

Many composers, however, do not hold full-time salaried positions and are only paid in royalties for their compositions that sell. According to ASCAP, the royalty rate for 2007 was $.091 per song per album sold. The $.091 is divided between the composer and the publisher, based on their agreement. If the album sold 25,000 copies in 2007, the royalties the composer and publisher received would be $2,275. Naturally, if this song is the only one the composer has that brings in income during this time, his or her annual earnings are extremely low (keep in mind that the composer receives only a percentage of the $2,275).

On the other hand, a composer who creates music for a feature film may have substantial earnings, according to the ASCAP. Factors that influence the composer's earnings include how much music is needed for the film, the film's total budget, if the film will be distributed to a general audience or have only limited showings, and the reputation of the composer. ASCAP notes that depending on such factors, a composer can receive fees ranging from $20,000 for a lower budget, small film to more than $1 million if the film is a big-budget release from a major studio and the composer is well known.

Musicians and singers employed in the motion picture and video industries earned mean hourly salaries of $37.70 in 2008.

Sound engineering technicians employed in the motion picture and video industries earned mean annual salaries of $60,600 in 2008, according to the U.S. Department of Labor.

The American Federation of Musicians of the United States and Canada has created pay scales for musicians and composers who perform or write music for motion picture and television films. Contact the federation for the latest rates.

Salaried sound workers receive typical fringe benefits such as paid vacation and sick days, health insurance, and the opportunity to participate in retirement savings plans. Freelance sound workers must pay for their own health insurance and other benefits. Freelance sound workers who belong to a union may receive some benefits as part of their membership package.

WHAT IS THE JOB OUTLOOK?

Overall employment in the motion picture and video industries is expected to grow about as fast the average for all industries through 2016, according to the U.S. Department of Labor. Competition for sound worker positions in the film industry is very strong. Sound workers with knowledge of filmmaking techniques will have better employment prospects than those with only a background in music or audio technology. Since it is very difficult to enter this career, many sound workers pursue related careers in other industries such as the performing arts, the music and recording industry, and other fields.

Employment for sound engineering technicians employed in the motion picture and video industries is expected to grow faster than the average for all careers through 2016.

Special and Visual Effects Technicians

SUMMARY

Definition
Special and visual effects technicians use technical and computer skills to create effects and illusions for motion pictures, theater productions, television broadcasts, and video games.

Alternative Job Titles
Computer animation specialists
Digital artists
Makeup effects specialists
Mechanical effects specialists

Pyrotechnic effects specialists
Special effects coordinators
Visual effects specialists and supervisors

Salary Range
$31,570 to $71,910 to $100,390+

Educational Requirements
Some postsecondary training

Certification or Licensing
Required for certain positions

Employment Outlook
About as fast as the average (special effects technicians)
Much faster than the average (visual effects technicians)

High School Subjects
Art
Computer science

Personal Interests
Entertaining/performing
Film and television

"Being able to do something that you really don't think is going to work and have it come out perfect or near perfect is always exciting," says special effects coordinator Geoff Martin. "We were doing a television series in San Diego and the 'gag' was that a fog bank had to come over a nine-foot rock wall, fall to the stream below, cross about 45 feet of water, get to the shoreline, rise vertically, and drop on an actor who was sitting with his back to the fog. This was to be shot outside at night over a real stream. I was on the far bank in the trees with the fog machine and couldn't see the set. I kept waiting for the screaming to start on the radio. The shot went on and on. When the first assistant director finally hollered 'cut!' I got on the radio and asked how it looked, knowing full well it probably looked really bad. His response—'It was perfect!' The only thing I did on that shot was to push the button on the smoker. We got the shot in one take! Ya' gotta love luck!"

WHAT DOES A SPECIAL OR VISUAL EFFECTS TECHNICIAN DO?

Special and visual effects technicians make what we see when we watch a movie, television broadcast, or theater production look and seem real. If a scene in a script calls for actors to walk down a 1920s Paris street, a Tyrannosaurus Rex to cause havoc in modern times, or a 25th-century spacecraft to "warp" in a blinding flash of light, it is the job of these technicians to make the viewer believe that it could really happen.

This article focuses on two types of effects technicians: *special effects technicians* and *visual effects technicians*. Both types of technicians create effects that amaze viewers as they watch movies, but they use different methods to go about creating movie magic. Special effects technicians deal with practical constructs and "in camera" effects—meaning those that are shot while the camera is rolling during a scene. Visual effects technicians use computer software programs to add or improve effects after a film is made. The following paragraphs provide more information on these two special effects fields.

Special Effects

Special effects technicians are crafts persons who build, install, and operate equipment used to produce the effects called for in scripts for motion picture, television, and theatrical productions. They read the script before filming to

---

To Be a Successful Special Effects Technician, You Should...

- be curious
- have basic mechanical ability
- be especially attentive to safety on the set
- be able to work long hours in varied environments
- be able to withstand stressful situations
- be physically strong
- be very observant
- be able to perform varied and complex skills
- be able to meet deadlines
- have good people skills

---

determine the type and number of special effects required. Depending on the effects needed for a production, they will mix chemicals, build large and elaborate sets or models, and fabricate required backdrops from materials such as wood, metal, plaster, and clay.

What's known generally as special effects is actually a number of specialized trades. There are companies—known in the industry as special effects shops or houses—that offer specialized services in such diverse areas as makeup, mechanical effects, and pyrotechnics. A special

To Be a Successful Visual Effects Technician, You Should...

- be very skilled at using visual effects software programs
- be willing to work long hours to meet deadlines when necessary
- have excellent observational skills
- have a good imagination
- be able to meet deadlines
- have excellent communication skills

effects shop might provide just one or a combination of these services, and the crafts persons who work at the shops are often skilled in more than one area.

Makeup effects specialists create elaborate masks for actors to wear in a film or theatrical production. They also build prosthetic devices to simulate human—or nonhuman—limbs, hands, and heads. They work with a variety of materials, from latex plastic to create a monster's mask, to human hair they weave into wigs, to plain cotton cloth for a costume. They are skilled at applying makeup and mixing colored dyes.

Mechanical effects specialists create effects such as rain, snow, and wind during movie productions. They may also build small sections of sets and backdrops that have an effect in them. They might also create moving or mechanized props,

such as a futuristic automobile for a science fiction film. Because of a production's budget constraints, they are often required to construct miniature working models of such things as airplanes or submarines that, on film, will appear to be life- or larger-than-life-sized. Mechanical effects specialists are usually skilled in a number of trades, including plumbing, welding, carpentry, electricity, and robotics. At some film studios, the construction department may be responsible for some of the more labor-intensive responsibilities of mechanical effects specialists.

Pyrotechnic effects specialists are experts with munitions and firearms. They create carefully planned explosions for dramatic scenes in motion pictures and television broadcasts. They build charges and mix chemicals used for explosions according to strict legal standards.

Most professionals working in the field of special effects offer their services as freelance technicians. Some also work for special effects shops. The shops are contracted by motion picture or television broadcast producers and theatrical productions to provide the effects for a specific production. After reviewing the script and the type and number of the special effects required, the shop will send a special effects team to work on the production, or hire freelance technicians to assist on the job. Depending upon their level of expertise, many freelance technicians work for several shops.

Often, nonunion team members are required to help out with tasks that fall outside an area of expertise during the production. This may involve setting up and tearing down sets, moving heavy equipment, or pitching in on last-minute design changes. Union technicians are contracted to provide a specific service and rarely perform work outside an area of expertise.

Visual Effects

Visual effects technicians use high-tech computer programs to create effects that are otherwise impossible or too costly to build by traditional means. They might create an elaborate castle on a mountaintop, a crowd scene set in ancient Rome, or a fierce monster with three heads and six mouths. They typically work in an office or animation studio, separate from the actual filming location. Because much of the technology they use is on the cutting edge of the industry, visual effects technicians are highly skilled in working with and developing unique computer applications and software programs.

Visual effects technicians often work as freelancers; some own their own businesses. Others may be employed as salaried workers by visual effects, animation, and film studios.

WHAT IS IT LIKE TO BE A SPECIAL OR VISUAL EFFECTS TECHNICIAN?

Some of Geoff Martin's credits as supervisor, foreman, or crew member include *Nights in Rodanthe*, *The Astronaut Farmer*, *North Country*, *The Mask of Zorro*, *The Longest Yard*, and *Spy Kids*. "The most satisfying aspect of our job," he says, "is seeing our work successfully being executed on camera, with no one getting hurt and having the director

happy with what he sees. Our job is taking an event or a thing that someone else has dreamt up and making it happen. To me, that's pretty exciting and fulfilling."

Geoff says that his primary duties constantly change as the process of making a film progresses. "Initially there is the script breakdown (to figure out what needs to be done effects-wise) and the budget," he explains. "Then we have to figure out if/what things have to be fabricated. Then comes the design phase—overseeing the actual fabrication, testing to make sure everything works according to plan, interfacing with the director to make sure you are giving him what he wants, getting all the 'gags' approved before they work on camera, and making sure that everything is done safely so that no one gets hurt. Once filming starts there is the constant budget monitoring and set attendance to make sure that all things are running smoothly and that our department is performing smoothly and professionally.

"Some of the secondary duties include hiring your crew," Geoff continues, "making sure they are working safely and that they are kept informed of any changes that may come along, and things always change. Paperwork is a big part of the job—revising scripts that come along and affect our department, signing timecards, preparing purchase orders. Going to meetings is also a major part of the job—whether it's production meetings, or interdepartment meetings, or budget meetings—there's a lot of meetings."

When asked to name drawbacks to his career, Geoff cites the working hours and conditions. "Sometimes the hours

Lingo to Learn

computer-generated image (CGI) A visual effect for a motion picture that was developed using complex computer software.

latex A malleable plastic used in the construction of masks and costumes for actors in film and theatrical productions.

matte Background paintings, of mountains or a futuristic city for example, which are used in movies in place of elaborate or costly sets.

on-location A site, usually outdoors, where the filming of a motion picture takes place. Filming may also take place on a set.

producer The individual, or group of individuals or a company, who arranges the financing for the filming of a motion picture, oversees the hiring and activities of all employees involved in a production, and determines the schedule for bringing the production to completion.

pyrotechnics The art of making and using fireworks and explosives.

shop A company that provides special or visual effects for motion pictures, theatrical productions, and television broadcasts.

storyboard A scene-by-scene script of a motion picture that indicates when and where special or visual effects are required.

tricks The term used for "special effects" by those who work in the motion picture industry.

ing filming, we are working days, then we go to nights, then back to days. That gets exhausting and is really hard on the body."

Steven Blasini is a visual effects supervisor and the co-owner (along with his wife) of BFX Imageworks, a visual effects studio in California that offers a variety of services, including visual effects, computer-generated animation, 3-D and 2-D compositing, script breakdowns, budgeting, and second-unit direction. Some of his film and television credits include *Fantastic Four*, *In Her Line of Fire*, *Phantom Below*, *Missionary Man*, and *Ice Spiders*. (Visit http://www.bfximageworks.com to learn more about Steven and his career.)

"For as long as I can remember," Steven recalls, "I've been intensely interested in film and 'special photographic effects' (as it was known back then). My older brother would take me to every single sci-fi extravaganza premiere and to every retrospective and re-release of all the older classic films. *Forbidden Planet*, *War of the Worlds* (the original), *Logan's Run*, *2001: A Space Odyssey*, the original *Star Wars*, and *Close Encounters of the Third Kind* were all inspirations for me. I would grab my Super 8mm film camera and go out to my backyard and experiment with all kinds of optical tricks to create illusions. I guess you can say it was 'in my blood.'"

Steven and his wife started BFX Imageworks in 2001. His employer at the time was moving its offices to Bulgaria, and Steven says that he had no desire to relocate—or continue to work for someone else. "We began our business with no money and no work," he recalls. "I put

get a little long and the working conditions get a little rough because of weather or terrain," he explains. "At times dur-

together two computers, one for myself and one for my wife, and we worked out of our loft apartment. Then when a single, small shot that was needed for a small indie film came along, we took it, and that began the flow. The money we earned on that small job allowed us to add computers and add software, so we began setting up a fledgling Render Farm, which is a cluster of separate computers connected via a local area network, each dedicated to generating each frame of a shot. Generally, when you are rendering CGI animation, especially when the end result is to go to film or high definition, each individual frame can take anywhere from a few seconds to a few days, which is why the dedicating of individual computers to each frame becomes a necessity in order to complete your work on time and on budget. This allowed us to take on larger projects that earned us more money and allowed us to add more resources. I believe it is a myth that you need capital to start a venture like what we did. We did it with no money. All you need is your dreams and the ability to forge ahead!

"Working in the field has been my lifelong dream," he continues, "and to see it realized, nothing compares to it. I love to create something out of nothing, to amaze people with visuals that are obviously not doable without artistry. It's also tremendously rewarding to have happy and satisfied clients come back to us for more and more work. We've had to do literally no advertising at all; our work comes from word of mouth exclusively. There are few things in life that can be that rewarding."

DO I HAVE WHAT IT TAKES TO BE A SPECIAL OR VISUAL EFFECTS TECHNICIAN?

"As I think about what my job entails," says Geoff Martin, "I realize how many skills are actually required. From the administrative end you have budgeting, design, record keeping, and hiring/firing. Then you have aspects of fabrication—welding, machining, carpentry, mold making, weapons fabrication, and training of employees. Basic mechanical ability is key from the standpoint of being able to figure out what needs to be built, what that item needs to do, and how to build it so that it works properly. Without this basic mechanical ability even the use of tools would become dangerous. Then you get into production (when the cameras are actually rolling), where you are dealing with the day-to-day operations of the effects department, the proper and safe use of explosives, the general safety of not only your crew but also of the actors and general crew when effects are involved. I have mentioned safety several times; it's very important. With the kind of things we do, things can go extremely bad extremely quickly, so you have to stay alert at all times so that people do not get hurt or worse—killed!"

Special effects technicians should also be good with people. "Being able to be diplomatic when dealing with directors, producers, other department heads, or your crew is very important," says Geoff. "It's easy to alienate people, and by doing so your job gets a lot harder.

"Being able to think 'outside of the box' is important because things are never what they appear to be," Geoff continues. "For example, in the movie *The Matrix* Neo had to be able to move faster than bullets and dodge them. If your thought process is conventional that shot would be impossible to get, but by a group of people thinking 'outside of the box,' you get the shot that was in the movie."

Depending on the production, mechanical effects specialists may find themselves knee-deep in mud in subzero temperatures, or working in a studio where they may have to wait hours inside a small, cramped space for their cue to perform an effect. Makeup effects specialists most often spend their days working in a trailer at a filming location or at a shop where they can construct the masks and prostheses needed for an actor's costume.

Because the majority of special effects technicians work as freelance or independent contractors, they must often provide their own tools and equipment when hired for a job. That requires them to have large cash reserves to purchase or rent equipment they'll need to perform an effect. Cash reserves are also important because getting work is largely dependent upon the needs of filmmakers and theatrical producers. Special effects technicians have to be able to budget the money they do make to weather the lean periods between jobs.

Steven Blasini says that visual effects technicians must have the ability to separate their egos from the work they are hired to create. "It is your art, to be sure, but it is their idea and their concept and most of all, they are paying for it," he says. "So, as hard as it can be, you have to really keep your ego in check and separate yourself from your work. It is very difficult to do, without a doubt. These creations are literally your babies and to have people reject or criticize or change your 'babies' can be easily taken as offensive, but it is not. It's a job. And you are a tool for their end product. Of course, you also have to be open, not only with thoughts you may have, but accepting of thoughts they may have."

Visual effects workers must also be able to meet deadlines. "I have had many a supremely talented animator work for me, but they have no concept of the deadline," says Steven. "So as they create their breathtaking art, if they end up taking too long and missing the deadline, well then, it matters little how great the shot was since it won't make it in the film."

Successful workers in this field have good observational skills. "You need to look at everything around you," Steven advises. "How does that light create a shadow on that rock? How much darker is it under that car in front of you, than around it. How does that bird's body react to the flapping of its wings as it flies? All of these are things you will undoubtedly have to re-create as a visual effect. And even if you create the baddest looking monster this side of *Alien*, if it doesn't blend well with the live-action footage, then it's useless. You should have a thorough understanding and appreciation of art. Drawing, painting, and sculpting skills are definitely a plus, as these all translate well into the visual effects medium. But most of all, be enthusiastic about your dream! That takes you anywhere!"

HOW DO I BECOME A SPECIAL OR VISUAL EFFECTS TECHNICIAN?

Education

High School

While companies that hire technicians in special or visual effects are more concerned with applicants' past experience than whether or not they have a high school diploma, high school is one of the best places to learn many of the skills required to become successful as a technician in effects.

High school courses in chemistry, mathematics, science, physics, art, shop, and electronics are important to learn the basic skills that special effects technicians use every day. Working on high school drama productions can also be helpful for learning lighting, set, and prop design.

Students who are interested in pursuing careers in visual effects should take computer science, animation, and other related classes.

Postsecondary Training

Some universities have film and theater schools that offer courses in special effects. Some special effects technicians major in theater, art history, photography, and related subjects. The bachelor's and master's of fine arts degrees offered at colleges across the country are studio programs in which you'll be able to gain hands-on experience in theater production and filmmaking with a faculty composed of practicing artists.

Many of the skills required to work in mechanical effects can be gained by learning a trade such as carpentry, welding, plumbing, or hydraulics and applying those skills by building sets or props for community theater productions.

There are also many schools that offer classes and degrees in animation. To find good schools offering animation and computer graphics programs, consult the Animation School Database of more than 900 schools around the world. The directory can be accessed for free at the Animation World Network's Web site, http://schools.awn.com.

Some of the visual effects technicians working today have not had any special schooling or training, having mastered graphics programs on their own. Many young technicians invest in software programs in order to learn their way around computer effects. Those who can demonstrate a great deal of talent and originality in addition to computer skills will have the most success.

Certification or Licensing

A mechanical special effects technician who works with fire and explosives generally needs a pyrotechnics operator's license issued by the state. A federal pyrotechnics license is also available.

Internships and Volunteerships

Since many of the skills needed to become a special effects technician are learned on the job, it is important for those interested in working in the field to get as much hands-on training as possible. And since employment is so competitive, working as a volunteer may be the best way to learn some of those skills.

Many small community theaters are so underfunded and understaffed that they must rely on volunteers to assist in prop construction and design, makeup, and simple mechanical effects. Student filmmakers often need volunteers to assist in their productions, and local haunted houses and amusement parks may have need for technicians.

For further information on volunteer positions and internships in theatrical productions, contact your local community theater.

Visual effects specialists can learn about internships and related opportunities through their college's career services office. They may also be required to participate in an internship at an animation studio or visual effects house as part of their degree program.

WHO WILL HIRE ME?

Networking is an important aspect of finding work in the film industry. The Internet Movie Database (http://www.imdb.com) is an extensive listing of professionals in many aspects of the industry. Another good resource is LA411.com, an online directory of film industry professionals. Aspiring visual effects technicians can visit http://vfxworld.com to obtain a list of potential employers.

Most technicians in special or visual effects are freelance or independent technicians who have started their own companies, or shops. Typically, a film or theater producer will hire a technician to provide the effects for a production. Depending upon the complexity of the required effects, the technician might then hire additional freelance technicians to assist on the job. The technician who was hired by the producer is considered the special or visual effects coordinator of the crew he or she assembles. It is not unusual for the coordinator on one job to be hired later as a crew member by the coordinator on another project.

As long as California remains the motion picture capital of the world, the majority of employment opportunities for technicians in special and visual effects will be found in that state. Opportunities are also available in New York City and, for visual effects specialists, in the Pacific Northwest.

WHERE CAN I GO FROM HERE?

Most special and visual effects technicians have worked for several years to develop a reputation that will enable them to find sufficient work to support themselves, so leaving the field usually isn't in their immediate career plans. Instead, trying to work on bigger, more elaborate, and challenging productions is their primary goal.

After gaining experience working for several special or visual effects shops and perfecting their skills working on different types of projects, technicians often start their own shops. Some shops have departments or subsidiary companies that build and sell equipment or proprietary software used for creating effects.

WHAT ARE THE SALARY RANGES?

The salaries for special and visual effects technicians can vary widely. Motion picture projects may pay hundreds of dollars a week, but technicians may go months between projects.

The U.S. Department of Labor (USDL) does not offer information on salaries for special effects technicians. It does report that median weekly earnings of all wage and salary workers in the motion picture and video industries were $593 in 2006.

Multimedia artists and animators who were employed in the motion picture and video industries earned annual mean salaries of $71,910 in 2008, according to the USDL. Salaries for all multimedia artists and animators ranged from less than $31,570 to more than $100,390. Technicians at some of the top effects houses can earn hundreds of thousands of dollars on a project.

Because most technicians work freelance, benefits aren't generally provided. Union members, however, can take advantage of health insurance and other benefits of membership.

WHAT IS THE JOB OUTLOOK?

Competition for jobs in film special effects houses is fierce. There is heavy competition in this field, and in general the plum jobs go to the best-trained candidates. While some technicians provide special effects for theater, few find the work steady or well-paying

---

Advancement Possibilities

Coordinators lead teams of special effects or visual effects technicians to provide effects for motion pictures, television shows, and commercials.

Owners of special effects shops operate their own business specializing in the fabrication, installation, and activation of equipment to produce special effects for television, motion picture, and theatrical productions.

Technical directors coordinate activities of radio or television studio and control-room personnel to ensure technical quality of picture and sound for programs originating in the studio or from remote pickup points.

---

enough to work in theater exclusively. Most supplement their incomes by providing effects for television commercials and industrial productions as well. "As long as movies are being made, there will be a need for special effects people," says Geoff Martin. "However, more and more effects are being done by computer. It's hard to say if it will ever get to the point where all effects are computer-generated or not. There are some effects, like rain or fire, that just don't look right being done by a computer. Perhaps someday they will figure that out also, but I don't think that we will ever just 'go away.'"

Employment of animators (which includes visual effects technicians) is expected to grow much faster than the average for all careers through 2016, according to the *Occupational Outlook Handbook*. Despite this prediction, competition for jobs is very strong since many people view this field as an exciting potential career path.

Stunt Performers

SUMMARY

Definition
Stunt performers are actors who perform dangerous scenes in motion pictures and other settings.

Alternative Job Titles
Stunt players
Stunt workers
Stuntmen
Stuntwomen

Salary Range
$7,500 to $50,000 to $100,000+

Educational Requirements
High school diploma

Certification or Licensing
Required

Employment Outlook
About as fast as the average

High School Subjects
Physical education
Theater

Personal Interests
Entertaining/performing
Film and television
Theater

"When I was age 13," says stunt professional Al Goto, "I saw a stuntman competition on an episode of CBS's *Wide World of Sports*. That was what first brought my attention to the stunt industry. I found it both interesting and challenging that these guys were able to crash and burn over and over the exact same way, and continue to get up! I thought, 'What a great job, these guys are basically the professional athletes of the film and television world.'"

WHAT DOES A STUNT PERFORMER DO?

Stunt performers work on a wide variety of scenes that have the potential for causing serious injury, including car crashes and chases; fist and sword fights; falls from cars, motorcycles, horses, and buildings; airplane and helicopter gags; rides through river rapids; and confrontations with animals, such as in a buffalo stampede. Although they are hired as actors, they only occasionally perform a speaking role. Some stunt performers specialize in one type of stunt.

There are two general types of stunt roles: double and nondescript. The first requires a stunt performer to "double"—to take the place of—a star actor in a dangerous scene. As a double, the stunt performer must portray the character in the same way as the star actor. A nondescript role does not involve replacing another person and is usually an incidental character in a dangerous scene. An example of a nondescript role is a driver in a freeway chase scene.

The idea for a stunt usually begins with the screenwriter. Stunts can make a movie not only exciting, but also profitable. Action films, in fact, make up the majority of box-office hits. The stunts, however, must make sense within the context of the film's story.

Once the stunts are written into the script, it is the job of the director to decide how they will appear on the screen. Directors, especially of large, action-filled movies, often seek the help of a *stunt coordinator*. Stunt coordinators are individuals who have years of experience performing or coordinating stunts and who know the stunt performer community well. A stunt coordinator can quickly determine if a stunt is feasible and, if so, what is the best and safest way to perform it. The stunt coordinator plans the stunt, oversees the setup and construction of special sets and materials, and either hires or recommends the most qualified stunt performer. Some stunt coordinators also take over the direction of action scenes. Because of this responsibility, many stunt coordinators are members not only of the Screen Actors Guild, but also of the Directors Guild of America.

Although a stunt may last only a few seconds on film, preparations for the stunt can take several hours or even days. Stunt performers work with such departments as props, makeup, wardrobe, and set design. They also work closely with the special effects team to resolve technical problems and ensure safety. The director and the stunt performer must agree on a camera angle that will maximize the effect of the stunt. These preparations can save a considerable amount of production time and money. A carefully planned stunt can often be completed in just one take. More typically, the stunt person will have to perform the stunt several times until the director is satisfied with the performance.

Stunt performers do not have a death wish. They are dedicated professionals who take great precautions to ensure their safety. Air bags, body pads, or cables might be used in a stunt involving a fall or a crash. If a stunt performer must enter a burning building, special fireproof clothing is worn and protective cream is applied to the skin. Stunt performers commonly design and build their own protective equipment.

Stunt performers are both actors and athletes. Thus, they spend much of their time keeping their bodies in top physical shape and practicing their stunts.

The working conditions of a stunt performer change from project to project. Their workplace could be a studio set, a river, or an airplane thousands of feet above the ground. Like all actors, they are given their own dressing rooms.

Careers in stunt work tend to be short. The small number of jobs is one reason, as are age and injury. Even with the emphasis on safety, injuries commonly occur, often because of mechanical failure, problems with animals, or human error. The possibility of death is always present. "I have lost friends in this business," says Al Goto. "There will be fatalities, as well as life-changing injuries; it's unfortunately a risk we know is out there. The largest number of deaths are from high falls. People on a movie set often see an air bag and think, 'I'll jump off of that building.' They don't understand that you need to hit the bag in the target zone and you need to land properly. If you fail to do either from a significant height, you will be having the rest of your meals through a feeding tube at best. High falls are no joke." Despite these drawbacks, a large number of people are attracted to the work because of the thrill, the competitive challenge, and the chance to work in motion pictures.

To Be a Successful Stunt Performer, You Should...

- be in excellent physical condition
- be able to follow instructions
- have confidence in your abilities
- be self-disciplined
- have good coordination
- be calm under pressure

WHAT IS IT LIKE TO BE A STUNT PERFORMER?

Al Goto has worked in the stunt industry since 1984. He has worked on hundreds of projects as a stunt performer, stunt coordinator, and second unit director—from action films such as *Windtalkers,* to comedies such as *Friends,* to music videos and commercials. Al has been nominated three times for World Stunt Awards. (Visit his Web site, http://www.algoto.com, to learn more about his career.) "Working as a stunt performer is a wonderful job," he says. "Where else are you able to do a high-speed car chase, crash the car, and have the police hold the traffic for you, while using someone else's vehicle? All the while getting paid! I have made great friends as we work extremely close as stunt players and have to have a lot of trust in one another. If I won the lottery, I would still be working in my profession. It's truly a privilege to do what you enjoy."

A typical day on the set for Al varies, depending on the project and other factors. "Normally," he says, "I will get to the set, check in with the assistant directors, grab breakfast from the catering truck, and then, depending on the show, I may need to meet with the director to do a 'walk thru' of the scene. Or on other occasions, I make certain that all of my gear and stunt players are present and ready to go. It really depends on the show and what the action for the day entails. Other times, it's prepping for upcoming action." Al typically works 12 hours a day (plus lunch) when working on a television show or film. "When I'm not on camera," he says, "often times we are rehearsing, prepping for upcoming action. Sometimes I'm breaking down the next script and dealing with other departments (i.e., wardrobe, hair, makeup, props, special effects, construction, art, set decorators, the production designer). If the action is 'light' on a show, there may be a lot of

The Toughest Stunts

Stuntman Tim Sitarz details the most challenging stunts to perform:

The hardest stunt to perform is a stunt that you know can really hurt you if you're off. You prepare and prepare, check and double check. But sometimes things don't go the way you want them to go. Knowing that and putting yourself into that position where you can get hurt makes things difficult. Also, difficult stunts are when you have to be so precise; for example, sliding a car into a $500,000 camera and stopping two feet away at 60 mph. If I'm off, I take out the camera and the camera operators, and I ruin the car. That is why stunt people practice everything all the time. We have to be on our toes with all stunts because things change every day. One day you're fighting, the next day you're falling off a horse, the next day you're driving, the next day you're being flung 40 feet backward after being shot by a plasma gun. You never know, so know it all.

'hanging out' until my scene is ready to shoot. Sometimes, this entails working with the actors, rehearsing, and teaching. I enjoy my job because it's not a 'typical' day. There is a lot of variety."

Tim Sitarz has worked as stunt performer and coordinator since the early 1990s. His long list of film and television credits include *Get Smart, Starsky & Hutch, CSI, 24, Jericho*, and *The Unit*. (Visit http://www.imdb.com/name/nm0803196 to learn more about Tim's career.) "When I was 10 years old," he recalls, "my family took a trip to California from Minnesota.

We went to Universal Studios, and I saw the Western Stunt Show. I saw a cowboy get shot and fall off a building onto a pad, and I leaned over to my parents and asked if he got paid for that. They said 'yes,' and I said, 'I'm going to do that someday.' Ever since then, I knew what I wanted to do. To this day, my friends from Minnesota still talk about me saying I wanted to be a stuntman and going for it. I'm living my dream!"

Tim says that being a stunt performer "is fun, challenging, and exciting. And when you're working the money is pretty good." He also says that there are a few downsides to the career. "A lot of stuntmen are out there, and there are not enough jobs," he says. "Not every movie or TV show has stunts in them. They don't shoot much in the United States anymore; a lot of shows go overseas for tax purposes." Tim also cites the physical abuse a stunt performer takes as a significant con. "I've had 11 concussions between 17 years of football and 16 years of stunts," he says. "I've broken many bones: my sternum twice, four ribs, femur, ankle, collarbone, wrist, and each foot twice. Stuntmen and stuntwomen do the dirty work; you fight in an alley in downtown Los Angeles, where a homeless person urinated two hours before. It's not what you see on *Entertainment Tonight* or *Extra*. We don't get to go to the red carpet events like you see on TV. I'm not in it for the glory, so that doesn't bother me much. Also, you sometimes have to fight with the producers to get paid for what the stunt is worth, yet they'll pay an A-list actor $40,000 a week. Another challenge is working with difficult actors or actresses."

DO I HAVE WHAT IT TAKES TO BE A STUNT PERFORMER?

Al Goto says that successful stunt performers are "level-headed, determined, mentally and physically tough, and good athletes."

"Stunt people are cool and calculated under pressure," says Tim Sitarz. "A good stunt person is athletic and not afraid to take chances, but smart chances. I don't jump off a bridge into water until I go check out the water and my surroundings. Stunt people have to be reliable. If a stuntman is jumping out a window when the building explodes and I have to catch him and I catch on fire, I can't put myself out first and leave him—then two people would be hurt. I catch him first, then put myself out. A good stunt person is honest, if they can't do something, be honest so no one gets hurt and production can get the shot. If you lie and screw up, people will know. You're only as good as your last job, and a bad name travels faster than a good one."

Stunt work requires excellent athletic ability. "A person should take martial arts and gymnastics," advises Tim. "You don't have to be the best, but know the basics and fundamentals. A person has to be in shape; not many overweight stunt people are out there. Actors and actresses work hard on their bodies to get noticed, so do stunt people because we have to double them." Many stunt performers were high school and college athletes, and some were Olympic or world champions. Qualities developed through sports such as self-discipline, coordination, common sense,

and coolness under stress are essential to becoming a successful stunt performer. As a stunt performer, you must exercise regularly to stay in shape and maintain good health. You should also have some understanding of the mechanics of the stunts you'll be performing—you may be working with ropes, cables, and other equipment.

Because much of the work involves being a stunt double for a star actor, it is helpful to have a common body type. Exceptionally tall or short people, for example, may have difficulty finding roles.

Important Skills

Students who attend classes at the United Stuntmen's Association International Stunt School learn the following skills:

- precision driving
- fire burns
- wire work
- weaponry
- air ram
- martial arts
- unarmed combat
- ratchet
- special effects
- foot falls
- stair falls
- high falls
- harness work
- rappelling

Source: United Stuntmen's Association

HOW DO I BECOME A STUNT PERFORMER?

Education

High School

In high school, take physical education, dance, and other classes that will involve you in exercise, weight lifting, and coordination. Participating in organized sports can help you develop the athletic skills needed for this profession. In a theater class, you'll learn to take direction, and you may have the opportunity to perform for an audience. Tim Sitarz advises students to take theater in school. "Even though you're a stunt person," he says, "you're still on camera, and you have to act. Many stunt roles require a line or two. I'm 6'4", 255 pounds. I play bouncers, thugs, and goons, and I get lines all the time. Additionally, play every sport you can, learn as much as possible, and don't limit yourself."

Postsecondary Training

There is no minimum educational requirement for becoming a stunt performer. Most learn their skills by working for years under an experienced stunt performer. A number of stunt schools, however, do exist, including the United Stuntmen's Association International Stunt School. You can also benefit from enrolling in theater classes.

Among the skills that must be learned are specific stunt techniques, such as how to throw a punch; the design and building of safety equipment; and production techniques, such as camera angles and film editing. The more a stunt performer knows about all aspects of filmmaking, the better that person can design effective and safe stunts.

Al Goto advises aspiring stunt performers to "stay in school, graduate from college (take film classes), and learn everything that you can in terms of athletic skills such as gymnastics, martial arts, firearms, motorcycles, car driving, and scuba diving. The more that you learn, the more you will have to offer. Whatever you do, if you can really excel in one thing to a professional level, that is a big help. You'll find when you get to Hollywood that there are professional cowboys, motocross riders, street bike riders, Olympic gymnasts, and world champion karate and mixed martial arts people. So if you have a professional-level skill, that is by no means a guarantee, but it's definitely an ice-breaker and a step in the right direction."

Certification or Licensing

There is no certification available, but, like all actors, stunt performers working in film and TV must belong to the Screen Actors Guild. Many stunt performers also belong to the American Federation of Television and Radio Artists. As a member of a union, you'll receive special benefits, such as better pay and compensation for overtime and holidays.

Internships and Volunteerships

It is difficult to gain experience as a stunt performer before you actually land a job in the field. Involvement in high school or college athletics is helpful, as is acting experience in a school or local theater. As an intern or extra for a film production, you may have the opportunity to see stunt people at work. Theme parks and circuses also make much use of stunt performers; some of these places allow visitors to meet the performers after shows.

WHO WILL HIRE ME?

Most stunt performers work on a freelance basis, contracting with individual productions on a project-by-project basis. Stunt performers working on TV projects may have long-term commitments if serving as a stand-in for a regular character. Some stunt performers also work in other aspects of the entertainment industry, taking jobs with theme parks and live stage shows and events.

Most stunt performers enter the field by contacting stunt coordinators and asking for work. Coordinators and stunt associations can be located in trade publications. To be of interest to coordinators, you'll need to promote any special skills you have, such as stunt driving, skiing, and diving. Many stunt performers also have agents who locate work for them, but an agent can be very difficult to get if you've had no stunt experience. If you live in New York or Los Angeles, you should volunteer to work as an intern for an action film; you may have the chance to meet some of the stunt performers, and make connections with crew members and other industry professionals. You can also submit a resume to the various online services that are used by coordinators and casting directors. If you attend a stunt school, you may develop important contacts in the field.

Tim Sitarz says that aspiring stunt performers need to be able to handle rejection. "It will take you at least five years of hustling (going set-to-set handing off your headshot and resume to the stunt coordinator) before you will start making a small living in stunts," he says. "Ninety percent of people who come to Los Angeles to be stunt people leave before one year has passed. Ninety percent of the remaining 10 percent leave in the following year because they can't get a job. Stunt people get jobs because the people who are hiring know they can get the job done right the first time. When you're new, no one knows what you can do, you're just hoping for that break to show your abilities. Try and get your union card from the Screen Actors Guild; no card, no job, no money."

WHERE CAN I GO FROM HERE?

New stunt performers generally start with simple roles, such as being one of 40 people in a fight scene. With additional training and experience, stunt performers can land more demanding roles. Some stunt associations have facilities where stunt performers work out and practice their skills. After a great deal of experience, you may be invited to join a professional association such as the Stuntmen's Association of Motion Pictures, which will allow you to network with others in the industry.

About five to 10 years of experience are usually necessary to become a stunt coordinator. Some stunt coordinators eventually work as a director of action scenes. These professionals are known as *second unit directors.*

Stunt Performer Spotlight: Manny Siverio

Manny Siverio has been a stunt coordinator, stunt performer, and second unit director since the early 1980s. He is the winner of the 2008 Taurus Stunt Award for Best Fire Gag (*American Gangster*). He has more than 300 film, TV, and video game credits, including *Supertroopers*, *We Own The Night*, *Ugly Betty*, *Max Payne 2* and *3* (video game), *Manhunt 1* and *2* (video game), *Girl Fight*, *Third Watch*, *Blade*, *Money Train*, *Men in Black*, *Dead Presidents*, *New York Undercover*, *Law & Order*, *Ransom*, *The First Wives Club*, *Dellaventura*, *Oz*, *Malcom X*, *The Super*, and *Out for Justice*. (Visit http://www.mannysiverio.com or http://imdb.com/name/nm0803371 to learn more about Manny and his work.) Manny discussed his career with the editors of *What Can I Do Now? Film*.

Q. What made you want to become a stuntman?

A. Two things come to mind. I've always been a very physical person, and Bruce Lee influenced my love for combat art forms. I've been involved in the martial arts since I was 10, and I got into being a physical fitness instructor in my early 20s. Not to mention the fact that I loved choreographing fight scenes. I always did. I still have Super 8 (film) footage of me in Puerto Rico doing a martial arts fight scene with some friends. I knew way back then that I wanted to get into the business. It was a great career concept for me. I would be getting paid to play and fake fight. In some of that early Puerto Rico fight footage, we were fighting on the roof of this one-story home. They were building another house right next door and there was this huge sand pile in between the two houses that was being used for mixing cement. Well, I quickly figured out that I could jump off the roof we were fighting on and land safely on the sand pile without getting hurt. So you can imagine that we incorporated that element into our fight scene. Nothing has changed for me since those early years in Puerto Rico—except for the fact that I now get paid to do that sort of stuff.

Q. What do you like least and most about working as a stunt performer?

A. Cons:
Paying your dues, paying your dues, and paying your dues. It's hard in the beginning. You're the new kid on the block and have to figure out how the game is played. You have to learn what makes you marketable and run with it. But you have to be careful that those very same skills that make you marketable don't end up defining you. For example, in the beginning I was the Latino or Hispanic stunt guy, and that card worked for me. It got me in some doors and allowed me to begin developing a reputation and get my name out there. But I was careful to not end up being seen as just a Latino/Hispanic stunt guy. If that happened, then people would only think of me when they needed a Hispanic stuntman. I made it a point to have people see me as a stuntman who *happens* to be Hispanic. The same thing goes if people just see you as a fight guy. They won't call you for any other gigs because they think you can only do fights. So my advice is don't end up being a one-horse man. Learn different aspects of stunt work. Take

driving and martial art classes, learn about rigging, high falls, etc. In other words, make yourself even more marketable.

Pros:

Once you start developing a reputation, then you've earned yourself a spot on what I like to call the Conga List. The Conga List is the list of people that each coordinator has when thinking of people to hire. Our business in many ways is incestuous. People like working with people they know and trust. And the more you work, the more people know you, and the more they learn to trust you. This brings us back to paying your dues. It's frustrating, but I wouldn't have it any other way.

Q. What are the most important qualities for stunt performers?
A. There are four qualities I respect.

- Number one: Be a team player, especially when working with several different stunt people on a show. It's almost like a military unit. Everyone is looking out for everyone else. I know that when I do a stunt I want those around me to double-check and triple-check everything as if they were the ones actually doing it. We have to get along and "play" together well. I know that I end up hiring people who fit in. If we're going to be spending this much time together, then being a team player is a must.

- Number two: Follow directions. We like people who do what they are told. In other words, follow directions and always pay attention. You have to be on top of your game.

- Numbers three and four: Know your limits and be honest. Know what you

can do and can't do and don't be afraid to speak up about it. If you get hurt because of a bad turn of events (or as I like to say, "zigging when you should have zagged"), then that's one thing. But if you get hurt because you just aren't the right person for the job or lied in order to get hired, then you can quickly expect your career to be a short one. This is a small business, and people talk to one another. I look at a person's resume whom I've never hired before, and I see for whom that person has worked. I won't rely on the resume (people have been known to beef up resumes). What I'll do is call another coordinator and ask for an honest opinion of what he or she thinks of you and your skills. I once had someone hand me a resume that listed he had worked on several shows that I coordinated. Needless to say that person will never work for me. If you lie on your resume, what else are you lying about?

Q. What is one of the most interesting or rewarding things that happened to you while working in this field?
A. One of the most rewarding things that has happened to me is becoming a respected member of the film community. I feel like I can walk on any film set in New York and people know who I am and respect my body of work. People trying to follow in any successful stunt person's career have to realize that this person did not become an overnight success. I keep telling people that I was an overnight success 30 years in the making. I've paid my dues, and I'm glad I did because it's given me the experience to deal with the pressure of filmmaking—

(continued on next page)

(continued from previous page)

the ability to adapt to curve balls thrown at me while on a job. But at the same time I realize that this experience doesn't mean that I know everything. You have to be willing to learn new things, know when to admit that you don't know something, and recognize a good idea when someone other than yourself presents it. Filmmaking is not a one-man activity. It's actually the result of a collaboration of many different people with different skill sets working together to make one person's vision come true. And if you become good at what you do,

then you can feel pride when well-known actors, directors, and producers stop and ask you for your opinion on something.

Q. Where do you see yourself professionally in five or 10 years?

A. I see myself still working in the business—hopefully working more as a second unit director, but never really abandoning coordinating totally. I can never really see myself retiring. I love what I do. I get paid to play, to go out there and run around playing cops and robbers or cowboys and Indians. There's nothing else I'd rather do until the day I die.

WHAT ARE THE SALARY RANGES?

Earnings for stunt performers vary considerably based on their experience and the difficulty of the stunts they perform. In 2007 the minimum daily salary of any member of the Screen Actors Guild (SAG), including stunt performers, was $759. Stunt coordinators who worked in television productions earned a daily minimum wage of $759, and a weekly minimum of $2,828. Though this may seem like a lot of money, few stunt performers work every day. According to the SAG, the majority of its members make less than $7,500 a year, but those who are in high demand can receive salaries of well over $100,000 a year.

Stunt performers usually negotiate their salaries with the stunt coordinator. In general, they are paid per stunt; if they have to repeat the stunt three times before the director likes the scene, the stunt performer gets paid three times. If footage of a stunt is used in another film, the performer is paid again. The more elaborate and dangerous the stunt, the more money the stunt performer receives. Stunt performers are also compensated for overtime and travel expenses. Stunt coordinators negotiate their salaries with the producer.

WHAT IS THE JOB OUTLOOK?

More than 7,700 stunt performers belong to the SAG, but only a fraction of those can afford to devote themselves to film work full time. Stunt coordinators will continue to hire only very experienced professionals, making it difficult to break into the business.

The future of the profession may be affected by computer technology. In more cases, filmmakers may choose to use special effects and computer-generated imagery for action sequences. Not only can computer effects allow for more ambitious images, but they're also safer. Safety on film sets has always been a serious concern; despite innovations in filming techniques, stunts remain very dangerous. However, using live stunt performers can give a scene more authenticity, so talented stunt performers will always be in demand.

"There is a vast amount of competition for work," says Al Goto. "There are always more stunt players than job opportunities. But if it is what you really want to do, I would go for it. You only live once. I went for it, it paid off, and I have no regrets for my decision. However, don't just become a stunt worker for money or fame. The most successful people in our line of work do it because they truly love what they do."

SECTION 3

Do It Yourself

So you're thinking about a career in film—good choice! Not only is the motion picture industry an exciting, rewarding, and highly respected field, it also holds many varied opportunities for employment. Although many film careers require advanced education and/or on-the-job experience, there are many film-related activities for people who are your age. Read on for some suggestions.

❏ READ BOOKS AND PERIODICALS

Looking for detailed information on film-related topics? If so, your high school or local library is a great place to start. There, you'll find books and periodicals about acting and directorial styles; famous actors such as Jimmy Stewart, Russell Crowe, or Halle Berry; film or screenwriting competitions; career options (such as film critic, actor, and director); and almost any other topic you can imagine. For a great list of books and periodicals about film, explore "Read a Book" in Section 4, What Can I Do Right Now?

❏ SURF THE WEB

You most likely use the Internet nearly every day of your life. You probably use it to help write term papers, to communicate with friends, and you may even have a page on MySpace or Facebook. But did you know that the Web also offers countless resources for those who are interested in film careers? You can surf the Web to find film associations, blogs, competitions, college programs, glossaries, studio infor-mation, movie reviews, worker profiles and interviews, and the list goes on and on. So surf the Web, and begin learning about the world of film! To help get you started, we've prepared a list of what we think are the best film sites on the Web. Check out "Surf the Web" in Section 4, for more info.

❏ JOIN AN ASSOCIATION

Although most film associations require members to be college students or working professionals, some associations offer membership to high school students or people with a general interest in film. For example, the American Film Institute (AFI, http://www.afi.com) is an organization that is committed to providing leadership in promoting and preserving the art of film, television, and digital media. AFI offers various classes and workshops to help educate filmmakers in the latest techniques and tools available, many of which are designed to help a specific group or discipline. There are different tiers of membership, starting with a Friend status all the way up to the highest level, the AFI Premier Circle. All tiers receive the AFI Online Catalog of Feature Films, discounts to industry publications, access to pre-ticket sales, and admission to AFI film festivals throughout the country. Visit "Look to the Pros" in Section 4 for more information on associations that offer student membership.

❏ VISIT A MUSEUM

Long before the invention of Dolby Digital Surround Sound, audiences relied on subtitles and exaggerated body language and facial expressions to help establish the mood and plot of a movie. These early films, known as silent films, were quite popular and paved the way for the movie industry, as we know it today. The Niles Essanay Silent Film Museum in Fremont, California, pays homage to the "Age of the Silver Screen."

Housed in a theater that silver screen greats Charlie Chaplin and Bronco Billy Anderson often visited to watch their movies, the museum has many artifacts related to the production of silent films. Its displays include movie posters, photographs, and items used for producing and promoting films. Silent films are shown in a special theater, with a silent film comedy festival scheduled annually. More importantly, the museum strives to raise awareness of the need to restore and preserve these priceless works of early filmmaking.

For more information regarding the museum, or to arrange a school tour of the facility, visit http://www.nilesfilm museum.org.

❏ TAKE A STUNT CLASS

Ever wonder how stunt men and women are able to fall from high buildings, run through a wall of flames, or duke it out in a street fight—and come out with hardly a scratch? Such feats are possible using techniques taught and trained at stunt schools or facilities.

One registered and licensed school known for its stunt training is the United Stuntmen's Association International Stunt School (http://www.stuntschool. com) in Washington State. Its program is designed to train individuals who are interested in pursuing a stunt performing career, as well as actors who wish to improve their delivery of basic stunts.

The training is composed of a three-week, 150-hour course. Instruction includes fire runs, stunt driving, high falls, and physical fighting. Many program graduates have started successful careers in film as well as participated in live stunt shows throughout the country. Applicants must be at least 20 years old, though admission is granted to younger students who show maturity and discipline.

Don't fret if you can't make it to the International Stunt School for training. There are many gymnastic, karate, judo, and mixed martial arts training schools in your area that can teach you basic skills that are used by stunt performers. Check your local yellow pages for more information.

❏ TAKE HIGH SCHOOL CLASSES

Many high schools offer film-related electives (some may even have dedicated film studies departments). Naperville North High School in Naperville, Illinois, for example, offers a Film Production class where students learn pre- and postproduction techniques during group projects. Students in Acting and Advanced Acting electives learn not only to memorize their lines, but also create unique characterizations and movements to give life to their performance.

Classes within the core curriculum can also help prepare you for a career in film. If you aspire to be a screenwriter, then take classes that have large writing requirements such as English and creative writing. Future actors and actresses can also hone their speaking skills with classes in speech or communications. Aspiring producers can take business and mathematics classes. Stunt performers will want to take as many physical education classes as possible.

❏ ATTEND A FILM FESTIVAL

While large, well-known festivals such as the Sundance Film Festival or the Cannes Film Festival attract industry heavyweights, their location and exclusivity may be out of your reach at this time. Instead, you may want to consider some of the smaller festivals, many of which are held in your own backyard.

One example of a local festival is the Seattle International Film Festival (SIFF, http://www.seattlefilm.com). It runs from the middle of May to June and showcases films that portray original, edgy stories with diverse cultural backgrounds. Films include features, documentaries, short films, and animations. Attendees can also benefit from many of the festival's educational programs and lectures from acclaimed directors and emerging filmmakers.

The SIFF also encourages entries from up-and-coming filmmakers, with a category specifically for teenagers. Accepted films are screened during the festival, with audiences that reach 140,000 viewers or more. To learn more about the festival or download a film submission application, visit the SIFF Web site

Some high schools even have film festivals. Maybe your high school is one of them. If not, you can always work with your drama teacher or film club adviser to start one. Here are the Web sites of a few high school film festivals to help you get an idea of what these festivals entail: http://utahhighschoolfilmfestival.com, http://burkefilmfest.com, and http://nwhsff.org.

❏ TAKE A DIRECTING/FILM CLASS

Do you dream of being the next George Lucas? Taking a community or park district class is an inexpensive way to learn what it takes to be a great director and screenwriter. Kids at the Orland Park District in the Chicago-area can take advantage of such a class, "Lights, Camera, Action" to create their own *Star Wars* movie. As directors and producers, kids work in teams to create a story line, write a script, and build sets and characters using *Star Wars* LEGOs. They use graphic editing techniques and stop-motion animation to film their vision, and add background noise and music to complete the movie. Each team presents their film during a screening at session's end.

❏ LIGHTS, CAMERA, ACTION!

Did you know Academy Award-nominated director M. Night Shyamalan got his start by making home movies? Follow his example, grab your dad's video camera, and create your own film! Think of the story you want to tell—is it a romance, action comedy, or gothic horror? Put your thoughts down on paper, including story line, dialogue, and background details—this will serve as your working script. Recruit your siblings, school friends, or kids in the neighborhood to serve as actors and actresses and assign roles accordingly. Enlist those too camera shy to take on behind-the-scenes jobs assisting with lights, extra cameras, sound effects, or props. There's a job for everyone!

You can turn your basement into a sound stage and create backgrounds as needed, or perhaps you'll want to go "on location" at a park or around the neighborhood. As director, you'll want to work with each actor so they understand your "vision" of the scene. Don't fret too much if your actors forget their lines—after all, some of the greatest movie scenes were made memorable with actors' improvisation. You'll want to reshoot or edit scenes, add background music, or perhaps even add special effects to create your final product.

No movie is complete without an opening night! Go all out by inviting your family and friends for a screening, pop some popcorn, roll out the red carpet, and enjoy your hard work!

❏ TOUR A FILM STUDIO

A tour is an interesting and entertaining way of getting into the back lot of a real film studio! Most large studios offer some sort of tours for fans—you can check the Internet for specifics such as location, hours, prices, and age requirements. Here are two popular tours:

Warner Bros. Studios. After viewing a short film covering the history of the studio, you'll take a ride on a 12-seat electric cart that whisks you through several areas of the studio. You'll visit back lot streets, sound stages, television show sets, and craft shops. Spring for the VIP tour and you'll witness new sets being created, watch a special effects demonstration, walk through the costume storage area, and perhaps even meet a real live star!

Sony Pictures Studios. This studio offers a walking tour that starts with a visit to the studio museum, which holds memorabilia from some of its most popular television shows and movies. Tour highlights include a visit to an on-site recording studio used to record and produce television theme songs and movie scores. A tour of the wardrobe department shows off well-known costumes from popular movies such as *My Best Friend's Wedding* or *Zorro*. Some lucky tour goers may even get a peek at sound stages used for popular games shows such as *Jeopardy* and *Wheel of Fortune.*

For booking information on these tours, contact http://www2.warnerbros.com/vipstudiotour and http://www.sonypicturesstudios.com.

❏ ENROLL IN A SUMMER PROGRAM

You can spend your summer vacation hanging around your friends...or you can spend it learning the ropes of the film industry. If you choose the latter, you may want to consider enrolling in a summer program specially designed to help you learn more about a career in filmmaking and production.

One such program, the iD Film Academy (http://www.internaldrive.com/film/), offers a two-week session that immerses students in all facets of the film industry. Students, ages 13 to 18, receive instruction in topics ranging from how to use film-editing programs and stop-motion animation to writing film scores. This summer program has locations in San Francisco and Montreal, Canada, which provide the background for many students' films and documentaries. Finished projects are screened at the end of each session. Don't worry—there is ample time provided for other activities such as sports or sightseeing.

Reel Voices (http://www.sdaff.org/education.php), a program sponsored by the San Diego Asian Film Foundation, gives students the knowledge and techniques needed for digital storytelling. Instruction includes video production workshops, media literacy classes, and reporting assignments. Industry professionals teach all classes. Teens receive a $500 award upon completion of their film, plus a screening during the annual San Diego Asian Film Festival. Some alumni of this summer program have even shown their work at major film festivals throughout the country.

There are many such teen programs offered in locations throughout the United States. Search the Internet for those located near your area, or ask your high school career counselor to help you find some.

See "Get Involved" in Section 4 for a comprehensive list of film-related summer programs.

❑ CONDUCT AN INFORMATION INTERVIEW/ JOB SHADOW A WORKER IN THE FIELD

Talking with film professionals and shadowing them for a day will help you learn more about the pros and cons of working in the field. (For example, you might learn that the life of an actor is not as glamorous as you think; many work 12- to 16-hour days during filming.)

An information interview is basically a conversation between you a film professional about his or her career. You may conduct this conversation in person or on the telephone. You can ask a director, for example, to detail her daily tasks, why she chose this specialty, what types of tools and other equipment she uses in her work, what personal skills are required, and so on. Here are a few basic rules when conducting an information interview: dress (if you are conducting the interview in person) and act appropriately, arrive or call on time, have written questions prepared, listen closely and don't interrupt the subject while he or she is talking, have a notepad and pen ready to record the subject's responses, don't overstay your welcome (if the subject has volunteered 20 minutes of his or her time, than stick to that time frame), and be sure to thank the subject both verbally and in writing (send a thank you via mail soon after the interview) for his or her time.

Job shadowing simply means observing someone while they do their job. In the case of a director, for example, you might shadow them as they work on film sets, in meetings with producers, and as they work closely with editors and composers to finish a film. Here are a few rules to follow when shadowing a worker: dress and act appropriately, arrive on time, take plenty of notes, pay attention (if the job seems boring, don't say so!), follow the ground rules established by the subject, and thank the subject both verbally and in writing for the opportunity.

Ask your drama teacher to help arrange an information interview or job shadowing opportunity. Perhaps one of your parents has a friend who is an animator, stunt performer, or art director you could job shadow. You could also take the initiative and call or email the public relations department of a film studio or film commission near you to see if they can refer you to someone.

❏ ACT UP

If you want to become a famous actor or actress, you'll need more than big dreams—you'll need the commitment to hone your craft, the stamina to create opportunities, and the personality to stand out from the crowd. Still interested? Then read on.

First you need to practice your acting skills. Enroll in acting classes—you can find workshops or acting schools in your area by looking in trade publications, the yellow pages, or even doing a search online. Consider trying out for school plays, church pageants, or community theater productions. It's important to get acting experience under your belt, so remember that no part is too small. Hiring a personal acting coach is also a good investment. He or she can help you learn many different aspects of acting—from body and facial expressions to how to portray different emotions by using your voice and actions. Acting coaches, as well as acting schools, are also privy to many upcoming auditions and casting calls.

You'll also need to create comp cards complete with headshots, personal information, and acting credentials—these are mandatory when you attend any audition. Professional photography can be costly, but don't skimp on this step. It's worth the investment as comp cards will often be the first impression you give to casting agents and directors. In the beginning, your comp card will list every school play and bit part you've ever taken, but with more experience, you can afford to delete and revise your resume to include only the best examples of your work. Have comp cards printed with different headshots, so you have a variety of styles and looks tailored to the type of audition.

Search for auditions—trade publications such as *Variety* list movies filming in your area, as well as stage plays and commercials. Don't wait for listings, however, be proactive and send your headshots and resumes to casting agents and directors. You may want to follow up with a postcard or phone call to keep your name and photo in the pipeline.

If possible, research the role for which you are auditioning. At the very least, prepare yourself for an open call by dressing appropriately. Be friendly, smile, and appear confident. You'll make a better impression by being "on," instead of being cocky.

While films, stage plays, and commercials are increasingly going on-location throughout the United States, Los Angeles and New York are considered the premier hubs of the industry. Are you prepared to move to these cities, or at the very least a large metropolitan area?

As a teenager, there are other considerations to being a professional actor or actress. Minors must have a legal work permit that allows them to work in the entertainment industry. Some states also mandate a special bank account be set up to hold any earnings in trust. Education can also be an issue. Since many casting calls and auditions are held during the day, students must work with their teachers to make up any assignments or exams missed during the school day. Child performers lucky enough to find steady employment often resort to private tutors or home schooling to help them meet academic requirements.

It's important to remember that acting is a tough field. While you may dream of being a leading man or woman someday, consider that some professionals make their living portraying character parts, and many more spend their entire careers waiting for that big break.

SECTION 4

What Can I Do Right Now?

Get Involved: A Directory of Camps, Programs, Competitions, and Other Opportunities

Now that you've read about some of the different film-related careers, you may be anxious to experience this line of work for yourself, to find out what it's really like. Or perhaps you already feel certain that this is the career path for you and want to get started on it right away. Whichever is the case, this section is for you! There are plenty of things you can do right now to learn about film-related careers while gaining valuable experience. Just as important, you'll get to meet new friends and see new places, too.

In the following pages you will find programs designed to pique your interest in film and start preparing you for a career. You already know that this field is complex and that to work in it you need a solid education. Since the first step toward a film-related career will be gaining that education, we've found nearly 50 organizations that provide programs that will start you on your way. Some are camps or special introductory sessions, others are actual college courses—one of them may be right for you. Take time to read over the listings and see how each compares to your situation—how committed you are to a career in a film-related field, how much of your money and free time you're willing to devote to it, and how the program will help you after high school. These listings are divided into categories, with the type of program printed right after its name or the name of the sponsoring organization.

❏ THE CATEGORIES

Camps

When you see an activity that is classified as a camp, don't automatically start packing your tent and mosquito repellent. Where academic study is involved, the term *camp* often simply means a residential program including both educational and recreational activities. It's sometimes hard to differentiate between such camps and other study programs, but if the sponsoring organization calls it a camp, so do we! Visit the following Web sites for an extended list of camps: http://www.kidscamps.com and http://find.acacamps.org/finding_a_camp.php.

College Courses/Summer Study

These terms are linked because most college courses offered to students your age must take place in the summer, when you are out of school. At the same time, many summer study programs are sponsored by colleges and universities that want to attract future students and give them a head start in higher education. Summer study of almost any type is a good idea because it keeps your mind and your study skills sharp over the long vacation. Summer study at a college offers any number of additional benefits, including giving you the tools to make a well-informed decision about your future academic career.

Competitions

Competitions are fairly self-explanatory, but you should know that there are only a few in this book because film-related competitions on a regional or national level are relatively rare. What this means, however, is that if you are interested in entering a competition, you shouldn't have much trouble finding one yourself. Your school counselor or drama teacher can help you start searching in your area.

Conferences

Conferences for high school students are usually difficult to track down because most are for professionals in the field who gather to share new information and ideas with each other. Don't be discouraged, though. A number of professional organizations with student branches or membership options for those who are simply interested in the field offer conferences. Some student branches even run their own conferences. This is an option worth pursuing because conferences focus on some of the most current information available and also give you the chance to meet professionals who can answer your questions and even offer advice.

Employment and Internship Opportunities

As you may already know from experience, employment opportunities for teenagers can be very limited, especially for jobs that require a bachelor's or graduate degree or those that can require a lot of on-the-job experience. Perhaps you might be able to find a job doing clerical work for a local film production company or work as an extra in a film. (Of course, you can work as an actor at any age if you have the talent.) If you can't land a film-related job, you may just have to earn your money by working at a mall or restaurant and get your experience in an unpaid position elsewhere. Bear in mind that, if you do a good enough job and the group you work for has the funding, this summer's volunteer position could be next summer's paid job.

Basically, an internship combines the responsibilities of a job (strict schedules, pressing duties, and usually written evaluations by your supervisor) with the uncertainties of a volunteer position (no wages [or only very seldom], no fringe benefits, no guarantee of future employment). That may not sound very enticing, but completing an internship is a great way to prove your maturity, your commitment to a film-related career, and your knowledge and skills to colleges, potential employers, and yourself. Some internships listed here are just formalized volunteer positions; others offer unique responsibilities and opportunities. Choose the kind that works best for you!

Field Experience

This is something of a catch-all category for activities that don't exactly fit the other descriptions. But anything called a field experience in this book is always a good opportunity to get out and explore the work of film professionals.

Membership

When an organization (such as the American Film Institute) is in this category, it simply means that you are welcome to pay your dues and become a card-carrying member. Formally joining any organization brings the benefits of meeting others who share your interests, finding opportunities to get involved, and keeping up with current events. Depending on how active you are, the contacts you make and the experiences you gain may help when the time comes to apply to colleges or look for a job.

In some organizations, you pay a special student rate and receive benefits similar to regular members. Many organizations, however, are now starting student branches with their own benefits and publications. As in any field, make sure you understand exactly what the benefits of membership are before you join.

Finally, don't let membership dues discourage you from making contact with these organizations. Some charge dues as low as $25 because they know that students are perpetually short of funds. When the annual dues are higher, think of the money as an investment in your future and then consider if it is too much to pay.

Seminars

Like conferences, seminars are often classes or informative gatherings for those already working in the field, and are generally sponsored by professional organizations. This means that there aren't all that many seminars for young people. But also like conferences, they are often open to affiliated members. Check with various organizations to see what kind of seminars they offer and if there is some way you can attend.

❏ PROGRAM DESCRIPTIONS

Once you've started to look at the individual listings themselves, you'll find that they contain a lot of information. Naturally, there is a general description of each program, but wherever possible we also have included the following details.

Application Information

Each listing notes how far in advance you'll need to apply for the program or position, but the simple rule is to apply as far in advance as possible. This ensures that you won't miss out on a great opportunity simply because other people got there ahead of you. It also means that you will get a timely decision on your application, so if you are not accepted, you'll still have some time to apply elsewhere. As for the things that make up your application—essays, recommendations, etc.—we've tried to tell you what's involved, but be sure to contact the program about specific requirements before you submit anything.

Background Information

This includes such information as the date the program or organization was established, the name of the organization that is sponsoring it financially, and the faculty and staff who will be there for you. This can help you—and your family—gauge the quality and reliability of the program.

Classes and Activities

Classes and activities change from year to year, depending on popularity, availability of instructors, and many other factors. Nevertheless, colleges and universities quite consistently offer the same or similar classes, even in their summer sessions. Courses like "Introduction to Film" and "Screenwriting 101," for example, are simply indispensable. So you can look through the listings and see which programs offer foundational courses like these and which offer courses on more variable topics. As for activities, we note when you have access to recreational facilities on campus, and it's usually a given that special social and cultural activities will be arranged for most programs.

Contact Information

Wherever possible, we have given the title of the person whom you should contact instead of the name because people change jobs so frequently. If no title is given and you are telephoning an organization, simply tell the person who answers the phone the name of the program that interests you and he or she will forward your call. If you are writing, include the line "Attention: Summer Study Program" (or whatever is appropriate after "Attention") somewhere on the envelope. This will help to ensure that your letter goes to the person in charge of that program.

Credit

Where academic programs are concerned, we sometimes note that high school or college credit is available to those who have completed them. This means that the program can count toward your high school diploma or a future college degree just like a regular course. Obviously, this can be very useful, but it's important to note that rules about accepting such credit vary from school to school. Before you commit to a program offering high school credit, check with your guidance counselor to see if it is acceptable to your school. As for programs offering college credit, check with your chosen college (if you have one) to see if they will accept it.

Eligibility and Qualifications

The main eligibility requirement to be concerned about is age or grade in school. A term frequently used in relation to grade level is "rising," as in "rising senior": someone who will be a senior when the next school year begins. This is especially important where summer programs are concerned. A number of university-based programs make admissions decisions partly in consideration of GPA, class rank, and standardized test scores. This is mentioned in the listings, but you must contact the program for specific numbers. If you are worried that your GPA or your ACT scores, for example, aren't good enough, don't let them stop you from applying to programs that consider such things in the admissions process. Often, a fine essay or even an example of your dedication and eagerness can compensate for statistical weaknesses.

Facilities

We tell you where you'll be living, studying, eating, and having fun during these programs, but there isn't enough room to go into all the details. Some of those details can be important: what is and isn't accessible for people with disabilities, whether the site of a summer program has air-conditioning, and how modern the facilities and computer equipment are. You can expect most program brochures and application materials to address these concerns, but if you still have questions about the facilities, just call the program's administration and ask.

Financial Details

While a few of the programs listed here are fully underwritten by collegiate and corporate sponsors, most of them rely on you for at least some of their funding. The 2009 prices and fees are given here, but you should bear in mind that costs rise slightly almost every year. You and your parents must take costs into consideration when choosing a program. We always try to note where financial aid is available, but really, most programs will do their best to ensure that a shortage of funds does not prevent you from taking part.

Residential vs. Commuter Options

Simply put, some programs prefer that participating students live with other participants and staff members, others do not, and still others leave the decision entirely to the students themselves. As a rule, residential programs are suitable for young people who live out of town or even out of state, as well as for local residents. They generally provide a better overview of college life than programs in which you're only on campus for a few hours a day, and they're a way to test how well you

cope with living away from home. Commuter programs may be viable only if you live near the program site or if you can stay with relatives who do. Bear in mind that for residential programs especially, the travel between your home and the location of the activity is almost always your responsibility and can significantly increase the cost of participation.

❏ FINALLY . . .

Ultimately, there are three important things to bear in mind concerning all of the programs listed in this volume. The first is that things change. Staff members come and go, funding is added or withdrawn, supply and demand determine which programs continue and which terminate. Dates, times, and costs vary widely because of a number of factors. Because of this, the information we give you, although as current and detailed as possible, is just not enough on which to base your final decision. If you are interested in a program, you simply must contact the organization concerned to get the latest and most complete information available or visit its Web site. This has the added benefit of putting you in touch with someone who can deal with your individual questions and problems.

Another important point to keep in mind when considering these programs is that the people who run them provided the information printed here. The editors of this book haven't attended the programs and don't endorse them: we simply give you the information with which to begin your own research. And after all, we can't pass judgment because you're the only one who can decide which programs are right for you.

The final thing to consider is that the programs listed here are just the tip of the iceberg. No book can possibly cover all of the opportunities that are available to you—partly because they are so numerous and are constantly coming and going, but partly because some are waiting to be discovered. For instance, you may be very interested in taking a college course but don't see the college that interests you in the listings. Call its admissions office! Even if the college doesn't have a special program for high school students, it might be able to make some kind of arrangements for you to visit or sit in on a class. Use the ideas behind these listings and take the initiative to turn them into opportunities!

❏ THE PROGRAMS
Acting and Performance Institute at the University of California—Los Angeles
College Courses/Summer Study

The University of California-Los Angeles (UCLA) offers a six-week residential Acting and Performance Institute for high school students who have a strong interest in theater and an interest in pursuing a career in the performing arts. Students who complete the program earn eight hours of college credit. Participants learn more about theater via performance training classes (which are held Monday through Friday), occasional guest speakers and field trips, and a final performance project. Morning sessions include Taiji Warm-Up, Acting

Technique, Scene Study, Improvisation, Movement for Stage, and Mask Work. In the afternoon, students take field trips to see professional plays, observe dress rehearsals, and participate in the filming of movies. Students ages 16 and over live in UCLA residence halls; those who are 15 and under can make supervised housing arrangements via other UCLA summer programs. No audition tape is required, but applicants must submit a letter of reference from a high school instructor that details their ability to participate in this rigorous program. Tuition for the institute is $2,225 (room and board is extra and rates depend on the type of housing a participant chooses). Financial aid is available to California residents. Contact UCLA for more information.

University of California—Los Angeles
Acting and Performance Institute
Summer Sessions and Special
  Programs
1332 Murphy Hall
Los Angeles, CA 90095-1418
310-267-4836
institutes@summer.ucla.edu
http://www.summer.ucla.edu/
  institutes/Acting&Performance/
  overview.htm

American Collegiate Adventures at American University
College Courses/Summer Study

American Collegiate Adventures (ACA) offers high school students the chance to experience and prepare for college during their summer vacation. Adventures, which last four weeks, are based at American

University in Washington, D.C. During the week, participants take college-level courses (for enrichment or college credit) that are taught by university faculty and visit other college campuses and recreation sites on weekends. Students live in comfortable en suite accommodations, just down the hall from an ACA resident staff member. Enrichment courses vary, but recently included Movie and Theatre Reviews and Creative Writing—perfect for those planning to pursue a degree in a film-related field. College credit courses are also available, but none currently focus on film-related topics. Tuition (which includes room and board) for the program is approximately $6,195. Contact American Collegiate Adventures for current course listings and application procedures.

American Collegiate Adventures
1811 West North Avenue, Suite 201
Chicago, IL 60622-1488
800-509-7867
info@acasummer.com
http://www.acasummer.com

American Collegiate Adventures at the University of Wisconsin
College Courses/Summer Study/ Employment and Internship Opportunities

American Collegiate Adventures (ACA) offers high school students the chance to experience and prepare for college during their summer vacation. Adventures are based at the University of Wisconsin in Madison; they vary in length from two to six weeks. On weekdays, participants take college-level courses (for enrichment or college credit) that are taught by university faculty. On weekends, they visit other regional colleges and recreation sites. All students live in comfortable en suite accommodations, just down the hall from an ACA resident staff member. Enrichment courses vary but recently included Get in Character!, Acting and Improv, Movie and Theatre Reviews, and Creative Writing. Students in the six-week program can also participate in law-, advertising-, and business-related internships (specialties that are in demand in the motion picture industry). A computer gaming program is also available; students interested in film and animation may find this to be an interesting option. Tuition (which includes room and board) for the two-week program is approximately $2,895; the three-week program, $4,395; the four-week program, $5,595; and the six-week program, $6,995. Contact American Collegiate Adventures for current course listings and application procedures.

American Collegiate Adventures
1811 West North Avenue, Suite 201
Chicago, IL 60622-1488
800-509-7867
info@acasummer.com
http://www.acasummer.com

American Film Institute
Membership

The institute offers a friend membership option for anyone who supports its goals. Members receive access to screenings, events, and discussions with filmmakers, as well as discounts on film festival passes and film magazines.

American Film Institute

2021 North Western Avenue
Los Angeles, CA 90027-1657
323-856-7600
http://www.afi.com

Arts Camp at Rocky Mountain College of Art + Design

Camps

Rocky Mountain College offers several summer arts camps for high school students who are interested in animation. Students in the 3-D Computer Animation Camp learn how to use AutoDesk's May software and state-of-the-art equipment to create the 3-D modeling and animation used in films, video and computer games, and television. (Note: There are other animation-related courses for students interested in working exclusively on computer and video games.) The student-to-teacher ratio for classes is 19-to-1. Tuition for the five-day course is $605; there is an additional lodging fee of $540 for students who plan to live in campus housing. A non-refundable application fee of $50 is also required. (Note: Lodging is only available for juniors and seniors.) Financial aid is available. Applicants must have a GPA of at least 2.0. Contact the Director of Continuing Education for more information.

Rocky Mountain College of Art + Design

Attn: Director of Continuing Education
Arts Camp
1600 Pierce Street
Lakewood, CO 80214-1433
800-888-2787
http://www.rmcad.edu/high-school-
programs/camps-and-workshops

Buck's Rock Performing and Creative Arts Camp

Camps

Buck's Rock Camp, about 85 miles from New York, has been in operation since 1942. It features more than 30 different activities in creative, performing, and visual arts. Activities include theater, video, costume, set design, lighting and sound design, clown/improv, and circus arts.

Buck's Rock Camp is for 11- to 16-year-old students who are artistic, talented, and independent. At camp, you make your own schedule and participate in as many activities as you want. Many students return to Buck's Rock year after year and go on to become counselors. If you're 16 to 18 years old, you can register for the Counselors-in-Training program and spend part of your day as a camper and part as a counselor. In this program, you receive a reduction in camp tuition.

Buck's Rock Camp has two four-week sessions, one six-week session, and one eight-week session. Contact the camp for current tuition costs. Campers stay in cabins, eat in the dining room, and enjoy a full schedule of evening activities. You can get financial aid to help with tuition, and Buck's Rock likes to help as many campers as possible. To apply to the camp, you must fill out an enrollment form and attend a personal interview. Visit the camp's Web site for more information.

Buck's Rock Performing and Creative Arts Camp

59 Buck's Rock Road
New Milford, CT 06776-5311
800-636-5218

info@bucksrockcamp.com
http://www.bucksrockcamp.com

Camp Ballibay

Camps

Camp Ballibay, established in 1964, offers programs (two to four weeks in length) in video, visual arts, theater, technical theater, radio, dance, music, rock and roll, and horseback riding for students ages six to 16. Campers stay in cabins and have access to a swimming pool, a riding area, tennis courts, sports fields, an infirmary, a camp store, and a dining hall. Tuition for this residential camp ranges from $1,965 to $4,380, depending on the length of the program. Contact Camp Ballibay for further information.

> **Camp Ballibay**
> One Ballibay Road
> Camptown, PA 18815
> 570-746-3223
> camp@ballibay.com
> http://www.ballibay.com

Camp Chi

Camps

Camp Chi, located near the beautiful Wisconsin Dells, features many activities, including art, athletics, cooking, media, outdoor adventure, performing arts, and water sports. Students interested in the media option can learn more about video. Camp Chi has its own video studio where students can produce and direct videos and movies, shoot and edit footage, write scripts, and show their work to fellow campers. In the media option, those interested in drama can participate in the Camp Play specialty in which they learn acting, singing, or stage production skills. At the end of camp, they put on a performance for the entire camp.

In addition to all the activities, the camp, which is operated by the Jewish Community Centers of Chicago, has a heated swimming pool, a spring-fed lake with waterfront activities, a climbing and rappelling wall, a roller hockey arena, rope courses, six tennis courts, and an animal farm. The staff-to-camper ratio is one to three. Camp Chi is for students ages nine to 16. You stay in cabins with built-in bunk beds. If you're 14 to 16 years old, Camp Chi offers a separate village just for teens. Cost of the camp ranges from $1,235 to $6,710, depending on age level and program. This cost includes everything but transportation to the site. Visit Camp Chi's Web site for more information.

> **Camp Chi**
> Summer Office:
> PO Box 104
> Lake Delton, WI 53940-0104
> 608-253-1681
> http://www.campchi.com
>
> Winter Office:
> 5050 Church Street
> Skokie, IL 60077-1254
> 847-763-3551
> http://www.campchi.com

Challenge Program at St. Vincent College

College Courses/Summer Study

The Challenge Program is just what its name implies. Challenge gives gifted, creative, and talented students in grades nine through 12 the opportunity to explore new and stimulating subjects that most high schools just can't cover. If you qualify for this program and are highly motivated, you will spend one week in July on the campus of St. Vincent College taking courses such as Beginner Star on the Stage, Video Magic, and A Star on the Stage. Should you choose, you may live on campus, meeting and socializing with other students who share your ambitions and interests. Resident students pay about $600 for the week, while commuter students pay closer to $500. A limited amount of financial aid is available. For more information about Challenge and details of this year's course offerings, contact the program coordinator. A similar Challenge program is available for students in the sixth through ninth grades; it is usually held one week before the high school session.

Challenge Program at St. Vincent College

Attn: Program Coordinator
300 Fraser Purchase Road
Latrobe, PA 15650-2690
724-532-6600
challenge@stvincent.edu
http://www.stvincent.edu/challenge_
  home

College Experience Program at Southern Methodist University
College Courses/Summer Study

Southern Methodist University (SMU) offers two programs for students interested in film and other fields: College Experience Program and Summer Youth Program.

Gifted and highly motivated high school students who have completed the 10th or 11th grade can participate in SMU's College Experience Program. The five-week residential program allows students to experience college-level instruction and earn up to six college credits. Students take two courses (such as Film and Television Genres and Politics and Film) from SMU's summer school schedule. Applicants must submit an academic transcript, recommendations, an essay, and PSAT, SAT, or ACT scores. Tuition for the program is approximately $2,470. An additional $1,600 for room and board and a nonrefundable registration fee of $35 are also required.

Students ages five through 18 can participate in enrichment workshops in a variety of fields via SMU's Summer Youth Program. There are several interesting classes for students who are interested in film and related subjects. Students entering grades seven through 11 can take 3D Animation Beginner or 3D Animation Advanced, while those entering grades three to eight might be interested in taking Acting Made Fun and Readers Theater. Each class in this nonresidential program lasts five days and costs $199.

Southern Methodist University

College Experience Program
PO Box 750383
Dallas, TX 75275-0383
214-768-0123

gifted@smu.edu
http://www.smu.edu/continuing_
  education/youth

Southern Methodist University

Summer Youth Program
5236 Tennyson Parkway
Plano, TX 75024-3526
214-768-5433
smu.youth.programs@smu.edu
http://smu.edu/education/youth/
  summeryouth

Collegiate Scholars Program at Arizona State University

College Courses/Summer Study/ Employment and Internship Opportunities

The Collegiate Scholars Program allows high school students to earn college credit during summer academic sessions. Students get the opportunity to explore careers and interact with college professors, as well as receive access to internships, mentoring programs, and research opportunities. Arizona high school seniors may apply, and they are evaluated for admission based on their "high school GPA and/or class rank, test scores, high school schedules, and involvement in other programs offering college credit." Some of the courses that will be of interest to students who would like to explore the world of film include Performance, Acting, and the Individual; Introduction to Film; Film History; Math for Business; and Public Speaking. Contact the Collegiate Scholars executive coordinator for information on program costs and other details.

Arizona State University

Collegiate Scholars Program
Attn: Executive Coordinator
480-965-2621
mark.duplissis@asu.edu
http://promise.asu.edu/csp

Discover Hopkins and Summer University at Johns Hopkins University

College Courses/Summer Study

Johns Hopkins University welcomes academically talented high school students to its two summertime pre-college programs: Discover Hopkins and Summer University.

Rising high school sophomores, juniors, and seniors are eligible to participate in the Discover Hopkins program, a for-credit intensive exploratory program that is typically held in July. There are two one-credit courses available in the Theatre, Film and Media section: Script Analysis and Modern Playwriting and the Theatre. Students in the six-day Script Analysis course study the three-act structure of the screenplay. According to the program's Web site, "The intended goal of the course is not to enable students to write a screenplay, though that may happen, but to give them the critical tools to be able to analyze a movie or screenplay from an informed artistic and commercial perspective." Modern Playwriting and the Theatre is two weeks in length. Students learn playwriting basics as "they write and workshop their own monologues, dialogues, scenes, and short plays." They also read and analyze plays by modern playwrights, attend talks by theater professionals, and take field trips to local theaters. Tuition for the Script Analysis course is $1,645, while the cost for Modern Playwriting and the Theatre is $2,055. Tuition includes room and board and academic and activities fees, but does not cover books or supplies. Financial aid is available.

Rising high school juniors and seniors who are interested in getting a jump on college can participate in the Summer University program. Participants live on Hopkins' Homewood campus for five weeks beginning in early July. Classes leading to college credit are available in more than 30 programs. Those interested in film should strongly consider enrolling in Shakespeare and (Teen) Film, Introduction to Business, American Comedy Classics, Watching the Detectives, and How the Kids Stole Hollywood: The Rise of the Independent Film. All participants in the Pre-College Program also attend workshops on college admissions, time management, and diversity. Students who live in the greater Baltimore area have the option of commuting. All applicants must submit an application form, essay, transcript, two recommendations, and a nonrefundable application fee (rates vary by date of submission). Tuition for residential students is $6,300 (for two courses, room and board, and up to six credits). Commuter students pay $630 per credit hour (books, supplies, meals, and special activities are not included in this price). Contact the Office of Summer Programs for more information on both programs.

Johns Hopkins University
Pre-College Program
Office of Summer Programs
Shaffer Hall, Suite 203
3400 North Charles Street
Baltimore, MD 21218-2685
800-548-0548
summer@jhu.edu
http://www.jhu.edu/~sumprog

Exploration Summer Programs: Senior Program at Yale University
College Courses/Summer Study

Exploration Summer Programs (ESP) has been offering academic summer enrichment programs to students for more than three decades. Rising high school sophomores, juniors, and seniors can participate in ESP's Senior Program at Yale University. Two three-week residential and day sessions are available. Participants can choose from more than 90 courses. Past film-related courses include A Stage of Your Own-Acting + Directing; Improv Underground-Guerilla Theater; Lights, Camera. . . Action!-Video Production; Explo Screen Writers Guild-Screenplay Writing; and No Business Like Show Business-Musical Theater. All courses and seminars are ungraded and not-for-credit. In addition to academics, students participate in extracurricular activities such as tours, sports, concerts, weekend recreational trips, college trips, and discussions of current events and other issues. Basic tuition for the Residential Senior Program is approximately $4,555 for one session and $8,390 for two sessions. Day session tuition ranges from approximately $2,100 for one session to

$3,820 for two sessions. A limited number of need-based partial and full scholarships are available. Programs are also available for students in grades four through nine. Contact ESP for more information.

Exploration Summer Programs
932 Washington Street
PO Box 368
Norwood, MA 02062-3412
781-762-7400
http://www.explo.org

The Film Music Society
Conferences/Membership

This organization, which "promotes the preservation of film and television music," offers membership to anyone who is interested in music that is used in film and television. Benefits include a subscription to the society's quarterly journal; discounts on books, collectibles and CDs; free members-only seminars and screenings; and discounted rates for conferences.

The Film Music Society
1516 South Bundy Drive, Suite 305
Los Angeles, CA 90025-2683
310-820-1909
info@filmmusicsociety.org
http://www.filmmusicsociety.org

Fresh Films
Competitions/Employment and Internship Opportunities/Field Experience

Fresh Films seeks to develop the next generation of filmmakers via what is considered to be the largest program of its type in the United States. Each summer, it "provides access to professional equipment, experienced instructors, and a complete filmmaking experience" in Chicago, New York, Detroit, Orlando, Dallas, Los Angeles, and other cities. Students write, direct, film, and edit movies that are entered into film contests and festivals and are critiqued by well-known film professionals such as John Lithgow, Sean Astin, Katherine Brooks, and Jeremy Coon, among others. Applicants for this weeklong program must be between the ages of 14 and 19 during production. They do not need to have any experience in filmmaking. There is no cost for the program, but participants must pay for their own transportation and housing.

Fresh Films also offers a Fresh Writers program for aspiring screenwriters between the ages of 14 and 24. And alumni of both programs can serve as interns during the next year's session. Visit the Fresh Films Web site to apply and for more information.

Fresh Films
c/o Dreaming Tree Films
4646 North Ravenswood Avenue,
  2nd Floor
Chicago, IL 60640-4510
773-334-8380 x111
alana@dreamingtreefilms.com
http://www.fresh-films.com

High School Honors Program/ Summer Challenge Program/ Summer Preview at Boston University
College Courses/Summer Study

Three summer educational opportunities are available for high school students interested in film and other majors. Rising high school seniors can participate in the High School Honors Program, which offers six-week, for-credit undergraduate study at the university. Students take two for-credit classes (up to eight credits) alongside regular Boston University students, live in dorms on campus, and participate in extracurricular activities and tours of local attractions. Recent classes include Screenwriting, Acting and Performance, and Video Production. The program typically begins in early July. Students who demonstrate financial need may be eligible for financial aid. Tuition for the program is approximately $4,120, with registration/program/application fees ($550) and room and board options ($1,897 to $2,055) extra.

Rising high school sophomores, juniors, and seniors in the University's Summer Challenge Program learn about college life and take college classes in a noncredit setting. The program is offered in three sessions. Students choose two seminars (which feature lectures, group and individual work, project-based assignments, and field trips) from a total of 15 available programs, including Mass Communication (which covers film, television, advertising, public relations, journalism), Business: From the Ground Up, and Creative Writing. Students live in dorms on campus and participate in extracurricular activities and tours of local attractions. The cost of the program is approximately $3,070 (which includes tuition, a room charge, meals, and sponsored activities).

Rising high school freshman and sophomores can participate in one-week Summer Preview Programs. The noncredit, commuter program introduces students to college life and a particular area of study, including film studies. A recent film studies seminar traced the character of the American teenager over the years through film. Tuition for the program is $1,100 (which includes tuition, textbooks, lunch, and activities). No financial aid is available.

Boston University High School Programs

755 Commonwealth Avenue,
  Room 105
Boston, MA 02215-1401
617-353-1378
buhssumr@bu.edu
http://www.bu.edu/summer/
  high-school-programs

High School Summer Institute at Columbia College Chicago
College Courses/Summer Study

Rising high school juniors and seniors and recent graduates can take courses in a variety of academic areas for college credit via Columbia's five-week High School Summer Institute. Academic areas of interest to readers of this book include Film and Video, Journalism, Radio, and Television. All courses are taught by regular Columbia College Chicago faculty, and most include field trips and hands-on experiences. Students who successfully complete their course(s) receive college credit from Columbia. Contact the institute for information on tuition; a limited number of scholarships are available. Contact the institute for further details. (Note: Columbia also offers a six-week Summer Arts Camp for children in grades three through eight.)

High School Summer Institute
Columbia College Chicago
600 South Michigan Avenue
Chicago, IL 60605-1900
http://www.colum.edu/Admissions/
  hssi/index.php

High School Summer Scholars Program at Washington University in St. Louis
College Courses/Summer Study

Rising sophomores and juniors can earn up to seven units of college credit by participating in the High School Summer Scholars Program. Two five-week sessions are available. More than 60 college courses are offered. Two film-related courses that were recently offered include Your Vision/Your Voice: Introduction to Media Literacy and Documentary Production and Race, Film, and American Politics: An Examination of the Impact of Race and Mass Media on Society. Students spend 16–20 hours each week in class; during the rest of the time, they do homework, participate in planned social activities, and explore the campus and the St. Louis area. Applicants must have a B+ average and have a combined SAT score of at least 1800, a combined PSAT score of 180, or an ACT or PLAN composite score of at least 25. Tuition for the program is about $5,935, which includes the classes, housing in a campus residence hall, three meals a day, and access to student health services. Financial aid is available. The average award is $2,300, and 80 percent of students receive financial aid. Contact the program director for more information, including details on application deadlines.

Washington University in St. Louis
High School Summer Scholars
  Program
Attn: Program Director
One Brookings Drive
Campus Box 1145, January Hall,
  Room 100
St. Louis, MO 63130-4862
866-209-0691
mhussung@artsci.wustl.edu
http://ucollege.wustl.edu/programs/
  highschool

Honors College Summer Scholars Program at Hofstra University
College Courses/Summer Study

Rising high school juniors and seniors can take part in the Honors College Summer Scholars Program at Hofstra University. The four-week program allows students to explore college life, learn about careers, and earn three transferable college credits. Students choose from one of three subject areas: drama, political science, and forensic science. Students who take the drama course, Fundamental of Acting I, learn the basics of acting through "exercises, improvisations, and scripted scene and monologue work." They also get to participate in performance opportunities and take field trips to New York City to see professional actors at work. Class sessions are held on Monday, Tuesday, Thursday, and Friday from 10:00 A.M. to noon. After a break for lunch, students might attend a lecture, take a field trip, or participate in a guided discussion. On Wednesdays, students explore career paths in their field of interest by taking field trips. Classes are taught by Hofstra professors. Students also participate in cultural and recreational activities and attend seminars and workshops that educate them about the college admission process, financial aid, and career development. Program participants live in the Honors College residence hall, which has a "courtyard, double and single occupancy rooms, lounges, cable TV, Internet access, washer/dryers, and common area bathrooms." There are a variety of entertainment opportunities available for students on evenings and weekends, such as movies, karaoke, comedy skits, dessert socials, trips to New York City, sporting events, and other attractions. The cost of the program is $5,800 (which includes tuition, excursions, residence hall accommodations, and meals Monday–Friday). Additionally, Hofstra advises students to bring approximately $500 to "cover incidental expenses and meals on their own during weekends and excursions." Books and course supplies will cost about $170. Financial aid is not available. The application deadline is typically April 15.

Hofstra University

Summer Scholars Admission Office
100 Hofstra University
Hempstead, NY 11549-1000
516-463-6600
http://www.hofstra.edu/Academics/
Colleges/HUHC/summerscholars

Idyllwild Arts Academy Summer Program

Camps

Since 1950, the Idyllwild Arts Academy has been offering students intensive opportunities to explore the arts. The academy's Youth Arts Center offers a variety of theater/film-

related classes for students ages 13 throu̇ 18, including Theatre Production, Acting for the Camera, Song and Dance, Filmmaking for High School Filmmakers, Computer Animation, and Screenwriting Workshop. Commuter and resident options are available. Most sessions last two or three weeks. Contact the academy for information on tuition and fees for room and board. Scholarships are available and are awarded on the basis of financial need and the artistic ability of the applicant.

Idyllwild Arts Academy Summer Program

52500 Temecula Road, Box 38
Idyllwild, CA 92549-0038
951-659-2171
http://www.idyllwildarts.org/
summer/summer.html

Interlochen Arts Camp

Camps

Interlochen, located near scenic Traverse City, Michigan, is one of the premier art camps in the United States for young people in grades three through 12. Opportunities are available in motion picture arts, theater arts, creative writing, dance, music, and visual arts. The Motion Picture Arts program is open to rising high school sophomores, juniors, and seniors and recent graduates. Participants choose either a screenwriting or production emphasis. The Theatre Arts program is open to students in grades three through 12. Participants at the high school level choose from one of the following programs: Musical Theatre Production, Musical Theatre Workshop, Musical Theatre Intensive Program, Repertory Theatre Production, and Theatre

Design and Technology. Campers stay in cabins with 10 to 18 other students and counselors and have access to a private beach, tennis courts, division headquarters, and laundry (students are required to do their own laundry). Extracurricular activities include concerts by well-known musicians, dances, viewing gallery exhibits, arts and crafts, films, sports, and outdoor activities. The tuition for this camp varies by program type and length, but includes classes, room and board, group instruction, and use of all recreational facilities. Financial aid is available based on the financial need and the artistic ability of the applicant. Applications for all programs are due in February. Contact the camp for more information.

Interlochen Arts Camp
Admissions Office
PO Box 199
Interlochen, MI 49643-0199
231-276-7472
admissions@interlochen.org
http://www.interlochen.org/academy

The International Animated Film Society: ASIFA-Hollywood
Membership/Volunteer Programs

This nonprofit organization offers volunteer opportunities and membership to anyone who is interested in animation. Visit its Web site for more information.

The International Animated Film Society: ASIFA-Hollywood
2114 Burbank Boulevard
Burbank, CA 91506-1232
818-842-8330
info@asifa-hollywood.org
http://www.asifa-hollywood.org

International Thespian Society
Competitions/Field Experience/Membership

The International Thespian Society is the student division of the Educational Theatre Association. It is the largest honor society for theater arts students in the world. It has clubs at more than 3,600 affiliated schools in the United States, Canada, and other countries. Students in grades six through 12 are eligible for induction into the society.

Students can participate in the International Thespian Festival, an "educational and performance event for middle and high school theatre…which features a variety of performances from some of the best high school theatre programs and hands-on workshops." They can also audition for the National Individual Events Showcase, a talent competition with six performance categories (duet acting, solo/duet/group musical theater, monologue, and mime) and eight technical categories (short film, costume design, costume construction, sound design, theater marketing, scenic design, stage management, lighting design). Students who are inducted into the society receive a variety of membership benefits. Some of the benefits received by high school-level inductees include a subscription to *Dramatics* magazine, eligibility for scholarships and grants, and discounts on products.

International Thespian Society
c/o Educational Theatre Association
2343 Auburn Avenue

Cincinnati, OH 45219-2815
513-421-3900
info@edta.org
http://www.edta.org/membership/
join

Internship Connection
Employment and Internship Opportunities

Internship Connection provides summer or "gap year" internships to high school and college students in Boston, New York City, and Washington, D.C. Internships are available for students who are interested in theater. As part of the program, participants learn how to create a resume, participate in a job interview, and develop communication and personal skills that are key to success in the work world. They also get the chance to make valuable contacts during their internships that may help them land a job once they complete college. The program fee for interns in New York or Washington is $2,500, and $2,000 for those in Boston. Contact Internship Connection for more information.

Internship Connection
17 Countryside Road
Newton, MA 02459-2915
617-796-9283
carole@internshipconnection.com
http://www.internshipconnection.
com

Learning for Life Exploring Program
Field Experience

Learning for Life's Exploring Program is a career exploration program that allows young people to work closely with community organizations to learn life skills and explore careers. Opportunities are available in arts and humanities, business, communications, and other fields. Each program has five areas of emphasis: career opportunities, service learning, leadership experience, life skills, and character education. As a participant in the Arts & Humanities program, you will learn about the demands and rewards of careers in the field such as film editor, entertainer, playwright, set designer, stage manager, hair stylist, camera operator, makeup artist, dramatics teacher, and theater manager.

To be eligible to participate in this program, you must be 15 to 20 years old *or* be 14 years old and have completed the eighth grade.

To find a Learning for Life office in your area (there are more than 300 throughout the United States), contact the Learning for Life Exploring Program.

Learning for Life Exploring Program
1325 West Walnut Hill Lane
PO Box 152079
Irving, TX 75015-2079
972-580-2433
http://www.learningforlife.org/
exploring

National High School Institute at Northwestern University
College Courses/Summer Study

The National High School Institute is the nation's oldest university-based program for outstanding high school students. It was established in 1931. The month-long program offers the following courses: Debate, Speech, Journalism, Music, Film & Video Production, and Theatre Arts. Students in the Film & Video Production program can take Production, Animation, or Screenwriting (which are five-week courses) or Acting on Camera (which last three weeks). The Theatre Arts program offers two courses: Theatre Arts, Design/Tech (a five-week course) and Musical Theatre (a seven-week course). The student-to-teacher ratio for these programs is 6-to-1. Applicants for the National High School Institute must be rising high school seniors, excel academically, and "meet a high standard of character, dependability, and intelligence." A variety of extracurricular activities are also available to students in the program, including tours, movies, shopping, sing-alongs, and outings to sporting and cultural events. Students live on campus in university residence halls, where they also take their meals. Costs range from approximately $2,850 to $6,500, depending on the program; these amounts include tuition, room, board, health service, field trips, and group events. Scholarships are available. The early admission deadline is typically in the beginning of March, while the regular admission deadline is in early April. Visit the program's Web site for more information.

Northwestern University
National High School Institute
617 Noyes Street
Evanston, IL 60208-4165
800-662-6474
nhsi@northwestern.edu
http://www.northwestern.edu/nhsi

New York Film Academy Film and Acting Camps for High School Students and Kids
Camps
Teens ages 14 through 17 who are interested in film, television, video, animation, and drama can participate in the following camps offered by the New York Film Academy: Film, Acting, Screenwriting, 3-D Animation, Musical Theatre, Broadcast Journalism, and Music Video. More than 20 specialized camps and classes are available under these categories. Camps are available for time spans of one, three, four, and six weeks. A 12-weekend film camp is also available. Camps are located at Millennium High School in New York City; Universal Studios in Los Angeles; Harvard University in Boston; Disney Studios in Florida; the National Film School of France in Paris; and locations to be determined in Florence, Italy. (Film and Acting Camps are also available to kids ages 10 through 13; they are located in New York City and Florida.) Classes typically run Monday through Friday, 9:00 A.M. to 6:00 P.M. On weekends, campers participate in planned activities and field trips. Instructors are film professionals who have MFAs from top film schools. Contact the academy for more information on tuition costs, room and board, and application deadlines.

New York Film Academy
100 East 17th Street
New York, NY 10003-2160
212-674-4300
film@nyfa.edu
http://www.nyfa.com/summer_camp/
  programs/filmmaking

Ohio Summer Honors Institute/ Residential Camps at Wright State University

College Courses/Summer Study

Ohio residents who are entering grades 10 or 11 may participate in the Ohio Summer Honors Institute at Wright State University. The Performance Theatre or Technical Theatre options will be of particular interest to students interested in drama. Only 15–25 spaces are available for these two-week residential programs, so it is a good idea to apply early. The application deadline is typically in early April. The all-inclusive cost for the program is about $500.

In addition to the Ohio Summer Honors Institute, students in grades six through nine can participate in weeklong residential camps. The following camps are available to students who are interested in drama, animation, and related fields: Digital Storytelling, Multimedia, Dramatic Theatre, and Young Writers–Creative Mind. For further details on these programs, contact the Office of Pre-College Programs.

Wright State University

Office of Pre-College Programs
3640 Colonel Glenn Highway
Dayton, OH 45435-0001
937-775-3135
precollege@wright.edu
http://www.wright.edu/academics/
 precollege

Pre-College Courses/Summer Session Credit/Theatre Bridge at Brown University

College Courses/Summer Study

High school students in the Pre-College Courses Program at Brown can take one or more interesting college-level courses. Classes, which last anywhere from one to four weeks, are held Monday through Friday. More than 200 classes are available; all are not for credit. Students spend three hours a day in class, and the rest of the time studying, interacting with professors and fellow students, and participating in cultural and social activities. Students with an interest in film and drama will find a wealth of fascinating courses, including The Art of the Film, Literature and Film, Digital Video Production, Creative Writing: Script and Stage, and History in Fact, History in Film: WWII–1980. These courses all last three weeks. There are also classes that will help you develop your communication or study skills or better prepare for the college admissions process, including Cracking the AP Code (one week), Putting Ideas Into Words (one week), Persuasive Communication (one week), Writing the Academic Essay (three weeks), and Writing the College Admissions Essay (one week). Program participants live in residence halls that are within walking distance of classes and other activities. Students who are interested in taking Pre-College Courses must have intellectual curiosity, be emotionally mature, and have a strong academic record. The following tuition rates are charged for Pre-College Courses: one week residential ($2,153), one week commuter ($1,652); two week residential ($3,265), two week commuter ($2,255); three week residential ($4,702), three week commuter ($3,200); four week residential ($5,454), four week commuter ($3,449). Housing and meals are included in the residential tuition. A limited amount of financial aid is available.

Rising high school seniors interested in film and drama can also take classes in the Summer Session Credit Program, including Shakespeare Rewrites Shakespeare and Art/Cinema. Each class lasts seven weeks. A commuter or residential option is available, although students who pursue the residential option must take two courses. The cost for one course for commuter students is about $3,200 and $5,990 for two classes. Tuition for residential students is about $9,200.

Brown University also offers Theatre Bridge, a six-week immersive theatre program for 10th- through 12th-grade students. Students take classes (except on Sunday) in text, improvisation, and movement. They spend much of their downtime rehearsing and preparing for classes. They also take field trips, have the opportunity to participate in cocurricular and recreational activities, and interact closely with theater faculty and students. At the end of the class, students put on a performance for staff and the public. Students live in Brown dormitories and eat in campus dining halls. The cost of the program is about $6,750 (which includes room and board). Some financial aid may be available.

Brown University
Office of Summer & Continuing Studies
42 Charlesfield Street, Box T
Providence, RI 02912-9063
401-863-7900
http://brown.edu/scs/pre-college/pre-college-courses.php

Pre-College Programs at the University of California—Santa Barbara
College Courses/Summer Study
The University of California-Santa Barbara offers two six-week programs for high school students who are interested in film and drama and other fields: Early Start and Academic & Enrichment. In the Early Start Program, students take two college-level courses to help them explore career options and prepare for college study. Students interested in film can take Intro to Cinema, Intro to Communication, or Shakespeare. Applicants must have completed the 10th, 11th, or 12th grades and have a GPA of at least 3.3 to be eligible for the program.

Students in the Academic & Enrichment Program take one for-credit course and one noncredit, skills-based enrichment course. Applicants must have completed the 10th, 11th, or 12th grades and have a GPA of at least 3.15 to be eligible for the program. A typical 1+1 pairing for students interested in acting might consist of Acting Through Improvisation (noncredit) and Introduction to Cinema (for credit).

Students in both programs live in Santa Cruz Residence Hall, which is located near the Pacific Ocean. The rooms feature high-speed Internet access. Other amenities in the residence halls and on campus include a recreation center, pool table, video games, multi-station computer center, and laundry room. The cost for either program is approximately $6,770 (which includes tuition, housing, three daily meals, and extracurricular activities). A nonrefundable application fee of $95 is also required.

University of California—Santa Barbara

c/o Summer Discovery
1326 Old Northern Boulevard
Roslyn, NY 11576-2244
805-893-2377
http://www.summer.ucsb.edu/
  precollegeprograms.html

Secondary School Program at Harvard University

College Courses/Summer Study

High school students who have completed their sophomore, junior, or senior years may apply to Harvard's Secondary School Program. The program is held for six weeks each summer, and participants earn college credit. Students who live on campus take either two four-credit courses or one eight-credit course for college credit. Commuting students may take two concurrent four-credit courses or one eight-credit course. Recent film-related courses include Shakespeare, Beginning Screenwriting, Introduction to Acting, Directing, Introduction to Film Theory, and various acting workshops. In addition to academics, students can participate in extracurricular activities such as intramural sports, a trivia bowl, a talent show, and dances. Tuition for the program ranges from $2,475 (per four-credit course) to $4,950 (per eight-credit course). A nonrefundable registration fee ($50), health insurance ($165), and room and board ($4,250) are extra. Contact the program for more information.

In addition to the aforementioned on-site offerings, Harvard also offers selected online classes to students who can't attend classes on campus.

Harvard University

Secondary School Program
51 Brattle Street
Cambridge, MA 02138-3722
617-495-3192
ssp@dcemail.harvard.edu
http://www.summer.harvard.
  edu/2009/programs/ssp

SkillsUSA

Competitions

SkillsUSA offers "local, state and national competitions in which students demonstrate occupational and leadership skills." Students who participate in its SkillsUSA Championships can compete in categories such as 3-D Visualization and Animation, Entrepreneurship, Prepared Speech, and Television (Video) Production. SkillsUSA works directly with high schools and colleges, so ask your guidance counselor or teacher if it is an option for you. Visit the SkillsUSA Web site for more information.

SkillsUSA

14001 SkillsUSA Way
Leesburg, VA 20176-5494
703-777-8810
http://www.skillsusa.org

Summer College Programs for High School Students at Cornell University

College Courses/Summer Study

Rising high school juniors and seniors and recent graduates who are interested in film can take On Camera: Studies in Film Analysis, a three-week residential program. Students in this program will learn how to creatively and critically analyze films. Students participate in lectures, discussions, regular film screenings, and screenwriting exercises. Some of the questions considered include "What is the relation of one scene to another?; What meanings are created by camera position and distance?; How does the duration of a shot or the angle of the lighting underline meanings?; Why does the camera tilt and pan, say, instead of zoom?; and How does a film draw us in, making us collaborators or voyeurs?" Students interact closely with professors, film professionals, and fellow students. These are regular undergraduate courses condensed into a very short time span, so they are especially challenging and demanding. Program participants live in residence halls on campus and get to take advantage of campus facilities. The cost for the program is $5,310 (which includes room and board). Applications are typically due in late April, although Cornell advises that submissions be made well in advance of the deadline; those applying for financial aid must submit their applications by April 1. Further information and details about the application procedure are available from the Summer College office.

Cornell University Summer College for High School Students

B20 Day Hall
Ithaca, NY 14853-2801
607-255-6203
http://www.sce.cornell.edu/sc

Summer College for High School Students at Syracuse University
College Courses/Summer Study

Students who have completed their sophomore, junior, or senior year of high school are eligible to apply to the Summer College for High School Students at Syracuse University, which runs for six weeks from early July to mid August. Commuter and residential options are available. The program has several aims: to introduce students to the many possible majors and study areas within their interest area; to help them match their aptitudes with possible careers; and to prepare them for college, both academically and socially. Students attend classes, listen to lectures, and take field trips to destinations that are related to their specific area of interest. All students are required to take two for-credit courses during the program and they receive college credit if they successfully complete the courses.

Students interested in drama can explore the field via the program's Acting & Musical Theater option, in which they take two classes: Drama 100: Elements of Performance and Drama 200: Basic Acting. Classes "aim to improve command of your body, mind, and voice, so that combined they become the expressive instrument of an actor."

Admission is competitive and is based on recommendations, test scores, and transcripts. The total cost of the residential program is about $6,995; the commuter option costs about $4,995. Some scholarships are available. The application deadline is in mid May, or mid April for those seeking financial aid. For further information, contact the Summer College.

Syracuse University
Summer College for High School
  Students
700 University Avenue
Syracuse, NY 13244-2530
315-443-5000
sumcoll@syr.edu
http://summercollege.syr.edu

Summer High School Institute at the University of Wyoming
College Courses/Summer Study

The Summer High School Institute is a three-week summer residential program that seeks to introduce high school students to college life and help them explore various academic fields. Participants are outstanding sophomores in Wyoming high schools who have been nominated by their teachers, counselors, or principals. Students take one humanities/social science course, one math/science course, and a personal growth seminar, which seeks to "help students develop positive interpersonal skills; share experiences; gain a better understanding of self, others, and the nature of human interaction; and provide the opportunity to form lasting friendships." Filmmaking 101, HSI Style is one humanities/social science course that would be of interest to those who want to explore the world of film. It examines the way film can be used to communicate accurate or biased information and the role it plays in influencing popular opinion. Students are introduced to career opportunities in the film industry, learn

filmmaking techniques, and produce a film documentary of their experiences in the class.

Participants live in campus residence halls and eat meals in dining rooms. There are a variety of extracurricular activities available such as a talent show, plays, concerts, recreational activities, and a sight-seeing trip to Denver, Colorado. The program is free, although students are responsible for transportation and should bring spending money for off-hour activities. Contact the institute for more information.

University of Wyoming
Summer High School Institute
1000 East University Avenue,
  Department 4147
101 Merica Hall
Laramie, WY 82071-2000
307-766-3005
hsi@uwyo.edu
http://www.uwyo.edu/hsi/info.
  asp?p=4695

Summer High School and William H. Cosby Future Filmmakers Workshop at New York University (NYU)
College Courses/Summer Study

High school students who are interested in film and drama can participate in two programs: the Summer High School and the William H. Cosby Future Filmmakers Workshop.

High school sophomores, juniors, and seniors in the four-week Summer High School program take college-level classes in New York City; Dublin,

Ireland; or Paris, France. Students earn up to six college credits upon completion of the program. Recent courses include Drama, Dramatic Writing, Film, and Photography in New York; Drama and Film in Dublin; and Drama in Paris. Students must stay in NYU-assigned housing. Applications are typically due in mid February. Tuition for New York-based programs is about $6,815. Participants also must pay the following fees: activities fee, $480; film narrative lab fee, $482; photography and imaging lab fee, $332; and room and board fee, unavailable at press time. Tuition for international-based programs is $10,267 and includes room and board and activities. An additional $527 fee is required for the filmmakers workshop lab and insurance. Application fees of $75 to $90 are also required. A limited number of need-based scholarships are available. Contact the Summer Programs Administrator for more information.

The William H. Cosby Future Filmmakers Workshop is available to "gifted students in the New York metro area (five boroughs of New York City, New Jersey, and Connecticut) who are traditionally underrepresented groups in the industry." Students learn about filmmaking through "screenings, discussions with professional filmmakers, and hands-on production of short student films." The program is free and meets for 12 weeks from February through May. The priority application deadline is typically in mid October. Contact the Director of Recruitment for more information.

New York University

Office of Special Programs
Attn: Summer Programs
  Administrator
721 Broadway, 12th Floor
New York, NY 10003-6807
212-998-1500
tisch.special.highschool@nyu.edu
http://specialprograms.tisch.nyu.edu/
  page/hsStudents.html

New York University

William H. Cosby Future
  Filmmakers Workshop
Attn: Director of Recruitment
721 Broadway, 8th Floor
New York, NY 10003-6807
212-998-1900
http://specialprograms.tisch.nyu.edu/
  object/FutureFilmmakers.html

Summer Program for High School Students at Columbia University
College Courses/Summer Study

Rising ninth through 12th graders who are interested in film and drama and other fields can participate in Columbia University's weeklong Summer Program for High School Students. Freshman–Sophomore Division courses include Understanding the Arts through Literature and Cinema and Introduction to Creative Writing. Junior–Senior Division courses include Digital Filmmaking: From Initial Concept to Final Edit; Theatrical Collaboration: the Actor, the Director, and the Playwright; Critical Focus on the Visual Arts; and Introduction to Business Finance and Economics. A course on college preparation is also available. Courses are rigorous, but are not available for college credit. During the week, students take classes from 10:00 A.M. to 12:00 P.M.; break for lunch and activities from 12:00 to 2:30 P.M.; and return to class from 2:30 to 4:30 P.M. In the evenings and on weekends, residential students participate in a wide variety of extracurricular activities, including on-campus events (such as parties, a talent show, a scavenger hunt, an open mike night, and organized sports) and off-campus excursions in and around New York City (such as guided walking tours, films, museums, concerts, restaurants, beaches, and amusement parks). Participants also have access to university libraries, computer labs, a fitness center, a student activity center, and other facilities. Commuter students pay approximately $3,400 per session. Residential students pay $6,225, which includes housing and dining. Both commuter and residential students pay an additional fee of $135 for activities and health coverage. The university also suggests that residential students bring an additional $700 in spending money. Contact the School of Continuing Education for more information.

Columbia University
Summer Program for High School
  Students
School of Continuing Education
203 Lewisohn Hall
2970 Broadway, Mail Code 4119
New York, NY 10027-6902
212-854-9666
hsp@columbia.edu
http://www.ce.columbia.edu/hs

Summer Scholars Institute at Pace University
College Courses/Summer Study

Rising high school juniors and seniors can participate in Pace University's Summer Scholars Institute, a two-week program that allows them to take college-level courses and get a taste of college life. Each major features two classes—one in the morning, and one in the afternoon. In the evenings, students participate in activities that help them learn how to write better college essays and applications, as well as explore the culture of New York City. Two majors are available for students who are interested in film/drama: On Broadway: Theatre & Acting and Film & Screen Studies. Students in the On Broadway: Theatre & Acting major take two interesting classes. Scenes and Monologues for Auditions features an interactive workshop that teaches students effective techniques for auditions. Audition Technique focuses on "sources for identifying appropriate auditioning opportunities, proper etiquette, and issues with agents, casting directors, and managers." Students in the Film & Screen Studies major take The Film Experience, which provides an overview of the basics of film and "explores how creative analysis of film intersects with issues of social significance." They also take Alfred Hitchcock, the Master of Suspense, a course that examines some of the legendary filmmaker's most popular films such as *Psycho* and *The Birds* and how effective screenwriting, camera techniques, and editing were used to make these masterpieces. The cost of the program is $1,000 for commuters (which includes one meal a day and social events) and $2,000 for residents (which includes room, two meals a day, and social events). Financial aid is available. Applications are typically due in mid June. Contact the program coordinator for more information.

Pace University
Summer Scholars Institute
Attn: Program Coordinator
Pforzheimer Honors College
W207E Pace Plaza
New York, NY 10038
212-346-1192
summerscholar@pace.edu
http://www.pace.edu/page.cfm?doc_
  id=17156

Summer Scholars Program at Furman University

College Courses/Summer Study

Rising juniors and seniors with strong academic skills who are interested in film/drama careers can take several interesting seminars. Students who take FUTube: Video for the Web! learn video, animation, design, and editing techniques to create videos for YouTube and other Web sites. They will learn how to use Apple iMovie, Apple Garage Band, Photoshop, Dreamweaver, digital video recorders, flatbed scanners, and other software and hardware. In the Theater: ACTion! seminar students learn how to use their bodies to communicate moods and emotions while acting. Students who take Writing About Film: Creative and Critical Eyes will learn about the "elements of film style: setting camera angle and movement, editing and sound."

They will also study the challenges and rewards of literary adaptation of classics such as Shakespeare's *Hamlet*. Tuition for each one-week program is $800 (which includes room, board, activities, and fields trips). Applications are typically due in June. Contact the Office of Enrollment for more information.

Furman University
Office of Enrollment
3300 Poinsett Highway
Greenville, SC 29613-0002
864-294-3231
mary.hearne@furman.edu
http://www.furman.edu/camps
  andconferences/camps.htm

Summer Scholars Program at the University of Notre Dame

College Courses/Summer Study

The Summer Scholars Program consists of more than 10 two-week classes for rising junior or senior high school students. Students who take Acting for Stage and Film: Acting Professionally learn how to act both on and off camera. They learn the importance of treating acting as an art (voice and movement, scene study, monologue preparation, script analysis, improvisation, and character studies) and a business (creating a resume, taking starter headshots, etc.). Those who take Film and Video Production: Making Movies Under the Dome learn about the history of motion pictures, study filmmaking, and produce and direct their own short film, which is screened at the end of the program. The application deadline for this mandatory residential program is typically in early

March. Tuition is about $2,500 (which includes room/board and meals), plus a $45 application fee. A limited amount of financial aid is available. Contact the Office of Pre-College Programs for more information.

University of Notre Dame
Office of Pre-College Programs
202 Brownson Hall
Notre Dame, IN 46556-5601
574-631-0990
precoll@nd.edu
http://precollege.nd.edu/
  summer-scholars

Summer Seminars at the University of Southern California
College Courses/Summer Study

Rising high school sophomores, juniors, and seniors who are interested in film and other subjects can get a taste of college life by participating in four-week Summer Seminars at the University of Southern California. Commuter and residential options are available. Past seminars include Acting Workshop, Basic Animation Techniques, and Playwriting. A typical schedule involves lectures from 9:00 A.M. to 12:00 P.M., a break for lunch, a workshop from 1:30 to 4:30 P.M., a study session from 4:00 to 6:00 P.M., dinner, and free time in the evening. A free College Application Process Workshop is also offered three times a summer to help students prepare to apply to college. In addition to classes, workshops, and studying, students participate in a variety of recreational activities (dancing, karaoke, a movie night) and field trips (the Hollywood Walk of Fame, a youth

symphony concert, Disneyland, Knott's Berry Farm, the J. Paul Getty Museum, the Santa Monica Pier, a Dodgers baseball game, or a visit to the beach).

Participants who choose the residential option stay in dormitories on campus that have a common hallway with bathroom and showers. Each room has analog phone ports, Ethernet ports, a Microfridge (a half-sized refrigerator with attached microwave), and cable TV hookup. Students must bring their own telephones, televisions, cables for Internet hookup, linens, and toiletry items. The cost of attendance for residential students is about $6,100 (and includes room and board, and lab, program, and health center fees). The cost of attendance for commuter students is about $4,295 (and includes a meal plan and lab, program, and health center fees). Financial aid is available. The application deadline is typically in late March.

**University of Southern
  California**
Continuing Education and Summer
  Programs
3415 South Figueroa Street,
  Suite 107
Los Angeles, CA 90089-0874
213-740-5679
summer@usc.edu
http://cesp.usc.edu

Summer Study at Pennsylvania State University
College Courses/Summer Study

High school students who are interested in film and other fields can apply to participate in the following Summer

Study programs: the College Credit Program and the Summer Enrichment Program. The six-and-a-half-week College Credit Program begins in late June and recently offered the following film/drama-related classes: The Art of the Cinema and Fundamentals of Acting. Students typically choose one college credit course (for three or four credits) and either an enrichment class/workshop (such as Computer Animation) or the Kaplan SAT or ACT prep class. Students who have completed the 10th, 11th, and 12th grades may apply. The noncredit Summer Enrichment Program offers three-and-a-half week and two-week options and recently featured film/drama-related classes such as Animaniacs: Introduction to Computer Animation; Move Over Spielberg: Digital Video/Film Editing; and All the World's a Stage: Theater. Students who have completed the 9th, 10th, and 11th grades are eligible for the program. Tuition for the College Credit Program is approximately $6,995, while tuition for the noncredit Enrichment Program is approximately $4,495 (three-and-a-half-week program) and $2,495 (two-week program). Limited financial aid is available. Contact the Summer Study Program for more information.

Pennsylvania State University
Summer Study Program
900 Walt Whitman Road
Melville, NY 11747-2293
800-666-2556
info@summerstudy.com
http://www.summerstudy.com/
  pennstate

Summer Term at the University of Maryland
College Courses/Summer Study

Rising high school juniors and seniors with a GPA of at least 3.0 may take one or more classes for credit in the University of Maryland's Summer Term program. Two six-week sessions and four three-week sessions are available. College credit is awarded to students who satisfactorily complete the course. Classes that would be of interest to students who want to pursue careers in film, theater, or drama include Introduction to the Theatre, Fundamentals of Theatrical Design, Acting: Foundations, and Play Directing. Participants live in residence halls at the University of Maryland and take their meals on campus or in selected College Park restaurants. A commuter option is also available. Contact the Office of Extended Studies for information on current tuition costs and application deadlines.

University of Maryland
Office of Extended Studies
Mitchell Building, 1st Floor
College Park, MD 20742
301-405-7762
http://www.summer.umd.edu

Summer Youth Explorations at Michigan Technological University
College Courses/Summer Study

Michigan Technological University (MTU) offers the Summer Youth Explorations program for students in grades six through 12. Participants attend weeklong sessions, choosing either to commute or to live on campus. Students undertake an exploration in one of many career fields through classes, field trips, and discussions with MTU faculty and other professionals. Students in grades nine through 11 who are interested in careers in film production can take Lights, Camera, Action! Film and Video Production, in which they will learn visual storytelling, video, and sound recording techniques to create a short documentary or fiction film. At the conclusion of the program, they will have the opportunity to have their film screened in the program's Summer Youth Showcase. The cost of the Summer Youth Program is $650 for the residential option, $395 for commuters. Applications are accepted up to one week before the exploration begins.

Summer Youth Explorations

Michigan Technological University
Youth Programs Office, Alumni
  House
1400 Townsend Drive
Houghton, MI 49931-1295
906-487-2219
http://youthprograms.mtu.edu/syp

Summerfuel at the University of California—Berkeley

College Courses/Summer Study

High school students who are interested in experiencing college life and learning about one or more of their favorite subjects can participate in the month-long Summerfuel program at the University of California—Berkeley. College credit is awarded to students who complete the program. Some recent courses include SAT Preparation, Creative Writing, Business & Entrepreneurship, Marketing & Advertising, Public Speaking, and Film

Studies. In the Film Studies class, students receive a "basic grounding in the theory, history, and criticism of film" and view a wide range of films. Classes are taught by university faculty. Noncredit mini-courses, such as Foreign Films & Food, are also available. In addition to course work, students participate in sports and other recreational activities, as well as take trips to a San Francisco Giants game, Alcatraz Island, area beaches, Six Flags Marine World, area colleges, and other local attractions. The cost for the residential program is $6,195. Participants live in a double room in one of the college's dorms and also have access to laundry machines, recreational facilities, computer labs, and the Foothill Dining Hall (students receive three meals a day during the week and two a day on weekends). All rooms have telephone and Internet access. Summerfuel programs are operated by Academic Study Associates, an organization that has been offering residential and commuter pre-college summer programs for young people for more than 25 years.

Academic Study Associates

ASA Programs
375 West Broadway, Suite 200
New York, NY 10012-4324
800-752-2250
summer@asaprograms.com
http://www.asaprograms.com/
  summerfuel

Summerfuel at the University of Massachusetts—Amherst

College Courses/Summer Study

High school students who are interested in experiencing college life and learning about one or more of their favorite subjects can participate in the month-long Summerfuel program at the University of Massachusetts—Amherst. College credit is awarded to students who complete the program. Some recent courses include Business & Entrepreneurship, Marketing & Advertising, Public Speaking, and Film Studies. In the Film Studies class, students receive a "basic grounding in the theory, history, and criticism of film" and view a wide range of films. Classes are taught by university faculty. In addition to course work, students participate in sports and other recreational activities, as well as take trips to a Boston Red Sox game, area beaches, Six Flags New England, and other local attractions. The cost for the residential program is $6,195. Participants live in fully air-conditioned, suite-style apartments. Summerfuel programs are operated by Academic Study Associates, an organization that has been offering residential and commuter pre-college summer programs for young people for more than 25 years.

Academic Study Associates

ASA Programs
375 West Broadway, Suite 200
New York, NY 10012-4324
800-752-2250
summer@asaprograms.com
http://www.asaprograms.com/
    summerfuel

Read a Book

When it comes to finding out about film, don't overlook a book. (You're reading one now, after all.) What follows is a short, annotated list of books and periodicals related to film. The books range from personal accounts of what it's like to be a stunt person to professional volumes on specific topics such as film editing or the history of film. Don't be afraid to check out the professional journals, either. The technical stuff may be way above your head right now, but if you take the time to become familiar with one or two, you're bound to pick up some of what is important to film professionals, not to mention begin to feel like a part of their world, which is what you're interested in, right?

We've tried to include recent materials as well as old favorites. Always check for the latest editions, and, if you find an author you like, ask your librarian to help you find more. Keep reading good books!

❏ BOOKS

Apel, Melanie Ann. *Cool Careers Without College for Film and Television Buffs.* New York: Rosen Publishing Group, 2008. Features interesting careers—such as actor, musician, and puppeteer—that do not require advanced education.

Boughn, Jenn. *Stage Combat: Fisticuffs, Stunts, and Swordplay for Theater and Film.* New York: Allworth Press, 2006. This book provides an overview of the ins and outs of stagecraft and step-by-step instructions for combat with and without weapons. It will teach you how to safely fall, tumble, engage in fights, and use swords.

Cowgill, Linda J. *Writing Short Films: Structure and Content for Screenwriters.* 2d ed. Los Angeles: Lone Eagle Publishing Company, 2005. An acclaimed screenwriter and teacher in various film schools, Cowgill cites numerous examples from films short and long to stress strategies for keeping your script on track, developing strong characters, and using compelling writing.

Crouch, Tanja L. *100 Careers in Film and Television.* Hauppauge, N.Y.: Barrons Educational Series, 2001. Focusing on behind-the-scenes positions as camera operators, film editors, art directors and more, the author talks to real-world film workers about their chosen careers.

Dancyger, Ken. *The Technique of Film and Video Editing: History, Theory, and Practice.* 4th ed. St. Louis, Mo.: Focal Press, 2006. This book provides a comprehensive look at the past and the future of film and video editing.

Debreceni, Todd. *Special Makeup Effects for Stage and Screen: Making and Applying Prosthetics.* St. Louis, Mo.: Focal Press, 2008. An encyclopedic resource that provides advice and tips on special effects makeup techniques and materials.

Desjardins, Christian, and Christopher Young. *Inside Film Music: Composers Speak.* Los Angeles: Silman-James Press, 2007. This book features 40 interviews with film composers, and will be interesting for both the professional composer and the average movie fan. Some of the composers interviewed include John Barry (*Dances with Wolves, Out of Africa, Goldfinger, Dr. No*); Gabriel Yared (*Cold Mountain, The Talented Mr. Ripley, City of Angels, The English Patient*); Mark Isham (*Freedom Writers, The Black Dahlia, Home for the Holidays, Quiz Show*); Marc Shaiman (*When Harry Met Sally, Ghosts of Mississippi, A Few Good Men, City Slickers, Misery*); and Alan Silvestri (*Back to the Future, Forrest Gump, The Polar Express*).

Dunne, John Gregory. *Monster: Living Off the Big Screen.* New York: Vintage Books, 1998. A mordantly funny insider's look at working in Hollywood and getting your scripts written, bought, and produced.

Ebert, Roger, and David Bordwell. *Awake in the Dark: The Best of Roger Ebert.* Chicago: University of Chicago Press, 2008. This "best of" book from the master of film criticism features

reviews of the best films of the past 38 years; essays on colorization, digital projection, and the movie-ratings system; and star interviews and profiles.

Edgar, Tom, and Karin Kelly. *Film School Confidential: The Insider's Guide to Film Schools.* New York: Perigee Trade, 2007. Provides reviews of the top film schools in the United States, and includes information on curriculum, student body, and program requirements.

Gibson, Bill A. *The S.M.A.R.T. Guide to Mixing and Mastering Audio Recordings.* Boston: ArtistPro Publishing, 2005. With technological advances making it increasingly easy for anyone to mix their own music, this guidebook provides the necessary information to help aspiring recording technicians mix and master audio recordings.

Gregory, Georgina, Ros Healy, and Ewa Mazierska. *Careers in Media and Film: The Essential Guide.* Thousand Oaks, Calif.: Sage Publications Ltd., 2008. Provides useful advice on pursuing a career in the film and media industries.

Hamlett, Christina. *Screenwriting for Teens: The 100 Principles of Screenwriting Every Budding Writer Must Know.* Studio City, Calif.: Michael Wiese Productions, 2006. This book provides useful tools, writing exercises, and advice that will help teens write their first screenplay.

Lanier, Troy, and Clay Nichols. *Filmmaking for Teens: Pulling Off Your Shorts.* Studio City, Calif.: Michael Wiese Productions, 2005. Two high school film teachers provide tips to help aspiring, young filmmakers make their first film.

Lowenstein, Stephen, ed. *My First Movie: Twenty Celebrated Directors Talk About Their First Film.* New York: Penguin Books, 2002. Prominent directors reminisce about the challenges and rewards of making their first films. Featured directors include Oliver Stone, Anthony Minghella, the Coen Brothers, Allison Anders, Mira Nair, Kevin Smith, Mike Leigh, P.J. Hogan, James Mangold, Neil Jordan, Ang Lee, and Pedro Almodovar.

Mayfield, Katherine. *Acting A to Z: The Young Person's Guide to a Stage or Screen Career.* New York: Back Stage Books, 2007. This book provides comprehensive information for kids about the world of acting—from the different styles of acting, to how to prepare for an audition or a rehearsal, to what to do if you hit the big time.

National Association of Schools of Theatre. *National Association of Schools of Theatre Directory.* Reston, Va.: National Association of Schools of Theatre, 2008. Lists accredited institutions and major degree programs in theater.

The New York Times. The New York Times Guide to the Best 1,000 Movies Ever Made. Rev. ed. New York: St. Martin's Griffin, 2004. Provides a comprehensive overview of the best dramas, documentaries, comedies, musicals, and thrillers ever made.

Nisbett, Alec. *The Sound Studio: Audio Techniques for Radio, Television, Film and Recording.* 7th ed. St. Louis, Mo.: Focal Press, 2003. A textbook for audio engineers, directors, writers, performers, and students, with an emphasis on general principles and understanding the importance of each operation and innovation in sound recording.

Pepperman, Richard D. *The Eye Is Quicker: Film Editing: Making A Good Film Better.* Studio City, Calif.: Michael Wiese Productions, 2004. A comprehensive overview of these key behind-the-scenes players in the film industry.

Pinteau, Pascal. *Special Effects: An Oral History-Interviews with 37 Masters Spanning 100 Years.* New York: Harry N. Abrams, 2005. Acclaimed special effects artists discuss makeup, animation, animatronics, modelmaking, computer tricks, and other techniques used in some of the most famous films in the history of the motion picture industry.

Price, David A. *The Pixar Touch.* New York: Vintage Books, 2009. The author takes readers inside Pixar Animation Studios, one of the most successful animation studios of all time and the creator of such classics as *WALL-E, Toy Story, Cars, Ratatouille, Finding Nemo,* and *The Incredibles.*

The Princeton Review. *Television, Film, and Digital Media Programs: 556 Outstanding Programs at Top Colleges and Universities Across the Nation.* New York: The Princeton Review, 2006. This book gives you the scoop on top programs and features interviews with well-known industry professionals.

Richards, Andrea. *Girl Director: A How-To Guide for the First-Time, Flat-Broke*

Film and Video Maker. Berkeley, Calif.: Ten Speed Press, 2005. Championing the female film director—from historical pioneers to tomorrow's leaders—this book encourages women of all ages to take their ideas to the next level by writing and directing their own work. With particular emphasis on teaching amateurs the step-by-step process involved in developing ideas, finding funding, and ultimately producing their own low-budget films, the book defines a wealth of essential industry terminology while highlighting examples of meaningful female contributions to this field.

Rickitt, Richard, and Ray Harryhausen. *Special Effects: The History and Technique.* 2d ed. New York: Billboard Books, 2007. This book traces the history of special effects in films, provides an overview of special effects techniques, and features profiles of well-known figures in the field.

Rizzo, Michael. *The Art Direction Handbook for Film.* St. Louis, Mo.: Focal Press, 2005. A well-known art director takes readers inside the world of art direction in the film industry.

Schneider, Steven Jay. *501 Movie Directors: A Comprehensive Guide to the Greatest Filmmakers.* Hauppauge, N.Y.: Barron's Educational Series, 2007. A team of film critics and historians details the best directors in history and what makes them so special. Some of the directors profiled include Woody Allen, Robert Altman, Ingmar Bergman, Tim Burton, Frank Capra, Joel Coen and Ethan Coen, Cecil B. DeMille, Walt Disney, Clint Eastwood, Federico Fellini, John Ford, Amy Heckerling, Alfred Hitchcock, Stanley Kubrick, Spike Lee, Otto Preminger, Martin Scorsese, Steven Spielberg, and Zhang Yimou.

Slone, Michael. *Special Effects: How to Create a Hollywood Film Look on a Home Budget.* Studio City, Calif.: Michael Wiese Productions, 2007. A helpful resource for the beginning filmmaker who wants to create dazzling special effects without breaking the bank.

Thomas, Tony. *A Wonderful Life: The Films and Career of James Stewart.* New York: Citadel Books, 2000. A comprehensive look at the life and times of the star of *It's a Wonderful Life, Mr. Smith Goes to Washington, The Philadelphia Story, Rear Window,* and other classics.

Thompson, Kristin, and David Bordwell. *Film History: An Introduction.* 3d ed. New York: McGraw-Hill Humanities/Social Sciences/Languages, 2009. Provides an overview of U.S. and world film history in every genre—from comedy and horror to documentary and drama.

Trottier, David. *The Screenwriter's Bible: A Complete Guide to Writing, Formatting, and Selling Your Script.* 4th ed. Los Angeles: Silman-James Press, 2005. Everything you need to know to write, submit, and sell a successful screenplay is included in this all-inclusive book appropriate for beginners through accomplished screenwriters. Formatting tips, marketing advice, character development, and a wealth of other topics are covered.

Vines, James. *Q & A: The Working Screenwriter: An In-the-Trenches Perspective of Writing Movies in Today's Film Industry.* AuthorHouse, 2006. Sixteen screenwriters provide practical advice and tips on breaking into and thriving in the field. Some of the screenwriters who are featured include Brent Maddock (*Tremors, The Wild Wild West, Short Circuit*), Katherine Fugate (*Carolina, The Prince and Me*), John Rogers (*The Core*), and David J. Schow (*The Crow, Texas Chainsaw Massacre 3*).

Walter, Mike S. *Hollywood Stuntman Comes Clean: What Hurts the Most?* Bloomington, Ind.: iUniverse Inc., 2007. An inside look at the ups and downs of life as a stuntman. Some of Walter's credits include *Twelve Monkeys, City Slickers 2: The Legend of Curly's Gold*, and *Roadhouse*.

Wolf, Steve. *The Secret Science Behind Movie Stunts & Special Effects.* New York: Skyhorse Publishing, 2007. An industry insider explains the science behind some of the movie's wildest and jaw-dropping special effects and stunts.

❏ PERIODICALS

Animation Magazine. Published 10 times annually by *Animation Magazine* Inc. (30941 West Agoura Road, Suite 102, Westlake Village, CA 91361-4637, 818-991-2884), this magazine covers all genres in which animation is used—movies, television, commercials, and more. Also included are school and job listings, making a subscription to this Web site/magazine invaluable to animation career seekers as well. Print and electronic subscriptions are available. Visit http://www.animationmagazine.net to read sample articles.

Below the Line. Published by *Below the Line* (6105 Melvin Avenue, Tarzana, CA 91356-1025, 818-888-5946, subscriptions@btlnews.com, http://www.btlnews.com), this newspaper bills itself as the editorial voice of the film crew and features interviews with industry professionals and articles about the field.

CARTOON. Published three times a year by the International Animated Film Society: ASIFA-Hollywood (2114 Burbank Boulevard, Burbank, CA 91506-1232, 818-842-8330, info@asifa-hollywood.org, http://www.asifa-hollywood.org), this magazine features articles about well-known animators, updates on chapter activities, and features on animation from around the world.

Cinefex. Published quarterly by *Cinefex* (PO Box 20027, Riverside, CA 92516-0027, 800-434-3339, http://www.cinefex.com), this magazine provides comprehensive coverage of motion picture special makeup and visual effects. It has been published since 1980.

CinemaEditor. Published quarterly by American Cinema Editors Inc. (100 Universal City Plaza, Verna Fields Building 2282, Room 190, Universal City, CA 91608-1002, 818-777-2900, http://www.ace-filmeditors.org/newace/mag_Main.html), this magazine highlights goings on in the field of film editing. Recent issues included career achievement award winner profiles, profiles of well-known editors, book reviews, and career profiles.

The Costume Designer. Published quarterly by the Costume Designers Guild (11969 Ventura Boulevard, 1st Floor, Studio City, CA 91604-2630, 818-752-2400, cdgia@costumedesignersguild.com), this magazine covers trends in the industry, the history of costumes in motion pictures, and union issues. Visit http://www.costumedesignersguild.com/cdg-magazine.asp to read sample issues.

Daily Variety. Published Monday through Friday by Reed Business Information (5900 Wilshire Boulevard, Suite 3100, Los Angeles, CA 90036-3659, 866-698-2743), this show-biz publication covers the latest breaking news in the entertainment industry and is delivered in print or online formats. Visit http://www.variety.com to read selected articles.

Directors Guild of America Monthly. Published by the Directors Guild of America (7920 Sunset Boulevard, Los Angeles, CA 90046-3300, 310-289-5333), this publication includes in-depth articles on guild activities. Electronic editions are available at http://www.dga.org.

Directors Guild of America Quarterly. Published by the Directors Guild of America (7920 Sunset Boulevard, Los Angeles, CA 90046-3300, 310-289-5333), this publication includes in-depth articles on areas of interest to film and television directors. Articles include director profiles, technology news, historic accomplishments in the field, and important trends to watch. Electronic editions are available at http://www.dga.org.

Dramatics. Published nine times annually by the Educational Theatre Association (2343 Auburn Avenue, Cincinnati, OH 45219-2815, 513-421-3900, info@edta.org), this publication for theater students and teachers offers "practical articles on acting, directing, design, and other facets of theater; profiles of working professionals that offer insights into theater careers; new plays; and book reviews." Two special issues list college theater programs and summer theater work and study opportunities. Visit http://www.edta.org/publications/dramatics to read sample articles.

Emmy. Published bimonthly by the Academy of Television Arts and Sciences (Attn: Subscription Department, 5220 Lankersheim Boulevard, North Hollywood, CA 91601-3109, 818-754-2800, http://cdn.emmys.tv/emmymag/index.php), this journal will interest general readers who seek profiles of people in the news and articles on trends and topics in the world of television.

Fangoria. Published 10 times annually by The Brooklyn Company (250 West 49th Street, Suite 304, 3rd Floor, New York, NY 10019-7454), this magazine is considered the bible of the world of horror entertainment. It features articles, book reviews, and interviews. *Fangoria* has been published since

1979. Visit http://www.fangoria.com to read sample articles.

FILMMAKER: The Magazine of Independent Film. Published quarterly by FILMMAKER (68 Jay Street, Suite 425, Brooklyn, NY 11201-8361, 212-465-8200, subscriptions@filmmakermagazine.com), this magazine features articles about "the most intriguing independent feature films that will be released in theaters over the subsequent three months." Print and online subscriptions are available. Visit http://www.filmmakermagazine.com to read a sample issue.

Film Music. Published by Global Media Online Inc. (23360 Valencia Boulevard, Suite E-12, Valencia, CA 91355-1700, 888-910-7888), this is a comprehensive resource for aspiring and professional film composers. Visit http://www.filmmusicmag.com to sign up for a subscription.

Film Score Monthly Online. Published by *Film Score Monthly* (6311 Romaine Street, Suite 7109, Hollywood, CA 90038-2617, 323-461-2240, http://www.filmscoremonthly.com), this online magazine features useful articles and resources for film composers—some of which are available for free.

The Hollywood Reporter. Published daily (Monday through Friday) by Nielsen Business Media Inc. (866-525-2150, subscriptions@thr.com), this industry news source has provided up-to-date information to industry professionals for more than 75 years, covering all topics related to the entertainment industry. The publication is available

in print and/or online subscriptions. Visit http://www.hollywoodreporter.com to read sample articles.

The Hollywood Scriptwriter. Published bimonthly (PO Box 3761, Cerritos, CA 90703-3761, 310-283-1630), this trade magazine for screenwriters, producers, and directors provides insightful articles on film industry happenings. Also included in the publication are listings of recommended books as well as contests and festivals for scriptwriters. Visit http://www.hollywoodscriptwriter.com to read sample articles.

Journal of Popular Film and Television. Published quarterly by Heldref Publications (1319 18th Street, NW, Washington, DC 20036-1802, 866-802-7059, heldref@subscriptionoffice.com, http://www.heldref.org/pubs/jpft/about.html), this scholarly title emphasizes U.S. popular film with a sociocultural analysis of film theory and criticism. Print and electronic editions are available.

Journal of the Audio Engineering Society. Published 10 times annually by the Audio Engineering Society (60 East 42nd Street, Room 2520, New York, NY 10165-2520, 212-661-8528, http://www.aes.org/journal), this peer-reviewed journal is devoted exclusively to audio technology. It contains the latest industry reports, society and product development news, and trade convention schedules.

MovieMaker. Published bimonthly (174 Fifth Avenue, Suite 300, New York, NY 10010-5965, 212-766-4100), this publication for independent filmmakers and mainstream Hollywood film professionals offers film reviews, tips on moviemaking, festival coverage, and profiles of actors, cinematographers, directors, editors, producers, and screenwriters. Recent articles include "25 Festivals Worth the Fee," "Tales from the Trenches: No Money? No Problem!," "Changing Lives at the Colorado Film School," "In Theaters Now," "Tales from the Trenches: Making Movies Is Back-Breaking Work," "Nicolas Cage Knows He's on Top," and "Write on at the Santa Fe Screenwriting Conference." Visit http://www.moviemaker.com to read selected articles.

On Writing. Published "occasionally" by the Writers Guild of America, East (555 West 57th Street, New York, NY 10019-2925, 212-767-7800, http://www.wgaeast.org/index.php?id=255), this publication for writers provides articles, essays, and commentary on the art of writing. The guild represents writers who write for film, television, radio, and news, and the publication caters to such writers. Issues may be downloaded for free as PDF files from the organization's Web site.

Perspective. Published bimonthly by the Art Directors Guild & Scenic, Title, and Graphic Artists (11969 Ventura Boulevard, 2nd Floor, Studio City, CA 91604-2619, 818-762-9995), this professional journal covers issues of interest to art directors and related professionals. Back issues of *Perspective* are available for free at http://www.artdirectors.org/?content=cm&art=perspective_magazine&section=25.

Pro Sound News. Published by NewBay Media (810 Seventh Avenue, 27th Floor, New York, NY 10019-5872, 212-378-0400, http://www.prosoundnews.com), this publication features headline news, product spotlights, and an industry calendar. Free to industry insiders, it covers topics of importance to those working in audio production. Students will find a complete directory of educational degree and certificate programs in audio technology that are available in the United States at the publication's Web site.

The Scenographer. Published bimonthly by Harman Publishing Ltd. (Registered Office, 1-5 Lillie Road, London SW6 1TX, U.K, mharman@thescenographer.com, http://www.thescenographer.com), this publication offers news and resources for "production designers, architects, set decorators, costume designers, exhibition crews, interior designers, specialized technicians, and anyone interested in art and design." Print and online editions are available.

The SCORE. Published quarterly by the Society of Composers & Lyricists (8447 Wilshire Boulevard, Suite 401, Beverly Hills CA 90211-3209, 310-281-2812), this newsletter features interviews with film composers and articles about breaking into the industry, technological trends, legal issues, and the history of the field. Visit http://www.thescl.com to read sample articles.

Screen Actor. Published quarterly by the Screen Actors Guild (5757 Wilshire Boulevard, Los Angeles, CA 90036-3600, 323-954-1600), this member publication provides updates on union activities and developments in the industry. Recent articles include "TV/Theatrical Contract Overview," "Greatest Performances of All Time," "State of the Industry," "Get Paid: From Financial Assurance to Residuals," and "20 Tips from 20 Actors: Things Every Great Actor Should Know." Visit http://www.sag.org/screenactor to read past issues.

Script. Published bimonthly by Final Draft Inc. (PO Box 90846, Long Beach, CA 90809-0846, 888-881-5861), this publication provides practical advice on screenwriting, interviews with top screenwriters, and information on developments in the film and television industries. Regular features include Writers on Writing, Scene Fix, Anatomy of a Scene, Book Reviews, Film Reviews, and Product Reviews. Visit http://www.scriptmag.com to read sample articles.

Videomaker. Published monthly by Videomaker Inc. (PO Box 4591, Chico, CA 95927-4591, 800-284-3226, customerservice@videomaker.com), this magazine is written for beginners and professional technicians with an emphasis on camcorders, desktop video, copywriting, animation software, reviews, and much more. Intended for those using video in hobbies, business, or education. Visit http://www.videomaker.com to read sample articles.

Weekly Variety. Published by Reed Business Information (5900 Wilshire Boulevard, Suite 3100, Los Angeles, CA 90036-3659, 866-698-2743), this show-biz magazine covers everything from film, music, theater, and television and includes the latest promotions and hirings within the industry, technology-related articles, and job listings. Appropriate for anyone interested in the business of show business, this magazine provides respected, up-to-date entertainment news. Visit http://www.variety.com to read selected articles.

Surf the Web

You must use the Internet to do research, to find out, to explore. The Internet is the closest you'll get to what's happening now all around the world. This chapter gets you started with an annotated list of Web sites related to film. Try a few. Follow the links. Maybe even venture as far as asking questions on a message board. The more you read about and interact with those in the field of film, the better prepared you'll be when you're old enough to participate as a professional.

Keep in mind that that URLs change all the time. If a Web address listed below is out of date, try searching on the site's name or other keywords. Chances are, if it's still out there, you'll find it. If it's not, maybe you'll find something better!

❏ THE LIST

Academy of Motion Picture Arts and Sciences
http://www.oscars.org

The academy was founded in 1927 by some of the most influential actors, directors, and studio heads of the time. It is an honorary membership organization that now has more than 6,000 members. Members vote to award Academy Awards, better known as Oscars, to those who have achieved excellence in filmmaking. Awards are given to actors, cin-ematographers, directors, screenwriters, and other film professionals, as well as given to the best film, animated feature, and films in other categories. Visit the academy's Web site for information on the Academy Awards, past winners, and the Student Academy Awards (for college students).

AMC Filmsite
http://www.filmsite.org

Given a thumbs-up by renowned film critic and columnist Roger Ebert, this site is a movie-lover's paradise! Movies are organized into diverse categories, including 100 Best Films, Best Chick Flicks, and Milestones in Film; all movie listings include a plot synopsis and cast listing. There's even an extensive list of Academy Award-winning films, actors and actresses, and directors dating back to the first awards given out in 1927. An added bonus is the Cinema's Best Question, a trivia quiz that might even stump Roger Ebert himself!

Association of Film Commissioners International
http://www.afci.org

At this organization's Web site, you can find links to more than 300 film commissions on six continents. For example, a search of the state of Colorado in the

United States locates four commissions: the Boulder County Film Commission, the Colorado Film Commission, the Colorado Springs Film Liaison Office, and the Glenwood Springs Film Commission. These commissions can provide valuable information on film-related job opportunities in particular areas, and you may be able to locate contact information of film professionals who might be willing to take a few minutes to participate in information interviews about their careers.

Back Stage
http://www.backstage.com

This site is the ultimate yellow pages for those wanting to break into show business. Check out the Pilot Season Guide, which lists dos and don'ts of the biz; College List, a resource that details undergraduate and graduate programs throughout the country; and also different sections on how to find the best photographers, create headshots, and determine photographic techniques to put you in the best light.

The many advice columns are also helpful—topics range from voice and movement training, to traveling for business, to the importance of withholding taxes from your acting checks. Don't leave the site without reading the blog section—this is where you'll learn the ins and outs of show business, from actors and actress already in the field.

College Navigator
http://nces.ed.gov/collegenavigator

College Navigator is sponsored by the National Center for Education Statistics, an agency of the U.S. Department of Education. At the site, users can _ for information on nearly 7,000 postsecondary institutions in the United States. Searches can be conducted by school name, state, programs/majors offered (including film/video), level of award, institution type, tuition, housing availability, campus settings, percentage of applicants who are admitted, test scores, availability of varsity athletic teams, availability of extended learning opportunities, religious affiliation, and specialized mission. Additionally, users can export the results of their search into a spreadsheet, save the results of their session, and compare up to four colleges in one view. This is an excellent starting place to conduct research about colleges and universities.

FilmFestivals.com
http://www.filmfestivals.com

Ever dream of attending film festivals all day, every day? It could be a reality, especially after visiting this site tagged as the premier online resource for film festivals worldwide. Large, well-known festivals such as Cannes and Sundance are listed, as well as smaller festivals with limited focus. Examples include the International Short Film Festival in Denmark, the Fespaco African Film Festival, and CamboFest—a Cambodian festival featuring video and animation. You can search festivals by location, size, calendar listing, or by the event's director or ambassador. If you want to do more than watch festival offerings, don't fret. Just click on the Festival Jobs section for a complete listing of employment opportunities for each event.

Filmmaking.net
http://www.filmmaking.net

Attention all new and independent filmmakers! This is the site for you—articles include information on how to write a script, how to distribute your short film, and current world market movie trends. Additional resources include a comprehensive film school database, a "toolshed" to download free filmmaking software, a marketplace to buy or sell equipment, and a Q&A section that details the most common filmmaking inquiries. Don't miss the forums where you can learn tricks of the trade, join a Web community geared toward your favorite film genre, or simply offer your opinions along with others in a newsgroup discussion forum.

GradSchools.com
http://www.gradschools.com

This site offers listings of graduate schools searchable by state. From the home page, use the drop-down menu to choose the field of study (such as communications), subject (such as radio, film, and television), and geographic location. Listings include basic program information, degrees offered, school Web site, and email contact.

How Stuff Works
http://www.howstuffworks.com

If you spend a lot of time wondering how stuff you use or see every day actually works, then this site should be on your short list of Web sites to explore, as it covers how "stuff," as varied and timely as tsunamis to identity theft to satellite radio, works. Complex concepts are carefully broken down and examined, including photos and links to current and past news items about the subject. Topics of interest for those interested in film careers include How Film Festivals Work, How Film Composers Work, and How Film Set Construction Works, among others.

The Internet Movie Database
http://us.imdb.com

You'll need a moment to adjust to the amount of information presented, sections to explore, or trailers to watch. Film, television, movie premieres, and DVD and Blu-ray—it's all here. Interested in what's coming to the big screen next Friday night? Just click on the movie trailer of your choice. Missed your favorite show on television? No worries, whether it's a drama or reality show, chances are you can read a recap of the episode—spoilers and all.

The coolest feature of this site is its search engine. Simply plug in a title, or even just a keyword, and you'll soon be reading a list of every television show, movie, or character containing that keyword. Click again and you can read a synopsis of a movie, trivia on an actor, or even the actor's Star Meter Rating.

Synopsis sections are contributed by "registered users," so be aware that some reviews may be biased. Nonetheless, this site is among the most popular of its kind, with 57 million visits each month by die-hard film and television followers worldwide.

Peterson's Summer Camps and Programs

http://www.petersons.com/
summerop/code/ssector.asp

This Web site offers great information about academic and career-focused summer programs. Finding a camp that suits your interests is easy enough at this site; just search Peterson's database by activity (Academics, Arts, Sports, Wilderness/ Outdoors, Special Interests), geographic region, category (Day Programs in the U.S., Residential Programs in the U.S., Travel in the U.S. and to Other Countries, Special Needs Accommodations), keyword, or alphabetically. By conducting a keyword search using the word *film*, you'll find a list of links to dozens of programs. Click on a specific program or camp for a quick overview description. In some instances you'll get a more in-depth description, along with photographs, applications, and online brochures.

RogerEbert.com

http://rogerebert.suntimes.com

Award-winning film critic and *Chicago Sun-Times* columnist Roger Ebert is a well-respected, and sometimes feared, figure in the movie industry. Read by a wide following, his reviews can help make or break a movie. Consider this site as the ultimate guide to movies—and more.

A wide range of movie reviews is listed, from big studio blockbusters to romantic chick flicks. All are listed with a synopsis, cast of characters, comprehensive review, and most importantly a star rating. Don't miss his One-Minute Reviews, an alphabetical listing of current movies all reviewed in one paragraph.

Additional features include a festival listing, movie glossary, and Answer Man—where Roger Ebert answers readers' burning questions on topics ranging from the merits of Blu-ray discs to disagreements on a bad movie review.

Screenwriter's Utopia

http://www.screenwritersutopia.com

Screenwriter's Utopia is the go-to destination for aspiring and professional screenwriters on the Web. Along with useful articles, news, forums, and contests, this Web site offers surveys, reviews, and suggestions for scriptwriters of all levels of experience. Want to get creative feedback from your peers regarding the television or film script on which you've been working? This site offers workshops and consultations on how to improve your work and how to better market it. Users will need to register (free) to gain access to the many features of this useful site. The Script Swap section allows you to read and comment on other's work and vice versa. Any serious wannabe film and television writer should visit this Web site to gain a better perspective on what is currently going on in the business.

So You Want to Be an Actor

http://www.redbirdstudio.com/
AWOL/acting2.html

You won't find fancy graphics, animation, or music at this Web site. This site is all about information, and it contains plenty of it. You'll find acting tips, directory listings of community theaters, and even acting industry links in the United States and Canada. Some of the more interesting sections include What Every Actor Needs To Know; The Casting Process; What About Scams?; The Language of Acting: A Glossary of Terms; Auditions Will Be Held for...(A Few Helpful Tips); And Help! I Got the Part! Now What? There are also links to acting and arts camps and film commissions. While the arrangement of this Web site may seem a little amateurish, it's full of informative tidbits—some very helpful, all entertaining.

Ask for Money

By the time most students get around to thinking about applying for scholarships, grants, and other financial aid, they have already extolled their personal, academic, and creative virtues to such lengths in essays and interviews for college applications that even their own grandmothers wouldn't recognize them. The thought of filling out yet another application fills students with dread. And why bother? Won't the same five or six kids who have been competing for academic honors for years walk away with all the really good scholarships?

The truth is that most of the scholarships available to high school and college students are being offered because an organization wants to promote interest in a particular field, encourage more students to become qualified to enter it, and finally, to help those students afford an education. Having a great grade point average is definitely a valuable asset. More often than not, however, grade point averages aren't even mentioned; the focus is on the area of interest and what a student has done to distinguish himself or herself in that area. In fact, sometimes the only requirement is that the scholarship applicant must be studying in a particular area.

❏ GUIDELINES

When applying for scholarships there are a few simple guidelines that can help ease the process considerably.

Plan Ahead

The absolute worst thing you can do is wait until the last minute. For one thing, obtaining recommendations or other supporting data in time to meet an application deadline is incredibly difficult. For another, no one does his or her best thinking or writing under the gun. So get off to a good start by reviewing scholarship applications as early as possible—months, even a year, in advance. If the current scholarship information isn't available, ask for a copy of last year's version. Once you have the scholarship information or application in hand, give it a thorough read. Try to determine how your experience or situation best fits into the scholarship, or if it even fits at all. Don't waste your time applying for a scholarship in drama if you hate reading Shakespeare and other playwrights.

If possible, research the award or scholarship, including past recipients and, where applicable, the person in whose name the scholarship is offered. Often, scholarships are established to memorialize an individual who majored in drama, film, or a related field, for example, but in other cases, the scholarship is to memorialize the *work* of an individual. In those cases, try to get a feel for the spirit of the person's work. If you have any similar interests, experiences, or abilities, don't hesitate to mention them.

Talk to others who received the scholarship, or to students currently studying in the same area or field of interest in which the scholarship is offered, and try to gain insight into possible applications or work related to that field. When you're working on the essay asking why you want this scholarship, you'll have real answers—"I would benefit from receiving this scholarship because studying film will help me become a better storyteller and filmmaker."

Take your time writing the essays. Make sure that you answer the question or questions on the application; do not merely restate facts about yourself. Don't be afraid to get creative; try to imagine what you would think of if you had to sift through hundreds of applications: What would you want to know about the candidate? What would convince you that someone was deserving of the scholarship? Work through several drafts and have someone whose advice you respect—a parent, teacher, or guidance counselor—review the essay for grammar and content.

Finally, if you know in advance which scholarships you want to apply for, there might still be time to stack the deck in your favor by getting an internship, volunteering, or working part time. Bottom line: The more you know about a scholarship and the sooner you learn it, the better.

Follow Directions

Think of it this way: many of the organizations that offer scholarships devote 99.9 percent of their time to something other than the scholarship for which you are applying. Don't make a nuisance of yourself by pestering them for information. Simply follow the directions as they are presented to you. If the scholarship application specifies that you should write for further information, then write for it—don't call.

Pay close attention to whether you're applying for a grant, a loan, an award, a prize, or a scholarship. Often these words are used interchangeably, but just as often they have different meanings. A loan is financial aid that must be paid back. A grant is a type of financial aid that does not require repayment. An award or prize is usually given for something you have done: built a park or helped distribute meals to the elderly; or something you have created: a musical composition, a design, an essay, a short film, a screenplay, or an invention. On the other hand, a scholarship is frequently a renewable sum of money that is given to a person to help defray the costs of college. Scholarships are given to candidates who meet the necessary criteria based on essays, eligibility, grades, or sometimes all three. They do not have to be paid back.

Supply all the necessary documents, information, and fees, and make the deadlines. You won't win any scholarships by forgetting to include a recommendation from a teacher or failing to postmark the application by the deadline. Bottom line: Get it right the first time, on time.

Apply Early

Once you have the application in hand, don't dawdle. If you've requested it far enough in advance, there shouldn't be any reason for you not to turn it in well in advance of the deadline. If it comes down to two candidates, your timeliness just might be the deciding factor. Bottom line: Don't wait, and don't hesitate.

Be Yourself

Don't make promises you can't keep. There are plenty of hefty scholarships available, but if they all require you to study something that you don't enjoy, you'll be miserable in college. And the side effects from switching majors after you've accepted a scholarship could be even worse. Bottom line: Be yourself.

Don't Limit Yourself

There are many sources for scholarships, beginning with your school counselor and ending with the Internet. All of the search engines have education categories. Start there and search by keywords, such as "financial aid," "scholarship," and "award." But don't be limited to the scholarships listed in these pages.

If you know of an organization related to or involved with the field of your choice, write a letter asking if they offer scholarships. If they don't offer scholarships, don't stop there. Write them another letter, or better yet, schedule a meeting with the executive director, education director, or someone in the public relations department and ask them if they would be willing to sponsor a scholarship for you. Of course, you'll need to prepare yourself well for such a meeting because you're selling a priceless commodity: yourself. Don't be shy, and be confident. Tell them all about yourself, what you want to study and why, and let them know what you would be willing to do in exchange—volunteer at their favorite charity, write up reports on your progress in school, or work part time on school breaks and full time during the summer. Explain why you're a wise investment. Bottom line: The sky's the limit.

One More Thing

We have not listed financial aid that is available from individual colleges and universities. Why? There are two reasons. First, because there are thousands of schools that offer financial aid for students who are interested in studying film or a related major, and we couldn't possibly fit them all in this book. Second, listing just a few schools wouldn't be helpful to the vast majority of students who do not plan to attend these institutions. This means it is up to you to check with the college that you want to attend for details on available financial aid. College financial aid officers will be happy to tell you what types of resources are available.

❏ THE LIST

Academy of Television Arts and Sciences

5220 Lankershim Boulevard
North Hollywood, CA 91601-3109
818-754-2800
ctasupport@emmys.org
http://www.emmys.org/foundation/
    collegetvawards.php

The academy offers the College Television Awards and the Fred Rogers Memorial Scholarship.

The College Television Awards competition rewards excellence in college (undergraduate and graduate) student film/video productions in the following categories: animation (all forms), children's, comedy, comedy series, commercial, documentary, drama, drama series, magazine, music (best composition), music (best use of music), and newscast. The first entry is free; subsequent entries are $25 per entry. All entries must have been "produced for school related classes, groups, or projects and, must be verified by a faculty member." First place winners receive $2,000; second place winners, $1,000; and third place winners, $500. There is also a $1,000 directing award, and a $4,000 Seymour Bricker Family Humanitarian Award.

College students who are pursuing degrees in early childhood education, child development/child psychology, film/television production, music, or animation may apply for one of three $10,000 Fred Rogers Memorial Scholarships. Applicants must have the ultimate goal of working in the field of children's media. Special consideration will be given to applicants from inner-city or rural communities.

American Legion Auxiliary
8945 North Meridian Street
Indianapolis, IN 46260-5387
317-569-4500
alahq@legion-aux.org
http://www.legion-aux.org/
    scholarships/index.aspx

Various state auxiliaries of the American Legion, as well as its national organization, offer scholarships to help students prepare for a variety of careers.

Most require that candidates be associated with the organization in some way, whether as a child, spouse, etc., of a military veteran. Interested students should contact the auxiliary for further information.

Army ROTC
800-USA-ROTC
http://www.goarmy.com/rotc/
    scholarships.jsp

The Army offers job opportunities for those interested in film, although "there is no guarantee a service member will receive the job they want." Students planning to or currently pursuing college study may apply for scholarships that pay tuition and some living expenses; recipients must agree to accept a commission and serve in the Army on active duty or in a reserve component (U.S. Army Reserve or Army National Guard).

Association on American Indian Affairs
Attn: Director of Scholarship
    Programs
966 Hungerford Drive, Suite 12-B
Rockville, MD 20850-1743
240-314-7155
lw.aaia@verizon.net
http://www.indian-affairs.org

Undergraduate and graduate Native American students who are pursuing a wide variety of college majors can apply for several different scholarships of $1,500. All applicants must provide proof of Native American heritage. Visit the association's Web site for more information.

CollegeBoard: Scholarship Search

http://apps.collegeboard.com/
cbsearch_ss/welcome.jsp

This testing service (PSAT, SAT, etc.) also offers a scholarship search engine at its Web site. It features scholarships worth nearly $3 billion. You can search by specific major (such as film) and a variety of other criteria.

CollegeNET: MACH 25- Breaking the Tuition Barrier

http://www.collegenet.com/
mach25/app

CollegeNET features 600,000 scholarships worth more than $1.6 billion. You can search by keyword (such as "film") or by creating a personality profile of your interests.

FastWeb

http://www.fastweb.com

FastWeb is one of the best-known scholarship search engines around. It features 1.3 million scholarships worth more than $3 billion. To use this resource, you will need to register (free).

Foundation for the Carolinas

Office of Scholarships
217 South Tryon Street
Charlotte, NC 28202-3201
704-973-4537
tcapers@fftc.org
http://www.fftc.org

The foundation administers more than 105 scholarship programs that offer awards to high school seniors and under-graduate and graduate students who plan to or who are currently pursuing study in a variety of disciplines. Visit its Web site for a list of awards.

GuaranteedScholarships.com

http://www.guaranteed-scholarships.
com

This Web site offers lists (by college) of scholarships, grants, and financial aid that "require no interview, essay, portfolio, audition, competition, or other secondary requirement."

Hawaii Community Foundation

1164 Bishop Street, Suite 800
Honolulu, HI 96813-2817
888-731-3863
info@hcf-hawaii.org
http://www.hawaiicommunity
foundation.org/scholar/scholar.php

The foundation offers a variety of scholarships for high school seniors and college students planning to or currently studying a variety of majors (including visual communication) in college. Applicants must be residents of Hawaii, demonstrate financial need, and attend a two- or four-year college. Visit the foundation's Web site for more information and to apply online.

Hispanic College Fund (HCF)

1301 K Street, NW,
  Suite 450-A West
Washington, DC 20005-3317
800-644-4223
hcf-info@hispanicfund.org
http://www.hispanicfund.org

The Hispanic College Fund, in collaboration with several major corporations, offers many scholarships for high school seniors and college students planning to or currently attending college. Applicants must be Hispanic, live in the United States or Puerto Rico, and have a GPA of at least 3.0 on a 4.0 scale. Contact the HCF for more information.

Illinois Career Resource Network

http://www.ilworkinfo.com/icrn.htm

Created by the Illinois Department of Employment Security, this useful site offers a scholarship search engine, as well as detailed information on careers (including film-related jobs). You can search for film-oriented scholarships based on major (such as film studies, playwriting and screenwriting, dramatic arts, etc.), and other criterion. This site is available to everyone, not just Illinois residents; you can get a password by simply visiting the site. The Illinois Career Resource Network is just one example of the type of sites created by state departments of employment security (or departments of labor) to assist students with financial- and career-related issues. After checking out this site, visit your state's department of labor Web site to see what it offers.

Imagine America Foundation

1101 Connecticut Avenue, NW,
  Suite 901
Washington, DC 20036-4303
202-336-6800
http://www.imagine-america.org/
  scholarship/a-about-scholarship.asp

The Imagine America Foundation (formerly the Career College Foundation) is a nonprofit organization that helps students pay for college. It offers three $1,000 scholarships each year to high school students or recent graduates. Applicants must have a GPA of at least 2.5 on a 4.0 scale, have financial need, and demonstrate voluntary community service during their senior year. Scholarships can be used at more than 500 career colleges in the United States. These colleges offer a variety of fields of study, including acting, business administration, cinematography and film/video production, and computer graphics. Visit the foundation's Web site for more information.

International Thespian Society

c/o Educational Theatre Association
2343 Auburn Avenue
Cincinnati, OH 45219-2815
513-421-3900
info@edta.org
http://www.edta.org/membership/
  join

The International Thespian Society is the student division of the Educational Theatre Association. It is the largest honor society for theater arts students in the world, with clubs at more than 3,600 affiliated schools in the United States, Canada, and abroad. Students in grades six through 12 are eligible to be inducted into the society. It offers scholarships and grants to inductees, and at least $25,000 is awarded annually. Auditions may be required for some scholarships. Contact the society for more information.

Marine Corps Scholarship Foundation

PO Box 3008
Princeton, NJ 08543-3008
800-292-7777
mcsfnj@mcsf.org
http://www.marine-scholars.org

The foundation provides children of marines and former marines with scholarships of up to $4,500 for postsecondary study. To be eligible, you must be a high school graduate or registered as an undergraduate student at an accredited college or vocational/technical institute. Additionally, your total family gross income may not exceed $80,000. Contact the foundation for further details.

National Endowment for the Arts (NEA)

1100 Pennsylvania Avenue, NW
Washington, DC 20506-0001
202-682-5400
support@grants.gov
http://arts.endow.gov/grants/apply/Media.html

The NEA was established by Congress in 1965 to support excellence in the arts. It offers grants to those who are involved in the "media arts—film, radio, and television—including the production, exhibition, distribution, and preservation of work; the provision of services to the field; and the training of artists." Visit the NEA Web site for a detailed list of available programs.

Navy: Education: Earn Money For College

http://www.navy.com/education

The Navy offers job opportunities for those interested in film, although "there is no guarantee a service member will receive the job they want." It offers several funding programs for college study. Students who receive money to attend college are typically required to serve a specific number of years in the Navy after graduation. Other students take advantage of programs that allow them to join the Navy and complete their degrees during their service obligation. Contact your local recruiter or visit the Navy's Web site for details.

Sallie Mae

http://www.collegeanswer.com/paying/scholarship_search/pay_scholarship_search.jsp

Sallie Mae offers a scholarship database of more than 3 million awards worth more than $16 billion. You must register (free) to use the database.

Scholarship America

One Scholarship Way
PO Box 297
Saint Peter, MN 56082-0297
800-537-4180
http://www.scholarshipamerica.org

This organization works through its local Dollars for Scholars chapters throughout the United States. In 2008 it awarded more than $219 million in scholarships to students. Visit Scholarship America's Web site for more information.

Scholarships.com

http://www.scholarships.com

Scholarships.com offers a free college scholarship and grant search engine (although you must register to use it) and financial aid information. Its database of awards features 2.7 million listings worth more than $19 billion in aid.

Scholastic
c/o Alliance For Young Artists &
  Writers
557 Broadway
New York, NY 10012-3962
212-343-6100
a&wgeneralinfo@scholastic.com
http://www.scholastic.com/
  artandwritingawards

Student artists and writers in grades seven through 12 are eligible to apply for Scholastic Art and Writing Awards of up to $10,000. Some of the categories for graduating high school seniors include animation, general writing portfolio, humor, and video and film. More than $20 million in scholarships have been awarded since the awards were founded in 1923. Visit Scholastic's Web site for a detailed overview of the various awards, competition levels, and application instructions.

United Negro College Fund (UNCF)
8260 Willow Oaks Corporate Drive
PO Box 10444
Fairfax, VA 22031-8044
800-331-2244
http://www.uncf.org/forstudents/
  scholarship.asp

Visitors to the UNCF Web site can search for information on thousands of scholarships and grants, many of which are administered by the UNCF. Its search engine allows you to search by major (such as business, communications, general, performing arts, and television production), state, scholarship title, grade level, and achievement score. High school seniors and undergraduate and graduate students are eligible.

U.S. Department of Education
Federal Student Aid
800-433-3243
http://www.federalstudentaid.ed.gov
http://studentaid.ed.gov/students/
  publications/student_guide/index.
  html

The U.S. government provides a wealth of financial aid in the form of grants, loans, and work-study programs. Each year, it publishes *Funding Education Beyond High School*, a guide to these funds. Visit the Web sites above for detailed information on federal financial aid.

Worldstudio/American Institute of Graphic Arts Scholarships
c/o American Institute of Graphic
  Arts
164 Fifth Avenue
New York, NY 10010-5901
scholarship@aiga.org
http://scholarships.worldstudioinc.
  com

High school seniors and college students planning to or currently pursuing undergraduate or graduate degrees are eligible to apply for scholarships in the following areas: advertising, animation, architecture, cartooning, crafts, environmental graphics, fashion design, film/theater design (including set, costume, and lighting design), film/video (direction or cinematography only), fine arts, furniture design, graphic design, illustration, industrial/product design, interactive design, interior design, landscape architecture, motion graphics, photography, surface/textile design, and urban planning. Applicants must have a GPA of at least 2.0 and demonstrate financial need.

Look to the Pros

The following professional organizations offer a variety of materials, including career information, lists of accredited schools, and salary surveys. Many also publish journals and newsletters with which you should become familiar. Some also have annual conferences that you might be able to attend. (While you may not be able to attend a conference as a participant, it may be possible to "cover" one for your school or even your local paper, especially if your school has a related club.)

When contacting professional organizations, keep in mind that they all exist primarily to serve their members, be it through continuing education, professional licensure, political lobbying, or just "keeping up with the profession." While many are strongly interested in promoting their profession and passing information about it to the general public, these busy professional organizations do not exist solely to provide you with information. Whether you call or write, be courteous, brief, and to the point. Know what you need and ask for it. If the organization has a Web site, check it out first; what you're looking for may be available to download, or you may find a list of prices or instructions, such as sending a self-addressed stamped envelope with your request. Finally, be aware that organizations, like people, move. To save time when writing, first confirm the address,

preferably with a quick phone call to the organization itself: "Hello, I'm calling to confirm your address. . . ."

❏ THE SOURCES

American Cinema Editors (ACE)
100 Universal City Plaza
Verna Fields Building 2282,
  Room 190
Universal City, CA 91608-1002
818-777-2900
amercinema@earthlink.net
http://www.ace-filmeditors.org

The ACE offers career and education information at its Web site, along with information about internship opportunities for college graduates, competitions, and sample articles from *CinemaEditor* magazine.

American Film Institute (AFI)
2021 North Western Avenue
Los Angeles, CA 90027-1657
323-856-7600
http://www.afi.com

Visit the institute's Web site for more information on workshops and membership and to view a movie on editing.

American Society of
Cinematographers
PO Box 2230

Hollywood, CA 90078-2230
800-448-0145
office@theasc.com
http://www.theasc.com

Visit the society's Web site for lists of tricks of the trade, recommended reading, and information on *American Cinematographer* magazine.

Art Directors Guild & Scenic, Title, and Graphic Artists

11969 Ventura Boulevard, 2nd Floor
Studio City, CA 91604-2619
818-762-9995
http://www.artdirectors.org

Visit this association's Web site for information on careers, to view a hall of fame, and to read sample articles from *Perspective* magazine.

Broadcast Film Critics Association

9220 Sunset Boulevard, Suite 220
Los Angeles, CA 90069-3503
310-860-2665
info@bfca.org
http://www.bfca.org

The association represents nearly 200 television, radio, and online critics in the United States and Canada. Visit its Web site for movie reviews and information on scholarships for college students.

Costume Designers Guild

11969 Ventura Boulevard, 1st Floor
Studio City, CA 91604-2630
818-752-2400
cdgia@costumedesignersguild.com
http://www.costumedesignersguild.com

This union represents costume designers in the film and television industries. Visit its Web site for information on the industry, to read copies of *The Costume Designer*, and to view costume sketches in an online gallery.

Directors Guild of America (DGA)

7920 Sunset Boulevard
Los Angeles, CA 90046-3300
310-289-2000
http://www.dga.org

Visit the guild's Web site to learn more about the industry and DGA-sponsored training programs and to read selected articles from *DGA Quarterly*.

The Film Music Society

1516 South Bundy Drive,
  Suite 305
Los Angeles, CA 90025-2683
310-820-1909
info@filmmusicsociety.org
http://www.filmmusicsociety.org

This organization "promotes the preservation of film and television music." Visit its Web site for more information.

International Alliance of Theatrical Stage Employees, Moving Picture Technicians, Artists and Allied Crafts of the United States, Its Territories and Canada

1430 Broadway, 20th Floor
New York, NY 10018-3348
212-730-1770
http://www.iatse-intl.org

This union counts film and television production workers among its craft members. Visit its Web site for information on education and training.

The International Animated Film Society: ASIFA-Hollywood

2114 Burbank Boulevard
Burbank, CA 91506-1232
818-842-8330
info@asifa-hollywood.org
http://www.asifa-hollywood.org

This nonprofit organization is "dedicated to the advancement of the art of animation." It offers membership to anyone who is interested in animation. Visit its Web site for details on membership benefits, *Cartoon* magazine, screenings, volunteer opportunities, and an animation hall of fame.

International Thespian Society

c/o Educational Theatre Association
2343 Auburn Avenue
Cincinnati, OH 45219-2815
513-421-3900
info@edta.org
http://www.edta.org/membership/join

The International Thespian Society is the student division of the Educational Theatre Association. It is the largest honor society for theater arts students in the world. It has clubs at more than 3,600 affiliated schools in the United States, Canada, and other countries. Students in grades six through 12 are eligible to be inducted into the society. Students can participate in the International Thespian Festival, an "educational and performance event for middle and high school theatre . . . which features a variety of performances from some of the best high school theatre programs, hands-on workshops, auditions for the National Individual Events Showcase, and scholarship and college auditions."

Motion Picture Association of America

1600 Eye Street, NW
Washington, DC 20006-4010
202-293-1966
http://www.mpaa.org

This is the trade association of the American film industry and home video and television industries. It operates the voluntary movie ratings system in cooperation with the National Association of Theater Owners.

National Association of Schools of Theatre

11250 Roger Bacon Drive, Suite 21
Reston, VA 20190-5248
703-437-0700
info@arts-accredit.org
http://nast.arts-accredit.org

Visit the association's Web site for information on accessing a print or online directory of theatrical programs and answers to frequently asked questions regarding education.

Online Film Critics Society (OFCS)

admissions@ofcs.org
http://ofcs.rottentomatoes.com

The OFCS is an international association of Internet-based film critics and journalists.

Producers Guild of America

http://www.producersguild.org

This is the leading professional organization for film and television producers. Visit its Web site for information about career options and to view profiles of producers.

Screen Actors Guild (SAG)

5757 Wilshire Boulevard, 7th Floor
Los Angeles, CA 90036-3600
323-954-1600
http://www.sag.com

This union represents more than 126,000 actors who work in motion pictures, television, commercials, video games, industrials, Internet, and all new media formats. Visit its Web site for more information on entering the field and to read a sample issue of *Screen Actor* magazine.

Set Decorators Society of America

7100 Tujunga Avenue, Suite #A
North Hollywood, CA 91605-6216
818-255-2425
sdsa@setdecorators.org
http://www.setdecorators.org

This organization represents the professional interests of set decorators who work in film and television. Visit its Web site for information on careers, publications, and membership for college students.

Society of Composers & Lyricists

8447 Wilshire Boulevard, Suite 401
Beverly Hills CA 90211-3209
310-281-2812
http://www.thescl.com/site/scl

This is a membership organization for "professional film/TV/multi-media music composers, songwriters, and lyricists." Visit its Web site for career resources, an online hall of fame, and information on membership for college students and *The SCORE*, its quarterly publication.

Society of Motion Picture and Television Engineers

Three Barker Avenue, 5th Floor
White Plains, NY 10601-1509
914-761-1100
http://www.smpte.org

This organization bills itself as the "leading technical society for the motion imaging industry." Visit its Web site for information on scholarships and membership for college students, publications, and links to useful resources.

Stuntmen's Association of Motion Pictures

10660 Riverside Drive, 2nd Floor, Suite E
Toluca Lake, CA 91602-2352
818-766-4334
info@stuntmen.com
http://www.stuntmen.com

This is a membership organization for stunt coordinators, stuntmen, and second unit directors in the film and television industries.

Stuntwomen's Association of Motion Pictures

818-762-0907
stuntwomen@stuntwomen.com
http://www.stuntwomen.com

This is a membership organization for stunt coordinators, stuntwomen, and action actresses. Visit its Web site to read profiles of its members.

United Scenic Artists Local 829

29 West 38th Street, 15th Floor
New York, NY 10018-5504
212-581-0300
http://www.usa829.org

This union represents scenic artists, scenic and production designers, art directors, costume designers, lighting designers, sound designers, projection designers, computer artists, industrial workers, and art department coordinators working in film, television, industrial shows, theater, opera, ballet, commercials, and exhibitions.

Visual Effects Society

5535 Balboa Boulevard, Suite 205
Encino, CA 91316-1544
818-981-7861
info@visualeffectssociety.com
http://www.visualeffectssociety.com

This nonprofit organization represents "visual effects practitioners including artists, technologists, model makers, educators, studio leaders, supervisors, public relations/marketing specialists, and producers in all areas of entertainment from film, television, and commercials to music videos and games." Visit its Web site for information about festivals and presentations and news about the industry.

Women in Film

6100 Wilshire Boulevard, Suite 710
Los Angeles, CA 90048-5107
323-935-2211
info@wif.org
http://www.wif.org

Women in Film's mission is to "empower, promote, and mentor women in the entertainment and media industries." Visit its Web site to learn about membership, internships, competitions, and financial aid for college students.

Writers Guild of America-East Chapter

555 West 57th Street
New York, NY 10019-2925
212-767-7800
info@wgaeast.org
http://www.wgaeast.org

Visit the guild's Web site to learn more about the film industry, read interviews and articles by noted screenwriters, access screenwriter tools and resources, read copies of *On Writing*, and find links to many other screenwriting-related sites on the Internet.

Writers Guild of America-West Chapter

7000 West Third Street
Los Angeles, CA 90048-4329
800-548-4532
http://www.wga.org

Visit the guild's Web site to access screenwriter resources and tools, read articles and interviews by well-known screenwriters, and find links to many other screenwriting-related Web sites.

Index

Entries and page numbers in **bold** indicate major treatment of a topic.